"This delightful book presents a year's daily r
Christian Desert tradition, with a very helpful
each date. It is a veritable pocket *Philokalia*, s
Way of the Pilgrim. Fr. David Keller has done ;
this very profound source of *lectio divina* for those seriously interested in
the spiritual path."

—Fr. John McGuckin
Professor of Byzantine Christian Studies
Columbia University

"A must-read for all who desire to form spiritually, Keller's rich and
profound work 'makes room' so that open pastors, leaders, parishioners,
and travelers can listen deeply and experience the overwhelming of God's
Spirit in silence and solitude. In *Desert Banquet*, Keller has indeed written
a wonderful resource for everyone who desires for the Holy One to come
near."

—The Rev. Kendrick E. Curry, PhD, MDiv
Senior Pastor, The Pennsylvania Avenue Baptist Church
Washington, DC

"David Keller offers much food for daily reflection on the wisdom sayings
of the ancient abbas and ammas of early Christianity, as also more
contemporary wise elders. Readers of *Desert Banquet* are led on a journey
to one's own heart, in moving monthly by means of themes of beginning
solitariness, through patient endurance in the grace of transformation
and dealing with the vices, to the fruit of Christ-consciousness, and
ending with the legacy of desert spirituality. Repeated stories take on
added dimensions for living the Gospel love command of love of God and
neighbor, as one is invited to ponder and practice these parables of early
Christianity. The feasting over a year's time on the delicacies of wisdom
ought to nurture a deeper and richer living of the Christian life."

—Mary Forman, OSB
Assistant Professor of Theology
College of Saint Benedict/Saint John's University
Collegeville, Minnesota

Desert Banquet

*A Year of Wisdom from
the Desert Mothers and Fathers*

David G. R. Keller

LITURGICAL PRESS
Collegeville, Minnesota

www.litpress.org

1	2	3	4	5	6	7	8

Library of Congress Cataloging-in-Publication Data

Keller, David G. R., 1937–
    Desert banquet : a year of wisdom from the Desert Mothers and Fathers / David G. R. Keller.
        p.   cm.
    ISBN 978-0-8146-3387-8 — ISBN 978-0-8146-3388-5 (e-book)
    1. Desert Fathers.   2. Devotional calendars.   3. Monastic and religious life of women—Middle East—History—Early church, ca. 30–600—Meditations.   I. Title.

BR190.K45 2011
242'.2
                                                                2011023397

For Emily,
who calls forth the holy and sacred
in everyday living for so many

and

For the monks of
Saint Macarius Monastery,
Wadi El-Natrun, Scetis, Egypt,
who welcomed me into their community,
offering food, a cell, worship, fellowship, and wisdom;
especially Abba Irenaeus, who became my guide and mentor.

In memoriam:
Abba Macarius the Great
(300–390 CE)
and
Abba Matta El-Meskeen
(1920–2006)
Two faithful lovers of souls

C O N T E N T S

PREFACE

An Inconvenient Journey

"And the Spirit immediately drove him out into the wilderness. He was in the wilderness forty days, tempted by Satan; and he was with the wild beasts; and the angels waited on him" (Mark 1:12-13).

In November 2006 I was invited to spend five days with the Coptic monks of St. Macarius Monastery in Scetis, Egypt, and then travel with Bedouins in the Sinai desert. It was a dream come true. For years I had studied the lives of the desert mothers and fathers and tried to integrate their wisdom into my personal life and ministry. My book describing the experiences that formed the context for their wisdom had just been published.* Yet I was reluctant to leave for Egypt.

My wife, Emily, and I had just moved from California to Ithaca, New York. The move had been exhausting for me, physically and emotionally, even though it was freely chosen and full of opportunities. The details of the transition and being "on the move" to a new location and home filled my days. Living out of boxes and endless arrangements prior to moving into a new home scattered the conventional rhythms of my life. It was an amazingly beautiful time in our lives, but I was suffering from the extended break from my usual physical and spiritual exercises. I wanted to sink into the patterns of "ordinary days," settle down with Emily into our new home, explore a new environment, and make new friends. There was so much to do and at the same time I longed for physical and mental rest.

But the call to the desert would not go away. What should I do? Emily encouraged me, saying, "Go, David. You must do this!" She

---

* David G. R. Keller, *Oasis of Wisdom: The Worlds of the Desert Fathers and Mothers* (Collegeville, MN: Liturgical Press, 2005).

was right, but it was not until I was thirty-six thousand feet above the Atlantic Ocean that I came face-to-face with my reservations about going into the desert. It simply was not *convenient*. When I realized how loudly fatigue, necessary tasks, and craving for normal routines were shouting for me to stay home, I discovered how much I *needed* the desert. Sometimes I have to be *driven* into the wilderness so that my mind and heart will listen and rest in God's presence and love. The desert can be anywhere, but it is always a place where I will be stripped of self-reliance and see myself honestly. This dying reveals who I really am. In this arid landscape God offers me food and healing for resurrection and when I least expect it, angels will come to wait on me.

Yet, the desert is not an end in itself. The person I become there is the person I am called to be when I return home.

ACKNOWLEDGMENTS

During eight years as steward of the Episcopal House of Prayer at Saint John's Abbey, Collegeville, Minnesota (1994–2002), I was able to study early monastic history with Sister Mary Forman, OSB, assistant professor of Monastic Studies at Saint John's School of Theology·Seminary, and Father Columba Stewart, OSB, now director of the Hill Museum & Manuscript Library at the abbey. Their scholarship, teaching, and encouragement gave me the confidence to write *Oasis of Wisdom: The Worlds of the Desert Fathers and Mothers*, published in 2005, and now *Desert Banquet*. I am grateful for their scholarship as well as the ways they continue to make the example and wisdom of the desert elders tangible in their lives.

In 2006 Bill Jamieson invited me to join him for a trek across Egyptian deserts with Rabia Tawfik and his Bedouin friends. We visited five ancient desert monasteries and experienced the Sinai desert firsthand by jeep, camel, and on foot. Rabia made it possible for me to spend five days at St. Macarius Coptic Monastery in Scetis. I'm grateful to Bill and Rabia for helping me experience a desert banquet with friends who call the desert home. And I will never forget Alaa Yehia Abed El-Al, who cared for me, a complete stranger, when I became ill in the desert.

My writing has been influenced by participants in courses, retreats, and seminars on the desert mothers and fathers that I have facilitated at the Episcopal House of Prayer in Collegeville; at Gladstone's Library (formerly Saint Deiniol's) in North Wales; and in the Oasis of Wisdom program in Asheville, North Carolina, that I direct with my wife, Emily Wilmer. Their questions, desire to enter a world so different from their own, comments, and suggestions have helped me see how much the desert tradition offers for life in the twenty-first century.

I want to thank Hans Christoffersen, publisher of the academic and trade markets at Liturgical Press, for seeing the promise of *Desert Banquet* and offering suggestions that have improved the manuscript. Stephanie Lancour, copy editor at Liturgical Press, has given invaluable and competent help in making hundreds of quotations and references as accurate as possible. Any omissions or errors are my own. And I am grateful for the creativity of Brother David Manahan, OSB, who designed the cover and caught the spirit of the book.

My wife Emily has helped me enter the desert, literally and figuratively, during the two years of reflection and writing that produced *Desert Banquet*. She and I have led courses and seminars on the desert elders together. Her support, patience, and helpful suggestions are woven into the book. I know there were times when she wanted to have equal time with Syncletica and John the Dwarf and give them "a word." Thank you, Emily!

Excerpts from the following works are used with permission:

RB 1980: The Rule of St. Benedict. Edited by Timothy Fry, OSB. Collegeville, MN: Liturgical Press. © 1981.

Dorotheos of Gaza: Discourses and Sayings. CS 33. Translated by Eric P. Wheeler. Kalamazoo, MI: Cistercian Publications. © 1977.

Evagrius Ponticus: The Praktikos & Chapters on Prayer. CS 4. Translated by John Eudes Bamberger, OCSO. Kalamazoo, MI: Cistercian Publications. © 1972.

The Lives of the Desert Fathers. CS 34. Translated by Norman Russell. Introduction by Benedicta Ward, SLG. Kalamazoo, MI: Cistercian Publications. © 1981.

The Sayings of the Desert Fathers: The Alphabetical Collection. CS 59. Translated by Benedicta Ward, SLG. Kalamazoo, MI: Cistercian Publications. © 1975.

The Syriac Fathers on Prayer and the Spiritual Life. CS 101. Translated by Sebastian Brock. Kalamazoo, MI: Cistercian Publications. © 1987.

The Way of Humility. MW 11. Translated by Andrew Louf, OCSO. Introduction by Lawrence S. Cunningham. Kalamazoo, MI: Cistercian Publications. © 2007.

The Lives of the Spiritual Mothers. Translated and compiled from the Greek of *The Great Synaxaristes of the Orthodox Church*. Buena Vista, CO: Holy Apostles Convent. © 1991. Used by permission.

John Cassian. *The Conferences*. Translated by Boniface Ramsey, OP. New York: Paulist Press. © 1997. Used by permission.

The Wisdom of the Desert Fathers. Fairacres Publication 48, ISBN-10 07283 0109; ISBN-13 978-0-7283-0034-7. © SLG Press, Convent of the Incarnation, Oxford, UK. Used by permission.

St. Macarius the Spiritbearer: Coptic Texts Relating to Saint Macarius the Great. Translated with introduction by Tim Vivian. Crestwood: St. Vladimir's Press. © 2004. Used by permission of St. Vladimir's Seminary Press.

The Life of Blessed Syncletica by Pseudo-Athanasius. Translated by Elizabeth Bryson Bongie. Toronto: Peregrina Publishing Co. © 1999. Used by permission.

Matericon: Instructions of Abba Isaiah to the Honorable Nun Theodora. Safford, AZ: Saint Paisius Serbian Orthodox Monastery. © 2001. Used by permission.

The following permissions were in process at the time of publication:

The Philokalia. Volume One. Translated and edited by G.E.H. Palmer, P. Sherrard and K. Ware. London: Faber & Faber. © 1979.

Writings from the Philokalia on Prayer of the Heart. Translated by E. Kadloubovsky and G. Palmer. London: Faber & Faber. © 1951.

INTRODUCTION

In 394 CE seven monks from Palestine visited men and women from various parts of the Roman Empire who had left conventional society to live in the desert. At Nitria, an isolated region west of the Nile River, they found a large community of hermits: *"We put in at Nitria, where we saw a great many anchorites. . . . Some applied themselves to contemplation, others to the active life. . . . Some of them invited us to a meal, others to learn about the virtues, and others to contemplation and the knowledge of God. Whatever ability each one had, he hastened to use it for our benefit. Indeed, how can one relate all their virtues, since one is totally unable to do them justice."*

These early Christians were seeking a closer relationship with God in the solitude of the desert. They had left what they experienced as futile aspects of society that distorted and abused human relationships, possessions, power, and virtues. They were not rejecting society or other human beings per se. Although they had various motives for fleeing to the desert, such as avoiding taxes, prosecution for crimes, arranged marriages, or obtaining spiritual "rewards" for living a holy life, most desired a life of prayer away from the distractions and unrestrained pleasures of the dominant society. They wanted to experience God's presence and find their way to heaven.

Instead of heaven, God gave them the desert. In their silence they experienced an intense struggle to overcome the influences of what they had left behind and move *toward* transformation of their lives. They learned that by opening themselves to God's presence they must also come to terms with their own lives. This self-knowledge was essential to letting go of control of the self they had created and make space for the transformation that would reveal their true self, in God.

Using This Book

"Ho, everyone who thirsts, come to the waters; and you that have no money, come, buy and eat! Come, buy wine and milk without money and without price. Why do you spend your money for that which is not bread, and your labor for that which does not satisfy? Listen carefully to me, and eat what is good, and delight yourselves in rich food" (Isa 55:1-2).

"[Jesus'] disciples replied, 'How can one feed these people with bread here in the desert?'" (Mark 8:4).

The Need for the Deserts of Our Lives

The wisdom of the desert elders is a banquet in a very unlikely place. Usually we do not look in barren wildernesses for rich food and drink that bring delight to body and soul. In the twenty-first century we are losing touch with the value of the wilderness as a mentor of the spirit. We prefer abundance to austerity and in the process are in danger of impoverishing our lives. Desert solitude and deep listening take us beyond our self-reliance and extend the boundaries of our experience and vision of ourselves and life itself. Is it possible for God to prepare a banquet in the deserts of our lives? It is worth the trip to discover for ourselves.

The Meaning of "Abba" and "Amma"

In Hebrew culture a name carries not only an identity but also the agency or active influence of the person named. To call a person by name is to enter into a relationship or continue an existing relationship. To address God by name is to acknowledge a genuine bond and recall God's prior actions that have formed and sustained that connection.

The Hebrew Scriptures use the term "father" twelve times to describe what God is like in both simile and metaphor. Female images are used as well. But Jesus' use of "Father" as a personal title was distinctive. Since he spoke Aramaic he used the word *abba*. "Ab" is the word a child uses for "father"; it is informal. In Middle Eastern cultures "abba" reflects an intimate, affectionate, respectful, and physical relationship. "Abb-a" may mean "my father" or "our father" depending on the context.

Among the thousands of people who fled to the desert and developed a variety of spiritual disciplines, some women and men emerged as wise *ammas* and *abbas*. The term abba or amma refers to these men and women whose lives, more than words, attracted disciples. They embodied an integration of love of God and neighbor. Their authority was acknowledged because the presence of Christ was tangible in their lives. Their wisdom evolved from their interior experience of God and the experiences of daily life. Like biological mothers and fathers, ammas and abbas formed intimate and lasting relationships with their disciples, and their teaching and influence have survived through thousands of sayings and personal narratives. *Desert Banquet* is a small sample of this rich tradition. Their wisdom is a banquet prepared from the crucible of experience.

The Desert Elders Are Faithful Guides, but We Must Do the Walking

Each month *Desert Banquet* emphasizes a unique aspect of the experiences of the desert fathers and mothers. These twelve themes will introduce readers to the diverse spiritual food that nourished and shaped their lives and personal transformation. Although these themes demonstrate common values and practices, there was no single rule of life except the common ingredient of the Great Commandment: love of God and neighbor. We can learn from this experience, but the abbas and ammas cannot live our lives for us. Every day of the year readers have the opportunity to reflect on a small part of this banquet and see what it brings forth in us. The value of this reflection is discernment, not imitation.

Keep This Desert Banquet in Context

Do not forget that the desert elders *chose* their austere life of prayer and never sought to impose their spiritual path on other people. Try to avoid looking at their way of life through the lenses of twenty-first-century social and religious values and practices. Look into these ancient lives and spiritual struggles for wisdom that transcends the centuries. Look beyond what may seem strange or offensive to you and discover a passion for life that will feed your body and soul.

Interiorized Monasticism

What can we learn from the desert elders that will assist us in our life with God? Each reader should answer this question for herself or himself. When monastic life is not romanticized or abused, it offers a manner of human life that is rich and authentic. Very few people are called to live in a monastic community, yet monastic life reminds us and inspires us to discover God's faithful presence in the lifestyle we have chosen. Monasticism is also an interior life of prayer and discipline that is the womb of our desires, words, actions, and relationships. The legacy of the desert mothers and fathers has a great deal to offer us as we discern how we may manifest an interiorized monasticism.

The desert tradition is a unique experience of Christian living. Its austere patterns of prayer and personal disciplines are freely chosen. Yet the minority of persons who follow Jesus Christ in this way manifest a dimension of human experience and spiritual maturity that can enrich, challenge, and inspire our lives today.

An Experiential Response

Although the purpose of this book is not didactic, readers are invited to discern specific ways that the lives and disciplines of the desert mothers and fathers may enrich their lives. Most contemporary persons do not have the time or personal calling to live as the desert elders lived. It would not be appropriate to mimic their lives. Yet walking through the desert for a whole year and tasting this banquet of wisdom may offer ideas and specific disciplines that will strengthen and guide your life with God. If you are attracted to a specific discipline, it will be wise to practice that discipline for a reasonable amount of time. This will help you discern its richness, even if difficult, and at the same time discover whether or not it is appropriate for you.

Travel Lightly

Desert Banquet is neither a study of the lives of the desert elders nor a "how-to" book on desert spirituality. It is an opportunity to reflect, one day at a time, on the wisdom of ancient and modern desert mothers and fathers. Enter the desert without expectations and let the Spirit speak.

Make the Journey Your Own

Desert Banquet is the result of the author's practice of *lectio divina* (holy reading) for a full year on the sayings of the desert elders. Each day I spent an hour in meditation on a different saying and writing a short reflection. I have spent twenty years studying this rich tradition. Although that research lies in the background, *Desert Banquet* is the child of silence and listening.

After you have read the saying* and reflection for each day, I invite you to spend some time in silence and continue to listen to the saying. Let it speak directly to you.

If you want to use the practice of *lectio divina*, a short method is described at the end of the book.

* The sayings are in italics throughout, and their sources can be found at the back of the book after the abbreviations.

JANUARY
Withdrawing from the World

As we have seen, thousands of men and women left the usual patterns of their relationships, activities, and responsibilities and fled to the deserts of Arabia, Egypt, Palestine, and Syria. Their fleeing was a rejection of the superficial values of late Roman society that emphasized materialism, unrestrained sexual pleasures, and self-serving power structures. Their aim was to *detach* themselves from a transient lifestyle that was committed to the surface of life and earthly resources that will pass away. At the same time their goal was to *attach* themselves to a life of prayer and offer themselves completely to God in solitude. They were not simply changing the venue of their lives. They were seeking transformation to a new way of life rooted in experience of God.

The Greek word for this kind of physical withdrawal is *anachoresis*. Many of the desert mothers and fathers were called *anchorites* because they lived in solitude, apart from conventional society and desert monastic communities.

Over the next three centuries the desert elders developed a disciplined lifestyle that included many forms of physical and mental prayer balanced with limited activities that earned money for food and alms for the poor. There was no predetermined plan for the forms of monastic life that evolved, but their common experiences of God led to three basic paths toward a vision of human life based on purity of heart, humility, and love of neighbor. Life in the desert and total dependence on God led to the formation of easily satisfied needs.

During this early phase of desert monasticism there were periods of intense persecution of Christians in the Roman Empire. "Red martyrdom" became the ultimate offering of a Christian's life to God. The lives of martyrs gave courage and inspiration to other Christians.

When the persecutions stopped and Christianity was accepted and later took root in the empire, people looked for an equivalent way to offer their lives to God. Leaving conventional society for a life of prayer in solitude became the new form called "white martyrdom."

Rejection of society's futility and "white martyrdom" form the primary context for January's focus on fleeing and withdrawal.

Always a Beginner

"Abba Poemen was asked for whom this saying is suitable, 'Do not be anxious about tomorrow.' (Matt. 6.34) The old man said, 'It is said for the man who is tempted and has not much strength, so that he should not be worried, saying to himself, "How long must I suffer this temptation?"' He should rather say every day to himself, 'Today.'"

We often carry into a new year the baggage of past expectations, failures, sinful behavior, and unfulfilled desires to embody love for others. "This year will be different and I will try harder!" Abba Poemen reminds us that life comes one day at a time. Although it is difficult to restrain from impatience with our failure to improve, he declares that God loves us even though we are unable to "fix" ourselves. Our anxiety can be transformed from a burden to an opportunity to turn toward God. If we begin each day with thanksgiving for life and a desire to rely on God's grace, our "suffering" will be replaced by the desire and trust that new life is possible.

Who Am I?

"While still living in the palace, Abba Arsenius prayed to God in these words, 'Lord, lead me in the way of salvation.' And a voice came saying to him, 'Arsenius, flee from men and you will be saved.'"

On the surface this answer to prayer seems like a denial of the goodness of human relationships and accomplishments. Arsenius was a famous fourth-century rhetorician, was tutor to the sons of Emperor

Theodosius I, and held a place of influence in the emperor's court. He dressed in the finest robes and was envied by many. Yet, like the rich young man who asked Jesus, "Good Teacher, what must I do to inherit eternal life?" (Mark 10:17), Arsenius sensed emptiness in the midst of the fullness of his ambitious life. His prayer articulated his helplessness in the midst of his great power. The response was an invitation to let go of attachment to the public benefits of his teaching and political influence. He could not yet see the cause of his anxiety. He must withdraw in order to find the path he desires.

JANUARY 3

From Speaking to Listening

"Having withdrawn to the solitary life he made the same prayer again and he heard a voice saying to him, 'Arsenius, flee, be silent, pray always, for these are the source of sinlessness.'"

Arsenius withdrew from the futility of a society and personal identity that scattered his soul. The centripetal force of living on the surface of life shredded his true identity and replaced it with toxic self-interest. The Greek word he used in his prayer for "salvation" literally means to experience abundant health. Simultaneously, he was fleeing from an intoxicating life and turning *toward* the healing he desired. The first step was *silence*. Solitude would create the space for a pattern of faithful *listening* to God and the centrifugal energy of the Spirit that would make transformation possible. The desert elders called this "resting in God." It is an environment of grace in which we place ourselves in God's hands in order to find ourselves and our reason for being alive. We cannot answer the questions, Who am I? and Why am I here? by ourselves.

JANUARY 4

Taking Time for Silence

"A brother questioned Abba Arsenius to hear a word of him and the old man said to him, 'Strive with all your might to bring your

interior activity into accord with God, and you will overcome exterior passions.'"

Arsenius had been told to flee and *be silent*. That must have been a tall order for a famous rhetorician. But during his years in solitude Arsenius learned that all speech and exterior activity have their origin in the heart, the psychic and spiritual center of every human being. Silence is the auditorium where the voice of God speaks to our hearts directly. This personal experience of God's Spirit enables us to bring our "interior activity into accord with God." We see God as God is and ourselves as God has created us to be. Silence is radical because it requires letting go of our efforts to control our lives. In that "death" we experience a fullness of life we cannot create for ourselves. Silence is the space where our unrestrained "passions" will be transformed into love of God and our neighbor.

Making Space for God

"[Abba Arsenius] also said, 'If we seek God, he will show himself to us, and if we keep him, he will remain close to us.'"

Arsenius was exhorted to flee, be silent, and *pray always*. His withdrawal from the busyness of palace life was not simply to "get away from it all." He was not exchanging one pattern of life for another. His deep longing was for *transformation*. This may seem odd for a person who had made it to the top. Twenty-first-century voices might say, "Get real, Arsenius!" That is precisely what he wanted, but he learned in his silence that it would not be one more achievement to add to his list. The path toward transformation depends on someone else. One of the earliest prayers of the desert elders is, "Bind my head and my heart in you, Holy One, and may I remain in your company this day." Each step toward reality is taken, one at a time, in the constant presence of God and relies on that relationship for everything.

Shedding Self-Reliance

"One day Abba Arsenius consulted an old Egyptian monk about his own thoughts. Someone noticed this and said to him, 'Abba Arsenius, how is it that you, with such a good Latin and Greek education, ask this peasant about your thoughts?' He replied, 'I have indeed been taught Latin and Greek, but I do not know even the alphabet of this peasant.'"

How long did it take for Arsenius to let go of the heavy burden of being in charge of his life and gain the freedom to sit at the feet of a peasant? He left the emperor's palace in 394 CE and died in his remote desert hermitage in 449. Toward the end of those fifty-five years, his companions in the desert gave a brief glimpse of how difficult it must have been: *"The old man used to say to himself: 'Arsenius, why have you left the world? I have often repented of having spoken, but never of having been silent.'"* The sacrifices of silence and listening are openings to newness of life. In our society it is often difficult to find silence or to listen. Many voices compete for our attention and in this mixture of words it is possible to miss what we may need to hear the most. Which voices should we trust? We tend to rely on our own experience and knowledge, yet, there are many twenty-first-century peasants speaking today. Can we be silent and listen?

Fleeing Is Not Trading Places

"It was revealed to Abba Anthony in his desert that there was one who was his equal in the city. He was a doctor by profession and whatever he had beyond his needs he gave to the poor, and every day he sang the Sanctus with the angels."

The desert mothers and fathers left the futility of conventional society in order to find solitude and seek God in the desert. Was this simply frustration with the people and places where they lived? Were they exchanging a flawed human existence for a more perfect spiritual way of life? For some, the answer was yes. But the majority learned that a change of venue, by itself, did not change their lives. Antony the Great was born in central Egypt and withdrew to the desert over one hundred years before Arsenius left Constantinople. His life of intense and austere solitude and prayer inspired many followers. Yet, his desert hermitage was not an end in itself because the place needing change was within him. The boundaries of God's grace have no limits. Where are our hermitages today?

Desire for Solitude Is Not Rejection of the World

"It was said of Abba John the Dwarf, that one day he said to his elder brother, 'I should like to be free of all care, like the angels, who do not work, but ceaselessly offer worship to God.' So he took off his cloak and went away into the desert. After a week he came back to his brother. When he knocked on the door, he heard his brother say, before he opened it, 'Who are you?' He said, 'I am John, your brother.' But he replied, 'John has become an angel, and henceforth he is no longer among men.' Then the other begged him, saying, 'It is I.' However, his brother did not let him in, but left him there in distress until morning. Then, opening the door, he said to him, 'You are a man and you must once again work in order to eat.' Then John made a prostration before him, saying, 'Forgive me.'"

Humor is often the chalice of wisdom we prefer not to drink. Singing with the angels may sound great, but our song is sung closer to home. Eventually, John the Dwarf's life of solitude prepared him to mentor novice monks in the hard work of caring for other people. In the Christian tradition there has always been a healthy tension between contemplation and action. Our desire for intimacy with God is a natural part of our lives and the gospels narrate Jesus' pattern of going off to pray alone early in the morning and in the evening. This was a constant pattern in his life of prayer. So it is easy to understand why John the Dwarf, like all "newcomers" to contemplative prayer, wanted to spend all his time in the presence of God and the angels. What he had not learned is that in Jesus' life intimacy with God was the womb that gave birth to his love of neighbor and his active engagement in the needs of the world. Prayer and action are soul mates.

People Are Not the Problem

"The same monk [Arsenius] used to say that there was a certain old man who had a good disciple. Through narrowmindedness he drove him outside with his sheepskin. The brother remained sitting outside. When the old man opened the door, he found him sitting, and he repented, saying, 'O Father, the humility of your patience has overcome my narrowmindedness. Come inside and from now on you are the old man and the father, and I am the younger and the disciple.'"

The easiest response to frustration with difficulties in human relationships and the superficialities of society is to "get away from it all." One of the hardest lessons the desert elders learned when they fled to the desert was that they could not flee from themselves. They left society and their possessions behind, yet arrived with lots of "old baggage." The more they encountered God without distractions, the more they learned about themselves and the need to unpack their own pride and faults. Transparent self-knowledge is difficult to embrace, but it leads toward humble patience. The desert elders sought heaven, but God gave them the desert's solitude; they would have to wait for heaven. In that solitude they had to come to terms with their "baggage" because as long as it remained it would stand in the way of what they truly desired. Knowing ourselves is the first step to embracing God.

Fleeing Leads to Surprising Places

"The old man was asked, 'What is the good of the fasts and watchings which a man imposes on himself?' and he replied, 'They make the soul humble. For it is written, "Consider my affliction and my trouble, and forgive all my sins." (Ps. 25.18) So if the soul gives itself all this hardship, God will have mercy on it.'"

Many people fled to the desert to escape taxes or punishment for crimes. Some found more than safety and anonymity. Moses the Robber did not have to flee *to* the desert. He lived there already, wandering in the vicinity of monastic sites stealing and committing murder.

Late in life he became a monk and a disciple of Isidore the Priest, an abba who "specialized" in difficult novices. Moses had much to leave behind and regret. These painful memories afflicted him so much he placed his helplessness to resolve them within a pattern of austere fasting and solitary nights of prayer. In this patient dependence on God his soul was healed and forgiven. He had fled into grace. Patience is not a popular virtue in the twenty-first century. We prefer rapid and efficient progress. What we miss in our haste is the opportunity for inner growth guided by God's grace.

The Desert Does Not Yield Its Treasure Easily

Amma Syncletica said, *"My children, all of us—male and female— know about being saved, but through our own negligence we stray away from salvation. First of all we must observe the precepts known through the grace of the Lord, and these are: 'You shall love the Lord your God with all your soul . . . and your neighbor as yourself' [Matt 22:37 and 39]. Whatever people say by the grace of the Spirit that is useful, therefore, springs from love and ends in it. Salvation, then, is exactly this—the two-fold love of God and of our neighbor. . . . Well, what do we need for the present moment? Obviously, austere asceticism and pure prayer."*

Syncletica's early life in the fourth century was lived in the shadow of Alexandria's esteemed Christian catechetical school. But in her prayer she learned that "useful" knowledge springs from experience of God. She reminds us that the disciplines of our life of prayer lead us from "our own negligence" toward a *desire* for love of God and our neighbor. We all have the freedom to "stray away from salvation." In the midst of daily distractions and temptations Syncletica advises us to focus on "austere asceticism and pure prayer." In this context "austere asceticism" means a freely chosen pattern of prayer and meditation on Scripture that will help us be good stewards of our souls. This will keep us from straying and preserve our desire for love.

Fleeing Is Not an End in Itself

"Amma Syncletica said, 'There are many who live in the mountains and behave as if they were in the town, and they are wasting their time. It is possible to be a solitary in one's mind while living in a crowd, and it is possible for one who is a solitary to live in the crowd of his own thoughts.'"

Beginning in the late third century thousands of men and women fled to the deserts of Arabia, Egypt, Palestine, and Syria. They were looking for a path leading directly to heaven but soon realized they must cope with the limitations of the desert. Stripped of conventional possessions, sources of food and water, and income, they developed an austere way of life, depending totally on God. Some lived as hermits and others in small or larger groups. There were varying degrees of austerity and some monks competed with others, taking pride in their degree of silence, solitude, and prayer. It was difficult to let go of attachment to these ascetic virtues and the path to heaven itself. The desert elders learned that when silence, prayer, and meditation become ends in themselves, they stand in the way of transformation. God calls us to faithfulness, not perfection.

Fleeing Is Not a Quick Fix

"Amma Syncletica said, 'In the beginning there are a great many battles and a good deal of suffering for those who are advancing towards God and afterwards, ineffable joy. It is like those who wish to light a fire; at first they are choked by the smoke and cry, and by this means obtain what they seek (as it is said: "Our God is a consuming fire" [Heb 12.24]): so we also must kindle the divine fire in ourselves through tears and hard work.'"

The desert mothers and fathers went to the desert seeking a life with God that was free from the distractions of conventional society. Syncletica began her withdrawal as a young woman by remaining in a room in her home for disciplined prayer. After her parents died, she gave the family's wealth to the poor and withdrew with her blind sister to a family tomb near the outskirts of the city of Alexandria to "kindle the divine fire." Soon other women joined her and others came to listen and learn from Syncletica's experience. Thus began a lifelong commitment to "advancing towards God." The "ineffable joy" did not come right away! It would take time. In our age of instant results we should not overlook the need for tears and hard work.

Having Second Thoughts

Abba Antony said, *"Having therefore made a beginning, and set out on the way to virtue, let us press forward to what lies ahead. And let none turn back as Lot's wife did, especially since the Lord said, 'No one who puts his hand to the plow and turns back is fit for the Kingdom of heaven.' Now 'turning back' is nothing except feeling regret and once more thinking about things of the world. But do not be afraid to hear about virtue, and do not be a stranger to the term. For it is not distant from us, nor does it stand external to us, but its realization lies within us, and the task is easy if only we shall will it."*

Antony struggled to let go of his attachment to the "things of the world" that interfered with his life with God. Exhausted from regrets, thoughts, temptations, and the discipline required for listening to God, "turning back" was an ever-present option. Often, when the disciplines of our life of prayer do not seem to be "working" or are taking too much time away from "practical things," we are tempted to return to "the way things were." In our frustration about lack of progress we can lose the trust we need to continue the journey. The "way to virtue" is a spiritual path that looks *forward* and must be chosen each new day. It "lies within us" and is always available whether we are hermits or not.

The Integrity of Conversations

"It was said of Abba Agathon that for three years he lived with a stone in his mouth, until he had learnt to keep silence."

Abba Agathon must have been quite a talker. Perhaps he had mastered the art of speaking and listening simultaneously. But his three-year discipline was not a repudiation of conversation. It was a statement about responsible use of words and the importance of silence. Idle speech can be harmful: *"It was said of Abba Ammoes that when he went to church, he did not allow his disciple to walk beside him but only at a certain distance; and if the latter came to ask him about his thoughts, he would move away from him as soon as he had replied, saying to him, 'It is for fear that, after edifying words, irrelevant conversation should slip in, that I do not keep you with me.'"*

Ammoes was not being rude. He knew that words, balanced with silence, have a powerful influence in a person's spiritual development. He wanted to reveal truth to his disciple by his actions as well as his speech.

JANUARY 16

The Gift of Food

Amma Syncletica said, *"Do not let yourself be seduced by the delights of the riches of the world, as though they contained something useful on account of vain pleasure. Worldly people esteem the culinary art, but you, through fasting and thanks to cheap food, go beyond their abundance of food. It is written: 'He who is sated loathes honey.' (Prov. 27.7) Do not fill yourself with bread and you will not desire wine."*

Syncletica was no prude, yet she knew the allure of Roman banquets in the city of Alexandria. Overabundance of expensive food among the wealthy was a popular source of esteem and lavish delight. But it was an empty abundance that hid the necessity of food under the veneer of vain pleasure. Syncletica reminds her disciples in the desert and in the city that moderation balances the need for food and a person's hunger for God. Neither is an end in itself. She knew that a person can be seduced to transform a basic need into unrestrained and vain pleasure. *"Abba Poemen heard of someone who had gone all week without eating and then had lost his temper. The old man said, 'He could do without food for six days, but he could not cast out anger.'"*

When Enough Is Enough

"They said of Abba Megethius, that if he left his cell and it occurred to him to leave the place where he was living he would go without returning to his cell. He owned nothing in this world, except a knife with which he cut reeds and every day he made three small baskets, which was all he needed for his food."

Abba Megethius had everything he needed for the life he had chosen. The wisdom of his poverty was that he had easily satisfied needs. He was a wandering desert abba and carried no more than his knife, some bread and water, and enough reeds to make three baskets a day. The baskets provided income for his food and alms for the poor. That is all he needed to be faithful to the work of God. His needs were integrated with the vocation he had chosen. Anything more would have been a distraction. At the same time, Megethius would never have claimed that his specific manner of life is a model for everyone. Every person must decide how to balance personal needs with the work of God they have chosen.

Stewardship of Sexuality

Amma Syncletica said, *"When moreover, we do confine ourselves to our houses, not even there should we be careless, but should maintain our vigilance. . . . The more we secure ourselves in chastity, the more we are plied with galling thoughts. . . . Even for women who live as solitaries (the Enemy) conjures up handsome faces and old relationships. . . . Giving your assent to these fantasies, moreover, is equivalent to sexual impurity in the world."*

The desert elders remained normal men and women when they withdrew to the desert, although they left behind their conventional responsibilities in society and personal relationships, including sexual relationships. In the desert their emotional and physical sexual urges and psychological gender identities did not cease. Whether they had been sexually active or chaste in their prior relationships, memories of old liaisons or temptations lingered and new temptations or fantasies

appeared. Loneliness or regrets created mental temptations and pro-
longed interior sexual impurity. Yet celibacy was an essential part of
their single-minded gift of self to God and galling thoughts distracted
them from this calling. Although there are many more sayings by male
abbas that refer to their need to avoid women, Syncletica is clear that
"handsome faces" were a temptation for ammas as well. Avoidance of
sexual relationships was freely chosen by the desert elders. Whether
or not a person is celibate, stewardship of sexual relationships, in fact
all relationships, is a fundamental responsibility.

JANUARY 19

Honoring the Body

*"Abba Gerontius of Petra said that many, tempted by the pleasures
of the body, commit fornication, not in their body but in their spirit,
and while preserving their bodily virginity, commit prostitution in
their soul. 'Thus it is good, my well-beloved, to do that which is written, and for each one to guard his own heart with all possible care.'"*

Seeking God in the desert did not include rejecting one's body and its
natural impulses. Some elders and early Christian theologians *did* view
human sexual activity as an evil aspect of human life. They advocated
abstinence as a higher form of prayerful living. Syncletica and Gerontius offered a different point of view based on their choice of monastic
chastity in a society where there were no restraints in the passionate
enjoyment of sexual pleasures. The desert elders' commitment to "bodily
virginity" affirmed that fornication, even "in their spirit," would blaspheme the sanctity of offering their bodies and souls to God in prayer. In
our relationships, too, we should honor the body "with all possible care."

JANUARY 20

When Crowds Scatter Our Souls

Abba Evagrius said, *"Restrain yourself from affection towards
many people, for fear lest your spirit be distracted, so that your interior peace may not be disturbed."*

Many of the desert elders were fleeing from the noise of Roman society. The noise of constant relationships, crowds, activities, and conversations scattered one's spirit and replaced its center with endless mind chatter. Abba Evagrius was a gifted scholar whose prayer was influenced by relationships and conversations with other abbas. He shared this wisdom in a remarkable book that has influenced Christian life and monastic prayer. Evagrius learned that the "noises" of life influence our life of prayer. He is advocating "restraint," not prohibition. Interior peace is not self-serving. It is the font of our words and actions and must be cared for. *"Snow can never emit flame. . . . A thorn bush can never produce a fig. Just so, your heart can never be free from oppressive thoughts, words, and actions until it has been purified internally. . . . Watch your heart always."*

Fleeing from Attachment

Abba Moses said, *"The monk must die to everything before leaving the body, in order not to harm anyone."*

Jesus of Nazareth was the exemplar for the desert elders. "For those who want to save their life will lose it, and those who lose their life for my sake will find it" (Matt 16:25). Possessions, food, speech, human sexuality, influence, passion for life, and seeking a life of prayer are all gifts. But they are not ends in themselves. It was difficult for monks to let go of personal attachment to these aspects of their lives and to their control of the outcome of life itself. Abba Moses said to Abba Poemen, *"If a man's deeds are not in harmony with his prayer, he labours in vain. The brother said, 'What is harmony between practice and prayer?' The old man said, 'We should no longer do those things against which we pray. For when a man gives up his own will, then God is reconciled with him and accepts his prayers.' The brother asked, 'In all the affliction which the monk gives himself, what helps him?' The old man said, 'It is written, "God is our refuge and strength . . ."' (Ps. 46.1)"*

Fleeing Is Not Avoidance of Life

"A brother said to Abba Anthony, 'Pray for me.' The old man said to him, 'I will have no mercy upon you, nor will God have any, if you yourself do not make an effort and if you do not pray to God.'"

On the surface Antony's response seems like a slap in the face. A fellow monk asked for help and is refused. But wait. Antony discerned that the brother was asking for an alternative to the self-knowledge and hard work to resolve his problem. He wanted a quick fix. Let God do it! Or at least Abba Antony. Antony does not abandon the monk but places his response in the context of his brother's willingness "to make an effort." Seeking God never means avoiding life's difficulties and challenges. *"When . . . Anthony lived in the desert he was beset by* accidie *[a lack of spirit], and attacked by many sinful thoughts. He said to God, 'Lord, I want to be saved . . . what shall I do in my affliction?' . . . Anthony saw a man like himself sitting at his work, getting up from his work to pray, then sitting down . . . then getting up again to pray. . . . He heard the angel saying to him, 'Do this and you will be saved.'"*

Fleeing Is Not Always Leaving Home

"Two Fathers asked God to reveal to them how far they had advanced. A voice came which said, 'In a certain village in Egypt there is a man called Eucharistus and his wife who is called Mary. You have not yet reached their degree of virtue.'"

The men and women who fled the futility of Roman society were not all hermits, anchorites, or living in monastic communities in the desert. Many, perhaps the majority, remained in or near their villages, towns, or cities. Like the desert elders, their single-minded intent was to seek God and love their neighbors. Their "fleeing" was from the conventional norms of family life, labor, sexual activity, and material possessions. Sometimes they sought solitude just outside their village. People valued their presence, prayer, and guidance. Eucharistus and Mary raised sheep and divided the profit in thirds among the poor, hospitality, and their own needs. During the day they wore ordinary clothes and hair shirts at night. They were celibate and slept separately. They served God where they were.

Fleeing Is Not Convenient

"A brother said to Abba Poemen, 'I want to go to the monastery, and dwell there.' The old man said to him, 'If you want to go to the monastery, you must be careful about every encounter and everything you do, or you will not be able to do the work of the monastery; for you will not have the right even to drink a single cup there.'"

Abba Poemen's advice does not sound welcoming, yet it is pastoral and practical. It is easy to romanticize the lives of the desert elders. They fled one form of life to embrace another, but their goal was not to "have it all." Although their desire for solitude was personal, even hermits did not relinquish their responsibilities for others. *"Abba Agathon said, 'If I could meet a leper, give him my body and take his, I should be very happy.'"* Agathon was willing to radically change his body and life of prayer for the sake of love. A brother said to Abba Poemen, *"'I have found a place where peace is not disturbed by the brethren; do you advise me to live there?' The old man said to him, 'The place for you is where you will not harm your brother.'"*

Fleeing Is an Interior Experience

"Abba Ammoun of Rhaithou came to Clysma one day to meet Abba Sisoes. Seeing that Abba Sisoes was grieved because he had left the desert, Abba Ammoun said to him, 'Abba, why grieve about it? What would you do in the desert, now you are so old?' The old man pondered this sorrowfully and said to him, 'What are you saying to me, Ammoun? Was not the mere liberty of my soul enough for me in the desert?'"

Sisoes's love for the desert was not affection for the desert itself but what the desert made possible. His flight to the desert became the venue for the liberation of his soul. In the desert Sisoes discovered another world: the world of God's presence. This new world freed him from the narrow world created by self-sufficiency and anxiety. Freed from peripheral concerns, Sisoes discovered himself and what it means to be human. It was hard to leave the place where such a gift had been given. His flight to the desert made his second "fleeing" possible. The desert and each monk's cell formed the physical "place" where, with God's grace, the "liberty of the soul" transformed the monk's life. Although Sisoes was sad to leave the desert, he did not leave what happened in his cell.

JANUARY 26

Fleeing Sheds New Light on Life

"When a person turns to what is good and abstains from evil and devotes himself to learning about himself and regrets the things he has done in times of careless indifference and seeks God with his whole soul, then the good God makes him sorrowful for what he has done."

Macarius the Great was an Egyptian camel driver who traded niter in the vicinity of the remote desert of Scetis southeast of Alexandria. He became a monk, influenced by Antony the hermit, settled in Scetis, and attracted many disciples. Macarius shared his personal experience of *repentance* as a fivefold action. He *turned* "to what is good," he *abstained* from the malign influences of his former life, he was devoted to *"learning about himself,"* and he *sought God* "with his whole soul." Finally he accepted the gift of *tears*, genuine sorrow for his "careless indifference." Macarius shows that *fleeing* casts new light on our lives, exposing what is false and contrary to goodness. This enlightenment creates a genuine desire for God and transformation.

Fleeing Is a Venue for Self-Discipline

"Many monks at the present time have been unable to persevere in quiet because they could not overcome their self-will. For this reason they live among men all the time, since they are unable to despise themselves and flee from the company of men, or to engage in battle. Thus they abandon quiet, and remain in the company of their neighbors, receiving their comfort thereby, all their lives."

Friends and companionship are spiritual gifts, in any setting. Abba Ammonas is writing to monks who have *chosen* an austere solitary life of prayer and are "unable to persevere in quiet" because they cannot overcome their need for constant companions. Self-discipline is the issue and not the goodness of friendship. Despising one's self, in this context, is recognizing that you cannot choose solitude and company of your neighbors at the same time. If you choose the comfort of companionship, you "abandon quiet." Once chosen, fleeing to quiet, regardless of duration, is a worthy "battle." Whether a monk is called to solitary or communal life, each requires a unique self-discipline. The choice will be difficult to maintain because the monk cannot "have it both ways." Ammonas points to the necessity of honest discernment of a person's vocation.

A Matter of Life and Death

Abba Antony said, *"Always have the fear of God before your eyes. Remember him who gives death and life. Hate the world and all that is in it. Hate all peace that comes from the flesh. Renounce this life, so that you may be alive to God. Remember what you have promised God, for it will be required of you on the day of judgement. Suffer hunger, thirst, nakedness, be watchful and sorrowful; weep, and groan in your heart; test yourselves, to see if you are worthy of God; despise the flesh, so that you may preserve your souls."*

There is nothing romantic about Antony's understanding of the need to flee. It requires "remembering" God as the source of life and that peace is not a commodity created and deployed by human power.

In Middle Eastern culture "hate" means "to turn away from." Antony's fleeing led him to a life of total dependence on God. His advice to "renounce this life" mirrors Jesus' exhortation to "die to self" and let go of attachment to things that will not last. Hunger, thirst, and nakedness taught him to have easily satisfied needs for the journey. Sorrow for his reliance on what could never feed his heart led him to renounce what endangered his soul's life. At the heart of this journey is self-knowledge. Knowing who we are is the first step toward transformation.

JANUARY 29

Fleeing to One's Self

"A sensible man who has prepared himself to be freed at the coming of Jesus knows himself in his spiritual essence, for he who knows himself also knows the dispensations of his Creator and what he does for his creatures."

Abba Antony's fleeing also led him to confront two questions: Who am I? and Why am I here? He learned that the human journey is lived simultaneously in multiple dimensions, all created by God. The easily visible dimensions are nature, human beings, and human societies. They are transient and limited. There is another dimension called "spiritual essence." God has made all things to be congruent with their original nature and God's "dispensations" or visitations enable us to discern these true natures. Antony's decades of silence prepared him to discover and experience his true self, his "spiritual essence" that is not transient. This self-knowledge freed him to see what is so often hidden within the surface of life and discover God's presence in all persons and things.

JANUARY 30

Why Bother?

"Three Fathers used to go and visit blessed Anthony every year and two of them used to discuss their thoughts and the salvation of their souls with him, but the third always remained silent and did

not ask him anything. After a long time, Abba Anthony said to him, 'You often come here to see me, but you never ask me anything,' and the other replied, 'It is enough for me to see you, Father.'"

"Abba Psenthaisius, Abba Surus and Abba Psoius used to agree in saying this, 'Whenever we listened to the words of our Father, Abba Pachomius, we were greatly helped and spurred on with zeal for good works; we saw how, even when he kept silence, he taught us by his actions. . . . We thought that sinners could not live devoutly, because they had been so created. But now we see the goodness of God manifested in our father, for see, he is of pagan origin and he has become devout; he has put on all the commandments of God. Thus even we also can follow him and become equal to the saints whom he himself has followed.'"

The "destination" of withdrawal to the desert is to make God tangible in our lives. What more can be said?

Fleeing Is Only the Beginning

"It happened that when Arsenius was sitting in his cell that he was harassed by demons. His servants, on their return, stood outside his cell and heard him praying to God in these words, 'O God, do not leave me. I have done nothing good in your sight, but according to your goodness, let me now make a beginning of good.'"

Arsenius did not have an inferiority complex. He realized that his desire for "goodness" was not simply a matter of personal will. He could not be the source of his own goodness. Arsenius probably began his withdrawal from life in the palace of Theodosius I by seeking "the solitary life" near Constantinople. It was his first step toward "the way of salvation." But it must have been too close to the abundance and relationships that stood in the way of "the beginning of good." Arsenius's act of withdrawal, by itself, could not change his life. "We are always beginners" acknowledges that we are not in control. The fleeing, solitude, and silence, by themselves, were not enough. God's presence was what Arsenius desired: "O God, do not leave me." This awareness expands the horizon of the path that leads toward transformation.

FEBRUARY

The Cell

Last month our focus was on *fleeing* to the desert. The desert is any place we find solitude from what distracts us from our life with God. We withdraw *from* what is futile and toxic and move *toward* the self-knowledge and prayerful discipline that opens our life to God's grace-filled transformation. The fleeing is a constant and dynamic aspect of our lives that will continue until the day we die. We are always a beginner.

In February we will focus on the *place* of transformation. The symbol and literal location of this place is *the cell*. It is the inner and exterior location where we open ourselves to *another world*. This world is a place of *struggle* between our attachment to aspects of life that are transient or futile and our longing for transformation. The cell is where we respond to Jesus' exhortation to "die to self" in order to find ourselves.

The desert elders placed great emphasis on the need to remain in the cell and be faithful to the austere spiritual disciplines the cell made possible. They would be the first to say that their disciplines are not for everyone. Some readers will find them unrealistic or unnatural. Try to remain open to what the cell and the disciplines embody and what you can learn from them. It is important for each reader to find his or her own cell and spiritual practice. The desert elders cannot live our lives for us, nor should we try to impose their experience on our lives. But they can offer guidance and accompany us as we discern our own forms of fleeing and cell.

Keep in mind that the cell is both an *inward* and *external* reality. We carry the environment of God's presence within us wherever we go. This inward cell is the "closet" Jesus exhorts us to enter as we pray.

It is the desert within. At the same time, we must choose a physical location, with as few distractions as possible, to incarnate the inner closet. It is the geographic desert.

The desert elders had a variety of cells. Some were in caves or included a cave with an outer structure. Others were tombs, abandoned forts, or freestanding hand-built dwellings. They used materials at hand that included rock, clay, and wood. Some monks in towns or cities used rooms in homes designated as cells. Regardless of location, the cell was always a place where the monk encountered God.

The Cell as Mentor

"A brother came to Scetis to visit Abba Moses and asked him for a word. The old man said to him, 'Go, sit in your cell, and your cell will teach you everything.'"

We are so afraid of missing something. Our cell phones, e-mail, iPods, BlackBerries, and pagers keep us always accessible. We crave entertainment and constant activity. Everywhere we go we find music, talking, and opportunities for information and visual stimulation. This is the age of information. We do not want life to be empty or to miss opportunities. There is nothing wrong with communication, conversation, entertainment, and opportunities for education and employment. At the same time it is possible to fill our lives with so many things that we empty life of its richness. In the midst of so much noise we may lose our ability to listen to each other and to life itself. We don't need experts to help us. We need some quiet and time to listen. Where is your cell? Find a place where you can be still and wait for wisdom.

Balancing Action with Waiting

"[Abba Anthony] said, 'Just as fish die if they stay too long out of water, so the monks who loiter outside their cells or pass the time with men of the world lose the intensity of inner peace. So like a fish

going towards the sea, we must hurry to reach our cell, for fear that if we delay outside we will lose our interior watchfulness.'"

Modern society is a place where "results rule." Diets, fitness, winning, positive financial returns, success in the workplace, and recreation consume our energies. No one will deny that these can be legitimate goals. But when they become sources of anxiety and physical and mental exhaustion, we "lose the intensity of inner peace." Then it is difficult for our souls to catch up with our minds and bodies. When multitasking blinds us to the spiritual dimension of our lives, we cease to be whole persons. Like fish "too long out of water" we can "hurry to reach our cell," wherever it is, and take time for "interior watchfulness." Waiting and looking are in danger of becoming lost arts in today's society. Although conventional wisdom says "there is no more time in the day," Antony exhorts us to "hurry to reach our cell."

FEBRUARY 3

Where Is Our Cell?

"One day Abba Daniel and Abba Ammoes went on a journey together. Abba Ammoes said, 'When shall we, too, settle down, in a cell, Father?' Abba Daniel replied, 'Who shall separate us henceforth from God? God is in the cell, and, on the other hand, he is outside also.'"

Daniel was a disciple of Abba Arsenius and was present at his death in 449 CE. Even though his abba, Arsenius, spent most of his time in his cell in an austere discipline of prayer, it is clear Daniel learned from his mentor that the cell is not an end in itself. The cell, indeed, is a place to "settle down" in God's presence with specific intention. But Ammoes expresses frustration about being on the move when he really wants to be in his cell. Daniel replies that God will be found in both places. The value of the cell, however, is that the experience of God in the cell, through watchfulness, will help us recognize God's presence outside the cell. We should not rely on some spiritual GPS to find God. Our own cell will give us firsthand experience.

What Happens in the Cell?

"A brother asked Abba Rufus, 'What is interior peace, and what use is it?' The old man said, 'Interior peace means sitting in one's cell with fear and knowledge of God, holding far off the remembrance of wrongs suffered and pride of spirit. Such interior peace brings forth all the virtues, preserves the monk from the burning darts of the enemy, and does not allow him to be wounded by them. Yes, brother, acquire it. Keep in mind your future death, remembering that you do not know at what hour the thief will come. Likewise be watchful over your soul.'"

Rufus describes the cell to his novice. First, the cell is a place of "interior peace" because it is a venue for "knowledge" or direct experience of God. Second, the cell is a place where a person can let go of a basic "attitude problem" that confuses one's self with God. To "fear" God is to be aware of the necessary difference between God and one's self. It is the realization that we are not the center of the universe and frees us from "pride of spirit" that prevents the flow of virtues within us. The cell is a place that holds self-knowledge and direct experience of God; it is both a place and what happens to a person in the place. As Abba Rufus describes, the "interior peace" within the cell "brings forth all the virtues." In other words, a person becomes what happens in the cell.

A Place of Struggle

"A brother asked Abba Rufus, 'What is interior peace, and what use is it?' The old man said, 'Interior peace means sitting in one's cell with fear and knowledge of God, holding far off the remembrance of wrongs suffered and pride of spirit. Such interior peace brings forth all the virtues, preserves the monk from the burning darts of the enemy, and does not allow him to be wounded by them. Yes, brother, acquire it. Keep in mind your future death, remembering that you do not know at what hour the thief will come. Likewise be watchful over your soul.'"

This saying is worth some more attention. The cell is a place of silence and listening. Although we usually think of prayer as directed toward God or responses from God, Rufus reminds us that "interior peace" is also the result of candid self-knowledge. *We* are present in the cell as well as God, and the deep listening reveals our desire to dwell on both the wounds of our lives and our self-satisfaction. These "burning darts" impede the movement of our souls toward God's grace. Unless these darts are released to God's grace through repentance, turning toward God, they will become a barrier to experience of God and personal transformation.

A Place to Value Life

"A brother asked Abba Rufus, 'What is interior peace, and what use is it?' The old man said, 'Interior peace means sitting in one's cell with fear and knowledge of God, holding far off the remembrance of wrongs suffered and pride of spirit. Such interior peace brings forth all the virtues, preserves the monk from the burning darts of the enemy, and does not allow him to be wounded by them. Yes, brother, acquire it. Keep in mind your future death, remembering that you do not know at what hour the thief will come. Likewise be watchful over your soul.'"

In our age that values youthfulness and sublimates the aging process, Rufus's comment about death seems off-the-wall. Is he morbid? Is he fatalistic? The wisdom of his exhortation to "keep in mind your future death" lies in the second part of his statement. If we are aware of our mortality, we will value the gift and sanctity of life, regardless of its longevity. Accepting the reality of death frees us from the desire to control every waking hour and "make the best of it." Interior peace transcends time. In our fast-paced society it is possible to take the health of our soul, our inner life, for granted or, even worse, to forget about it. Being aware of our mortality will help us be good stewards of our soul.

A Place of Resurrection

Amma Alexandra said, *"From early morn to the ninth hour I pray hour by hour, spinning the flax the while. During the remaining hours I meditate on the holy patriarchs and prophets and apostles and martyrs. And having eaten my bread I remain in patience for the other hours, waiting for my end with cheerful hope."*

Alexandra gives a vivid picture of life in her cell and demonstrates the integration of her work and her prayer. Spinning flax is more than linen thread; a mundane task of a solitary woman living in a tomb becomes a prayerful liturgy. Labor, too, is a venue for grace and self-offering. In her spare time she directs her thoughts away from herself toward God's presence in the example and wisdom of other faith-filled women and men. Her cell is also a workshop for spiritual formation and, when her work is done, becomes a place for patient "waiting for my end with cheerful hope." Her labor, meditation, and waiting bring the realm of eternity into time and space so that contemplation of her death is emptied of fear.

Balancing Solitude and Community

Theodore of Pherme said, *"The man who has learnt the sweetness of the cell flees from his neighbor but not as though he despised him."*

The cell is not an escape from life or other people. Modern society conditions us to remain connected with other people all the time. Cell phones, text messaging, and e-mail are great innovations in communication, but being in constant "touch" with others can deprive us from being in touch with ourselves. The "sweetness of the cell" is intimacy with the One who loves us unconditionally. We can be "who we are" without the expectations or judgments placed on us by others or ourselves. Seeing ourselves as God sees us helps us see others as God sees them. Amma Sarah prayed often that *"my heart may be pure towards all"* and Abba Poemen said, *"Teach your mouth to say that which you have in your heart."* The "sweetness of the cell" is the source of civility, honest dialogue, and valuing our neighbors for themselves and not simply for our benefit. They are with us in the cell.

Learning to Depend on God

Abba John the Dwarf said, *"I am like a man sitting under a great tree, who sees wild beasts and snakes coming against him in great numbers. When he cannot withstand them any longer, he runs to climb the tree and is saved. It is just the same with me; I sit in my cell and I am aware of evil thoughts coming against me, and when I have no more strength against them, I take refuge in God by prayer and I am saved from the enemy."*

Everyone has a dark side. Abba John was honest enough to realize he was capable of evil. In his cell "wild beasts and snakes" in the form of thoughts, unrestrained passions, and possibilities for behavior that could harm others and distract him from seeking God were so great that he had "no more strength against them." When he had one foot across the threshold into sinful behavior, his cell became a tree of life whose branches offered a place where he could "take refuge in God by prayer." Regardless of its location, the cell is a constant reminder of our need to depend on God when we sense the presence of darkness. The key is to *want* to ask God for help and not rely on ourselves.

A Place of Vision

Abba John the Dwarf said, *"I am like a man sitting under a great tree, who sees wild beasts and snakes coming against him in great numbers. When he cannot withstand them any longer, he runs to climb the tree and is saved. It is just the same with me; I sit in my cell and I am aware of evil thoughts coming against me, and when I have no more strength against them, I take refuge in God by prayer and I am saved from the enemy."*

John's image of sitting *under* the tree and then *climbing the tree* is rich. In his cell he is like a man sitting under a tree. He is on the same plane as the wild beasts and snakes that personify his strong temptations and evil thoughts. He allows the psychic energy of these images to sap the strength of his self-created ego. John, as the John he creates, has "no more strength against them." As long as he relies on the ego he controls, he is helpless against this negative energy. Climbing the tree extends his vision. He yields control to God's grace and is freed from the negative energy. John, who knew the psalms well, mirrors the first verse of Psalm 46: "God is our refuge and strength, a very present help in trouble."

FEBRUARY 11

A Place Where I Learn Who I Am

Abba Alonius said, *"If a man does not say in his heart, in the world there is only myself and God, then he will not gain peace."*

Abba Alonius is not promoting a self-centered "me and God" spiritual path. In the most direct possible terms, and from his own experience, he declares that the cell is a place of complete transparency before God. In the cell we cannot escape from God or ourselves. This is why the desert elders told their novices to "stay in your cell." It takes persistence and time to "say in one's heart," "I really want to be here." The intensity of awareness of God and one's self in the cell is as if "there is only myself and God" in the whole world. This directs our attention to God and ourselves without the external expectations and patterns of behavior that are sources of fear and anxiety. We need the spacious and grace-filled environment of God's direct and loving gaze to be honest about the self we have created to cope with our experience of life. We will begin to "gain peace" as we are able to see ourselves as God sees us.

Seeing as God Sees

Abba Alonius said, *"If only a man desired it for a single day from morning till night, he would be able to come to the measure of God."*
"He also said, 'If I had not destroyed myself completely, I should not have been able to rebuild and shape myself again.'"

Abba Alonius is not talking about "measuring up" or getting "fixed" through a self-help program. He had learned that sooner or later we have to come face-to-face with ourselves and decide whether we want to remain a self-created person or not. Conventional society admires a self-made person while Alonius is recommending self-destruction. Is he the ultimate masochist? The issue for Alonius is *vision.* Our vision of ourselves is limited to what our ego desires and needs to sustain itself. The "measure of God" is what God sees in us and desires for us. If we desire what God desires for us, we must be willing to let go of our efforts to be a self-made person. Then the effort "to rebuild and [re]shape" takes place in our life with God.

Two Temples

Abba Evagrius said, *"Allow the Spirit of God to dwell within you; then in his love he will come and make a habitation with you; he will reside in you and live in you. If your heart is pure you will see him and he will sow in you the good seed of reflection upon his actions and wonder at his majesty. This will happen if you take the trouble to weed out from your soul the undergrowth of desires, along with the thorns and tares of bad habits."*

Evagrius mirrors an image from St. Paul. In our deepest being we are "the temple of the living God" (2 Cor 6:16). But Evagrius's own experience taught him that we tend to obscure this part of our original nature with "the undergrowth of desires, along with the thorns and tares of bad habits." The cell is an outward temple of solitude where "reflection upon [the Spirit's] actions and wonder at his majesty" will reveal our inner temple and "allow the Spirit of God to dwell within [us]." But first we must "take the trouble" to enter the outer temple and spend time "weeding" the garden of our soul and purify its soil with "the good seed of reflection." Then in the same way we inhabit our physical cell, whatever and wherever it is, God "will come and make a habitation" within us.

Paying Attention

"Abba John [the Dwarf] gave this advice, 'Watching means to sit in the cell and always be mindful of God. This is what is meant by the saying, "I was on the watch and God came to me."'"

What happens in our outer temple? Abba John reminds us that our cell, regardless of its location, is a place for intentional "watching." What does he mean? In our fast-paced world it is easy to miss things. Images on TV flash before our eyes and rarely remain on screen for more than a second or two. There are endless demands for our attention and our minds are constantly at work. It is necessary to be personally attentive to people and things that matter the most. How do we decide where our attention should go? Our energies will flow in that same direction. Time in our cell will help us "always be mindful of God" as we discern our priorities and values. It is like the rotating beacon directing an aircraft toward an airport. If we avert our attention from God, where will we be? Where do we want to be?

Firsthand Experience

"Abba John [the Dwarf] gave this advice, 'Watching means to sit in the cell and always be mindful of God. This is what is meant by the saying, "I was on the watch and God came to me."'"

The cell is a place for direct experience of God. It is where we go intentionally to be "on the watch" so that wherever we are God's presence will be transparent. Being on the watch in the outer temple awakens us to the reality of God within. When Abba John says, "God came to me," he recognizes that we can keep God at a distance. God is not "out there" in a physical sense. God is always within us and all around us. It is we who place God outside our awareness. The desert elders took Jesus seriously: "Abide in me as I abide in you. Just as the branch cannot bear fruit by itself unless it abides in the vine, neither can you unless you abide in me" (John 15:4). This is an invitation, not a command, to experience the One who is the source of life. It is an opportunity to choose life over barrenness.

Resisting Distractions

"Abba Sisoes was sitting in his cell one day. His disciple knocked on the door and the old man shouted out to him saying, 'Go away, Abraham, do not come in. From now on, I have no time for the things of this world.'"

This saying demonstrates why the desert elders have been criticized as being antisocial. It is clear that Abba Sisoes wanted to remain quiet in his cell and lost patience when his disciple came to ask a question. His shouting and anger show how difficult it was for him to remain watchful in his cell and attentive to the needs of his brother monk. This tension exists in every person's life of prayer, especially when we really need some time to ourselves. In his anger Abba Sisoes shouts that he has "no time for things of this world." He probably got over it, but his anger came from a deep need to remain faithful to his experience of God as the source of his transformation. His experience underlines the importance of being stewards of our need for solitude in the midst of caring for other people.

A Place of Companionship

Abba Paul the Great said, *"Keep close to Jesus."*
This may be the shortest saying in the collection of the wisdom of the desert elders, yet it takes us to the heart of their way of life. They were more interested in experience and example than words.

Whether they lived in towns, cities, or deserts, their aim was to form an alternative society embodying the Great Commandment to love God and their neighbor. They learned, first, to desire their own transformation, and the key to this new life is to "keep close to Jesus." Keep it simple! Abba Paul's wise words echo St. Paul: "As you therefore have received Christ Jesus the Lord, continue to live your lives in him, rooted and built up in him and established in the faith, just as you were taught, abounding in thanksgiving" (Col 2:6-7). The cell is a place where companionship with Jesus sustains our lives along the path toward transformation. The roots of that relationship will build a society based on love.

Transparent Walls

"It was also said of [Abba Ammonas] that, coming to the town one day to sell his wares, he encountered a sick traveler lying in the public place without anyone to look after him. The old man rented a cell and lived with him there, working with his hands to pay the rent and spending the rest of the money on the sick man's needs. He stayed there four months till the sick man was restored to health. Then he returned in peace to his cell."

The cell does not limit our vision of the world. Ammonas was a disciple of St. Antony and after his abba's death, he lived in Antony's isolated mountain cave for years. The stone walls that surrounded his prayer formed a place that expanded his heart so that when he "encountered a sick traveler" near a town, he rented a cell and cared for "the sick man's needs." Seeing his neighbor's need, Ammonas became the love he had experienced in the solitude of his own cell. In the words of Abba Evagrius, he was *"a man who is separated from all and who is in harmony with all."* The cell helps us see and feel what lies beyond it in a different way. Rather than isolating us from the world, the cell is a womb giving birth to compassionate engagement with the world.

A Silent Workshop

Abba John Cassian said, *"This I say is the end of all perfection—that the mind, purged of every carnal desire may daily be elevated to spiritual things, until one's whole way of life and all the yearnings of one's heart become a single and continuous prayer."*

The cell is a workshop of God's grace wherein the whole person—body, mind, soul, and spirit—is mentored by the Spirit. In the solitude and silence our true self begins to emerge as our heart yearns for "the end of all perfection." Abba John sat at the feet of many desert elders and collected their wisdom. He learned that "carnal desire" stands in the way of perfection, our movement toward completion in God (*perfactio*). Carnal desires may lead to unrestrained misuse of natural and sacred bodily functions, such as gluttony and fornication. Abba John exhorts us to empty our minds of these desires so that our hearts will yearn for the authentic spiritual integrity in all aspects of our lives. He reminds us that "one's whole way of life" can be an undivided prayer.

A Place of Self-Emptying

Abba Poemen said, *"If you take little account of yourself, you will have peace wherever you live."*

At first glance Abba Poemen seems to be promoting self-deprecation, with peace as the reward. As always, we are invited to look deeper. One person cannot create peace. It is a mutual relationship with people "wherever you live." Poemen is suggesting that self-assertion will inhibit the way we relate to our neighbors. He is not suggesting we have a lack of initiative. He is pointing to a core value and attitude that will bond us with others. Taking "little account of yourself" is a way of seeing ourselves that frees us to see other people without using ourselves as the benchmark. In the cell we have an opportunity to see the personal pride that inhibits peace. At the same time, the cell slows us down enough to let God transform our self-promotion to genuine love. This self-emptying eliminates the space between us and other people. It will help us depend on God more than ourselves.

Taking the Cell Everywhere

"Abba Moses asked Abba Silvanus, 'Can a man lay a new foun-dation every day?' The old man said, 'If he works hard, he can lay a new foundation at every moment.'"

It is easy to become the creation of our aspirations and activity. Sometimes fulfilling these expectations and the pressures of daily work are so consuming that we leave our spirits behind. Our horizon shrinks to the surface of what must be done. We spiral into a vortex of what is happening in front of our eyes. Abba Silvanus suggests that whether our goals are worthwhile or disappointing, there is a "new foundation" in "every moment" that guides and transcends our work. If we carry our cell with us throughout each day, reflection will help us "lay a new foundation every moment." Silvanus reminds us that neither work nor prayer should be set in stone. The mystery of God's life in us is never "accomplished." When our spirits "work hard" to discern the foundation of God's presence in all things, we will embrace ever-new possibilities rather than satisfaction.

A Place of Loneliness

Amma Theodora said, *"However, you should realize that as soon as you intend to live in peace, at once evil comes and weighs down your soul through accidie [listlessness, lack of energy], fainthearted-ness, and evil thoughts. . . . It dissipates the strength of soul and body, so that one believes one is ill and no longer able to pray."*

Time in the cell is rarely all bliss. It can be hard work and at other times it seems as though nothing is happening. Since we pray with mind, body, and spirit, Amma Theodora describes the psychosomatic consequences of our frustrations. When we do not experience "prog-ress" or awareness of God's presence, impatience, loneliness, and laziness set in. We can identify with the Hebrews in the Sinai wilder-ness when they cried out to Moses, "Is the Lord among us or not?" (Exod 17:7). At times like this we are tempted to leave our cell and let go of its solitude and silence. Theodora has some difficult advice:

"But if we are vigilant, all these temptations fall away . . . for the wise [person] practices perpetual prayer." Part of the vigilance is trusting, through "perpetual prayer," that our discouragement and listlessness will not last forever.

The Stature of Waiting

"Abba Poemen often said, 'We do not need anything except a vigilant spirit.'"
Abba Poemen agrees with Amma Theodora. Wise persons will value "a vigilant spirit," especially when our solitude seems empty and we lose resolve. Neither the cell nor silence is an end in itself. Both provide opportunities for an attitude of waiting. Poemen and Theodora learned that persistence in prayer enlarges our experience of God's transformative power. Wakefulness and expectation strip us of our need to control the outcomes of prayer and reflection. They help us resist the temptation to fix ourselves. Abba Poemen reminds us that vigilance is not limited to the cell. *"If three men meet, of whom the first fully preserves interior peace, the second gives thanks to God in illness, and the third serves with a pure mind, these three are doing the same work."* The "work" is looking for and relying on God's presence, whether our lives are empty or full, in solitude, during illness of body or mind, or while doing activities.

A Place of Refuge

Abba John the Dwarf said, *"I am like a man sitting under a great tree, who sees wild beasts and snakes coming against him in great numbers. When he cannot withstand them any longer, he runs to climb the tree and is saved. It is just the same with me; I sit in my cell and I am aware of evil thoughts coming against me, and when I have no more strength against them, I take refuge in God by prayer and I am saved from the enemy."*

We have seen this saying before and it is worth repeating. Sometimes the cell is overcrowded. Abba John the Dwarf is transparent about the "evil thoughts coming against me" and his helplessness to overcome them. Our "wild beasts and snakes" become specific in desires, decisions, and behavior. Others are less clear, hidden in tempting rationalizations or inaction. Abba John reminds us that watchfulness inside or outside our cell will help us be honest about self-serving motives and behavior. When we "cannot withstand them any longer," we will look beyond ourselves and "take refuge in God by prayer." Acknowledging our weakness helps us rely on God's strength. This is a refrain we will hear over and over again from the desert elders because each day brings new challenges.

FEBRUARY 25

Contemplation in a World of Action

Abba Antony said, *"Just as fish die if they stay too long out of water, so the monks who loiter outside their cells or pass their time with men of the world lose the intensity of inner peace. So like a fish going towards the sea, we must hurry to reach our cell, for fear that if we delay outside we will lose our interior watchfulness."*

Antony was speaking to monks who were called to intense solitude and silent prayer as parts of a unique vocation. Most of us are not called to monastic life, yet we too must learn to balance our active and responsible lives with contemplative prayer. Antony is not criticizing men and women "of the world," nor is he saying that we do not live holy lives. He reminds us that if we "loiter" in idle conversations or hyperactivity, we will dissipate spiritual energy and wisdom that center our lives in God's presence. "Intensity of inner peace" and "interior watchfulness" are sources of our soul's health *and* responsible stewardship of our lives in the world. Contemplation and action are colleagues.

Limiting Our Options

Amma Syncletica said, *"If you find yourself in a monastery do not go to another place, for that will harm you a great deal. Just as the bird who abandons the eggs she was sitting on prevents them from hatching, so the monk or nun grows cold and their faith dies, when they go from one place to another."*

Some of us have too many options: superstores, internet surfing, broadband TV channels, self-help programs, and an endless variety of spiritual paths and resources. My options include endless music CDs, books, retreats, minicourses, hiking, astronomy, and travel. Just like my hobbies, it is tempting to craft a continuous personal spiritual path based on my current needs or interests. Amma Syncletica urges us to find a spiritual home and remain committed to its way of life as a vital complement to our personal prayer. If we "go from one place to another," we forfeit the environment of life in a faith community that will give birth to spiritual vitality and challenge us to develop fruits of the Spirit. Fewer options will help us enter into the lives of other people.

Rich Soil for Bearing Fruit

Abba Moses said, *"The man who flees and lives in solitude is like a bunch of grapes ripened by the sun, but he who remains amongst men is like an unripe grape."*

Abba Moses is speaking about fruitfulness. Our society tends to evaluate tasks and success in terms of productivity. While it is important to be good stewards of time, money, and personal effort, productivity is not always the best way to evaluate progress. Moses is speaking to monks whose vocation is solitude. He knows their vocation will not bear fruit if they spend too much time in the towns and cities. By limiting interaction with surrounding society and spending time in their cell, they will begin to manifest fruits of the Holy Spirit. Their fruitfulness will be manifested in what kind of person they become rather than mastery of their monastic disciplines. At the same time they can be productive through work, hospitality, study, care of the poor, and teaching. What are we becoming in our efforts for productivity and success? Are we fruitful?

What Takes Place in Your Cell?

"A brother came to Scetis to visit Abba Moses and asked him for a word. The old man said to him, 'Go, sit in your cell, and your cell will teach you everything.'"

We end February repeating Abba Moses' word. Every morning is a new birth of our life with God. Abba Gregory of Nyssa lived in a city in Cappadocia. He was a philosopher, mystic, and bishop. Abba Gregory taught that when the soul is simple and unified with God, it is fulfilled. Its great desire is to be with God, who alone is lovable. God's love is dynamic and will transform the soul in a never-ending process filled with ever-new discoveries.

Your cell is where you will make endless discoveries. Where is your cell? When can you spend time there? What hinders or supports your time there? What do you do in your cell? What is it like to be alone with God? What are you becoming in your cell? What happens when you return from your cell to the rest of your life?

MARCH

Praxis: Caring for One's Soul

At the heart of the lives of the desert elders was the Great Commandment. "You shall love the Lord your God with your whole soul, and your neighbor as yourself." Abba Pachomius declared to the monks in his monasteries that the greatest vision he had ever seen was the presence of the living God in a human being. The presence of God makes love possible because God is love. It sounds easy, but it is not. The abbas and ammas knew themselves well enough to realize that there would have to be many changes in their lives before this kind of love could be tangible in their lives. Amma Syncletica put it this way: "My children, all of us—male and female—know about being saved, but through our own negligence we stray away from the path of salvation. . . . Salvation, then, is exactly this—this two-fold love of God and of our neighbor. . . . Well, what do we need for the present conflict? Obviously, austere asceticism and pure prayer."

As always, Syncletica gets right to the point. But what are "austere asceticism and pure prayer"? Asceticism has its roots in the Greek word *ascesis*, meaning a pattern or discipline of caring for something. It also referred to training and exercise to achieve a certain goal. If a person is to love God and neighbor with his or her "whole soul," then asceticism is caring for the soul. A person who cares for her or his soul in this way is an "ascetic." The desert elders also called this discipline "praxis." In the Greek culture of their day, praxis meant an action or discipline that is practiced habitually. Praxis is what happens when a person is caring for the soul, and in the desert it took many forms. Its venue was usually in the monk's cell.

The desert fathers and mothers learned from their own experience that praxis is never an end in itself. Although it is an essential part of human transformation, it is not the goal. This was a hard lesson to learn and many of the desert monks, male and female, got caught up in trying to be more competent in their praxis than other monks. Another danger was thinking that certain practices were better than others and constituted the "right way." The wiser monks knew from experience that this led to pride and vainglory and damaged the soul. The goal of praxis is love of God and neighbor.

Another important aspect of praxis was the realization that it included the whole person, body, mind, and spirit. The venue for transformation was human daily life, not some "other worldly" sphere. Praxis did not deny either the sanctity of human flesh or the material world. Therefore, praxis was both external practices as well as an interior movement leading to what the elders called "purity of heart." Purity of heart is total openness to God's movement in one's life and nonattachment to material things or desired outcomes. It is a dying to self in order to find one's self in God.

Yet praxis was not only a personal discipline, even for the hermits. It was both a personal and communal experience. Most often hermits were mentored by an abba, amma, or life in a community before seeking a solitary life. Other monks lived in communities where they shared common praxis that contributed to all and had opportunities for their own personal disciplines. This month we will focus on the variety of ways praxis was woven into the lives of the desert elders, its difficulties, joys, and contributions to human transformation in Christ.

MARCH 1

Caring for One's Soul

Abba Macarius suggests disciplines for prayer in a monk's cell. In March we will reflect on these practices in more detail.

"When you get up in the morning each day, make it the beginning of your life as a monk; practice every virtue and every commandment of God; fearfully practice perseverance and patience; demonstrate a love of God and a love of people with a humble heart and bodily humility . . . with prayers and supplications and groans, with purity of tongue while humbly guarding your eyes, without anger, in peace, without returning evil to an evildoer, without passing judgment on those in need, without thinking of yourself in anything, placing your-

self below every creature . . . with renunciation of material things and fleshly things, with the struggle of the cross, with spiritual poverty, with good free will and bodily asceticism, with fasting and repentance and tears . . . with pure counsel and the tasting of good goodness, quietly at midday; with manual work, with vigils, with numerous prayers, with hunger and thirst, with frost and nakedness and afflictions . . . and the acquisition of your tomb . . . placing your death near you day after day."

Reflect on these disciplines and virtues carefully. What questions arise? What inspires you?

The Whole Person

" . . . with the struggle of the cross, with spiritual poverty, with good free will and bodily asceticism, with fasting and repentance and tears . . ."

Macarius gives a profile of praxis that integrates body, mind, and spirit. He exhorts his brothers to rise early and *"acquire the beginning of every virtue and every commandment of God."* This difficult task involves an honest release of psychological, physical, and spiritual energies. It requires nothing less than *"all the fervor of your soul and body."* Macarius learned that living "with the struggle of the cross" is an experience with movements in vertical and horizontal directions. Our inner path toward transformation and eternal union with God is traveled simultaneously along the outward path of our daily life and relationships. Macarius shows that this twofold journey is reflected psychologically, through interior distress and tears; physically, through fasting and keeping vigil; and spiritually, through patience and humility. These few examples demonstrate that praxis is a way of life.

A Balance of Virtues

"A brother asked Abba Poemen, saying, 'Can a man put his trust in one single work?' The old man said to him that Abba John the Dwarf said, 'I would rather have a bit of all the virtues.'"

The younger brother was excited about his monastic vocation. He wanted to concentrate his effort on one aspect of praxis, either through attraction to it or from a strong sense of personal need. In either case, he wanted to "put his trust in one single work." It is tempting to build our lives of prayer on a single practice and, like a mandala, design everything else around that center. This decision can limit possibilities for our spiritual growth and vitality, especially if we are beginning or renewing our intention for disciplined prayer. Abba John advises us to consider "a bit of all the virtues." The danger in choosing "one single work" is that we deprive ourselves of balanced opportunities for the Spirit to enrich and mentor our whole being. A crucial virtue is nonattachment to control of the process of our transformation.

Praxis Is Not the Goal

Amma Syncletica said, *"My children, all of us—male and female—know about being saved, but through our own negligence we stray from the path of salvation. First of all we must observe the precepts known through the grace of the Lord, and these are: 'You shall love the Lord your God with your whole soul, and your neighbor as yourself.' In these precepts the first principle of the Law is preserved, and it is on this Law that the fullness of grace depends. The expression of the principle is brief, indeed, but its importance in this matter is great and unlimited, for all advice to help the soul depends on these precepts. . . . Whatever people say by the grace of the Spirit, therefore, that is useful springs from love and ends in it. Salvation, then, is exactly this—this two-fold love of God and of our neighbor. . . . Well, what do we need for the present conflict? Obviously, austere asceticism and pure prayer."*

The center of the desert elders' lives was the Great Commandment, "for all advice to help the soul depends on these precepts." Praxis is the servant of love and the soul's health. Syncletica spent a lifetime learning and sharing this advice. She grew up in the large and cosmopolitan city of Alexandria in a devout Christian family and in the shadow of the great Christian catechetical school. As a young woman she chose the solitary life in a room in her home and when her parents died, she sold her property, gave the proceeds to the poor, and went to live in a family tomb on the outskirts of the city with her blind sister. Her whole life was a form of praxis, yet her focus was always the Great Commandment.

Praxis Is Unique to Each Person

"Abba Abraham went to see Abba Ares. They were sitting together when a brother came to the old man and said to him, 'Tell me what I must do to be saved.' He replied, 'Go, and for the whole of this year eat only bread and salt in the evening. Then come back here and I will talk to you again.' The monk went away and did this. When the year was over he came back to Abba Ares. Now by chance it happened that Abba Abraham was there again. Once more the old man said to the brother, 'Go, and for the whole of this year fast for two days at a time.' When the brother had gone, Abba Abraham said to Abba Ares, 'Why do you prescribe an easy yoke to all the brethren, while you impose a heavy burden on this brother?' The old man replied, 'How I send them away depends on what the brethren came to seek. Now it is for the sake of God that this one comes to hear a word, for he is a hard worker and what I tell him he carries out eagerly. It is because of this that I speak the word of God to him.'"

Praxis is not the same for every person. Its design and intensity depend on each person's need, opportunity, and ability. It is tempting to design or seek a "packaged" path to spiritual transformation. The twenty-first century is filled with self-help programs, popular authors with good ideas and advice, and retreat centers offering a variety of resources for spiritual growth. Although there is great treasure to be found, the assumption is often that "one size fits all." Even theological schools offer quality education for ministry that is usually the same for all students. The wisdom of Abba Ares is that he knew the personal characteristics of this young brother and what he "came to seek." The brother needed to learn patience and Ares saw that, for now, an austere praxis was best suited to help him learn that being "saved" would not happen overnight.

Seeking Guidance

Abba Dorotheos of Gaza said, *"I have told you all this so that you may know how much rest and tranquility a man may have—and that with all security—by not settling anything by himself, but by casting everything that concerns himself on God and on those who, after God, have power to guide him. Learn then, brothers, to enquire; be convinced that not to set one's own path is a great thing. This is humility, this is peace of soul, this is joy!"*

Although praxis of prayer is deeply personal, it is not lived in isolation. Hermits like Antony began their praxis in the company of an experienced mentor. As desert monastic life evolved into communities of monks living a shared life, monks who desired the hermit life were required to live with faithfulness in their community before receiving permission to live as hermits. As we begin or renew the pattern of our praxis of prayer, it is wise to "enquire" what God desires and seek practical advice from an experienced mentor. The give-and-take between mentor and novice as well as life in a community takes the focus away from self-sufficiency. A strong desire for transformation is a good thing, but it must be tempered by the humility of learning from others. Although it is tempting, "not to set one's own path is a great thing."

Vigils

Abba Evagrius said, *"Let us make provision for protecting this power of our soul by praying to Christ in our nightly vigils."*

Watchfulness was the heart of the desert elders' praxis. They made space within themselves to experience God's presence and the movement of God's grace. They were willing to wait but disciplined their bodies to avoid physical distractions, developed methods to remain attentive, and tried not to rush the process. They used the Bible and chanting to open their hearts.

"Then, after having eaten, they sit and listen to the father's teaching on all the commandments until the first watch of the night. At this point some of them go out into the desert and recite the Scriptures by heart throughout the night. The rest remain where they are and worship God with ceaseless hymnody until daybreak."

Although most of us cannot stay up all night, there is value in learning verses from the Bible by heart and repeating them quietly or singing a favorite hymn to make space in our hearts. The emphasis is not on words but what takes place within us as we read, chant, or recall a passage from memory. The foundation of the praxis of vigils is the pattern of recitation that turns our attention and hearts to the movement of God's presence. During vigils we assume an attitude of waiting without controlling the outcome.

MARCH 8

The Mind Descending into the Heart

"For the heart directs and governs all the other organs of the body. And when grace pastures the heart, it rules over all the members and all the thoughts. For there, in the heart, the mind abides as well as all the thoughts of the soul and all its hopes. This is how grace penetrates throughout all parts of the body."

Keeping vigils is more than repeating words. As we recite or chant there is an interior movement of our deepest desire for God that flows from the mind and the body into the heart. The mind and all the members of our body house our thoughts, memories, anxieties, joys, temptations, and physical strengths and weaknesses. The activity of our mind and the consciousness of our body's tiredness or pain can distract our openness to God's presence. The words of Scripture and the chanting bring the activities of our mind and body into the heart. The desert elders believed the heart is the physical, psychic, and spiritual center of our being. So often the mind takes "front seat" in our lives and our lives are scattered by what we are thinking or doing. As "grace pastures the heart" we can be led beyond distractions toward experience of God.

Standing in the Need of Prayer

Abba Evagrius said, *"When you stand up for prayer, do not begin in a slovenly way, lest you perform all your prayer in a slack or slovenly and wearied way. Rather, when you stand up, sign yourself with the sign of the cross, gather together your thoughts, be in a state of recollection and readiness, gaze upon him to whom you are praying, and then commence."*

The desert elders used their bodies in prayer. They employed several postures, but standing was a favorite during the night vigil. They paid attention to disciplined posture for attentiveness rather than austerity. After a day's work and normal evening tiredness, it is easy to "begin in a slovenly way." But our purpose is not to "get through" our time of prayer but to "gaze upon him to whom you are praying." Evagrius has some practical advice. Stand with good posture. Center your body, mind, and heart by making the sign of the cross. Gather your thoughts and "be in a state of recollection and readiness." Like Jesus, the Jew, the desert elders understood prayer as a very personal and active engagement with God. It was an interpersonal encounter. Our whole being looks toward God who is already gazing at us.

Beyond Words and Sound

Abba John of Damascus said, *"Therefore, the Apostles saw Christ bodily and what He endured and His miracles and they heard His words; we also long to see and to hear and to be blessed. They saw face to face, since He was present to them bodily, even as we hear His words through books and are sanctified in our hearing and through it we are blessed in our soul, and venerate and honor the books, through which we hear His words. . . . For this reason Christ assumed body and soul, since human kind consists of body and soul; therefore also baptism is twofold, of water and the Spirit; as well as communion and prayer and psalmody, all of them twofold, bodily and spiritual, and offerings of light and incense."*

The desert elders repeated Bible verses and chanted verses from the psalms, knowing that repetition was not an end in itself. Through the bodily motion and sound "we are blessed in our soul" and eventually meet Christ "face to face." We become different people. We may not be aware of the change because it is not our work. It is Christ at work in us. Often it is difficult to trust that anything is "happening." Yet Abba John reminds us that our entire being is involved in our life with God. Although the risen Christ is not with us in bodily form, he is indeed present through our "offerings of light and incense" and his words, still alive through books, "are sanctified in our hearing and through it we are blessed in our soul."

MARCH 11

The Letter and the Spirit

Maximus the Confessor wrote, *"And let him through an informed study of Holy Scripture wisely get past its letter and rise up to the Holy Spirit, in whom are found the fullness of all goodness and the treasures of knowledge and the secrets of wisdom. If anyone is shown to be interiorly worthy, he will find God engraved on the tablets of his heart through the grace of the Spirit, and with face unveiled will see as in a mirror the glory of God, once he has removed the veil of the letter."*

Maximus was born in 580 CE near Constantinople and became a monk and philosopher whose contemplative life was influenced by abbas Evagrius and Macarius. His "desert" was usually in a city. As a scholar he knew the importance of the contents of the Bible, but as a monk his evening vigils "removed the veil of the letter" and led him to "find God engraved on the tablets of his heart." His recitation led him not only to goodness and wisdom but also "through the grace of the Spirit" to find "the glory of God" within himself. Maximus reminds us that it is possible to live very busy and responsible lives and at the same time "find God engraved on the tablets" of our hearts. If we take time to listen to God's presence in Holy Scripture, we will be able to recognize that same voice in all the other aspects of our lives. The face of God within us reveals God's face everywhere.

Passion rather than Accomplishment

"Abba Lot went to see Abba Joseph and said to him, 'Abba, as far as I can I say my little office, I fast a little, I pray and meditate, I live in peace and as far as I can, I purify my thoughts. What else can I do?' Then the old man stood up and stretched his hands towards heaven. His fingers became like ten lamps of fire and he said to him, 'If you will, you can become all flame.'"

Abba Lot gives us a vivid picture of a desert monk's praxis. He says his daily prayers, he fasts, he prays and meditates during vigils, he redirects his attention from harmful thoughts to contemplation of God, and he does his best to live in peace with his brother monks and neighbors. And yet, he feels his praxis is incomplete. "What else can I do?" Abba Joseph realizes that Lot's yearning will not be satisfied by increasing his prayerful activities. Lot is "doing" enough. What he lacks is passion. "If you will, you can become all flame." The "ten lamps of fire" remind us that when our praxis is filled with passionate desire for God, we experience transformation. Praxis is not simply "getting the job done."

Living Water in the Desert

Abba Nesteros said, *"Hence, the successive books of Holy Scripture must be diligently committed to memory and ceaselessly reviewed. This continual meditation will bestow on us double fruit. First, inasmuch as the mind's attention is occupied with reading and preparing to read, it cannot be taken captive in the entrapment of harmful thoughts. Then, the things that we have not been able to understand because our mind was busy at the time, things that we have gone through repeatedly and are laboring to memorize, we shall see more clearly afterward when we are free from every seductive deed and sight, and especially when we are silently meditating at night. Thus, while we are at rest and as it were immersed in the stupor of sleep, there will be revealed an understanding of hidden meanings that we did not grasp even slightly when we were awake."*

The Bible was the heart of the study, teaching, and meditation of the desert elders. It was a sacred well full of living water for thirsty souls. Nesteros speaks of the "double fruit" of memorizing and meditating on the Bible. Focusing attention on a biblical text will take the place of other distracting and potentially harmful and "seductive" thoughts. This freedom will lead to new understanding of a text because we will be able to give it our full attention. It will then become such a part of our consciousness that even in our sleep it will continue to speak. For the next few days we will reflect on the praxis of meditation and study of the Bible.

The Gift of Holy Reading

Abba Nesteros said, *"Hence, the successive books of Holy Scripture must be diligently committed to memory and ceaselessly reviewed. This continual meditation will bestow on us double fruit. First, inasmuch as the mind's attention is occupied with reading and preparing to read, it cannot be taken captive in the entrapment of harmful thoughts."*

Abba Nesteros speaks about two disciplines that helped the desert elders focus their attention on the Bible. The first is reading. He speaks of "preparing to read" and being "occupied with reading." By the end of the third century literate monks had access to most books of the Bible and taught illiterate monks to read so that they too could meditate on biblical passages. Some monks studied and read on their own, while others were guided by their amma or abba. The reading was done aloud, involving body, mind, and speech in meditation. It released the mind from being "taken captive in the entrapment of harmful thoughts" so that it could listen to God's voice. In today's society listening is becoming a lost art. Even in our worship we lose the power of the spoken word by following lessons in printed bulletin inserts rather than giving full attention to the spoken word.

The Gift of Memorization

"Then, the things that we have not been able to understand because our mind was busy at the time, things that we have gone through repeatedly and are laboring to memorize, we shall see more clearly afterward when we are free from every seductive deed and sight, and especially when we are silently meditating at night."

In the monasteries of Abba Pachomius each day began with morning prayer, where long portions of the Bible were read as the monks listened while weaving baskets, mats, or rope. Part of the reading would be memorized and become the focus of meditation for the day. The desert elders memorized portions and entire books of the Bible and used them for meditation while working and during their nightly vigils. Today we are also losing the art of memorization in the midst of TV, minicomputers, and the internet. Our minds are scattered by competing messages. We are suspicious of rote learning, yet our minds and souls yearn for spiritual food to carry us through each day. Carrying a memorized or written verse to repeat throughout the day will help keep us centered in the midst of what each day brings.

Meletē

Abba Isaac said to Abba John Cassian, *"The formula for this discipline and prayer that you are seeking, then, shall be presented to you. Every monk who longs for the continual awareness of God should be in the habit of meditation on it ceaselessly in his heart, after having driven out every kind of thought, because he will be unable to hold fast to it in any other way than by being freed from all bodily cares and concerns. . . . This, then, is the devotional formula proposed to you as absolutely necessary for possessing the perpetual awareness of God: 'O God, incline unto my aid; O Lord, make haste to help me.'"*

Meletē is the practice of repeating a verse or short phrase throughout the day, usually aloud. The desert elders used meletē for "continual awareness of God" in the midst of distractions caused by "every kind of thought" and "all bodily cares and concerns." This simple practice, done silently or aloud at different times, can help us remain centered on God's presence in the midst of distractions and responsibilities that consume our attention. The "formula" reminds us to always seek God's help and reminds us that we are never without God's presence. This simple practice destroys the myth that there is not enough time in the day for meditation. It enables us to pause several times each day to become mindful of what is most fundamental in life.

An Interior Conversation

"Then, the things that we have not been able to understand because our mind was busy at the time, things that we have gone through repeatedly and are laboring to memorize, we shall see more clearly afterward when we are free from every seductive deed and sight, and especially when we are silently meditating at night. Thus, while we are at rest and as it were immersed in the stupor of sleep, there will be revealed an understanding of hidden meanings that we did not grasp even slightly when we were awake."

The disciplines of reading aloud, meletē, and memorization formed the foundation of the desert elders' contemplative life. They were not ends in themselves because they led a monk beyond the words of a specific biblical text toward an inner conversation where the Word enabled the monk to "see more clearly." Saint Benedict, whose Rule for monastic life became a foundation for later monastic life throughout the world, calls this practice "listening with the ear of the heart." The outward praxis created an inner environment for attentiveness to God's voice. Abba Nesteros uses the analogy of sleep to refer to an inner state, not focused on literal meanings, that opens us to "an understanding of hidden meanings."

Inner Pastures

"For the heart directs and governs all the other organs of the body. And when grace pastures the heart, it rules over all the members and the thoughts. For there, in the heart, the mind abides as well as all the thoughts of the soul and all its hopes. This is how grace penetrates throughout all parts of the body."

It is time to return to these words of the Syrian Abba Pseudo-Macarius. He summarizes the integrity of praxis, especially contemplative experience of the Bible. Saint Paul reminds Christians that "we have the mind of Christ" (1 Cor 2:16). Although this seems audacious, Macarius declares that the mind of Christ is closer than we "think." But it is not an object we seek and grasp. It is an *inner experience.* As we are rooted and grounded in contemplative experience of the Bible, "grace pastures the heart," the center of our body, mind, emotions, energies, thoughts, and actions. This contemplative listening opens our heart to the mind of Christ, already present, and our whole being is led by grace to make Christ tangible in our words and actions.

Supplications, Prayers, Intercessions, and Thanksgivings

Abba Isaac, echoing St. Paul, said, *"I urge first of all that supplications be made."* He also said, *"Prayers are those acts by which we offer or vow something to God. . . . We pray when we renounce this world and pledge that, dead to every earthly deed and to an earthly way of life, we will serve the Lord with utter earnestness of heart. . . . In the third place there are intercessions, which we are accustomed to make for others when our spirits are fervent, beseeching on behalf of our dear ones and for the peace of the whole world. . . . Finally, in the fourth place there are thanksgivings, which the mind, whether recalling God's past benefits, contemplating his present ones, or foreseeing what great things God has prepared for those who love him, offers to the Lord in unspeakable ecstasies."*

Abba Isaac describes four *specific ways* that reading, memorization, and meletē lead us beyond words so that "we shall see more clearly." In the realm of the heart our yearnings become congruent with "the mind of Christ" and are articulated through "unspeakable" prayers. Supplications, prayers, intercessions, and thanksgivings form the foundation of the desert elders' life with God. These four practices are a path toward embracing "the mind of Christ." Without a doubt, Isaac is applying St. Paul's exhortation to Christians in Philippi to the lives of monks: "Do not worry about anything, but in everything by prayer and supplication with thanksgiving let your requests be made known to God" (Phil 4:6). We will look at each practice in the next four days.

Supplications

Abba Isaac said, *"'I urge first of all that supplications be made.' A supplication is an imploring or a petition concerning sins, by which a person who has been struck by compunction begs for pardon for his present or past misdeeds . . . [this] first kind of prayer seems to pertain more especially to beginners who are still being harassed by the stings and by the memory of their vices."*

Why should supplications be "first of all"? Abba Isaac speaks from personal experience. Awareness of vices and sins can be a serious barrier to our relationship with God. Sometimes it is hard to pray when we are "being harassed" by these memories, especially if we are new to prayer or have given up. Isaac urges us to let awareness of sins coupled with "compunction" (genuine sorrow for "present or past misdeeds") *become* our prayer. As difficult as it may be, this supplication will free us to expand our experience of prayer and grow in love of ourselves, others, and God. This demonstrates the deep psychological integrity in the wisdom of the desert elders. Our relationships with God, ourselves, and others will not progress if we "hang on" to the dysfunctions and failures of the past. Isaac must have remembered Jesus' words: "But the one to whom little is forgiven, loves little" (Luke 7:47).

Prayers

"Prayers are those acts by which we offer or vow something to God. . . . We pray when we renounce this world and pledge that, dead to every earthly deed and to an earthly way of life, we will serve the Lord with utter earnestness of heart."

Abba Isaac is not referring to prayers articulated with words. The words of the Bible, repeated in meditation, are physical, both in their written form and in the sound of the monk's voice. Yet these physical words mirror the presence of the One they describe and lead the monk to *encounter* God. "Prayers are those acts" in which the monk actually meets and becomes formed by the One who is present in the words he has been reciting or chanting. In this form of prayer a person offers or vows "something to God." By letting go of attachment to "an earthly way of life" (yet remaining in the world), we offer ourselves to God "with utter earnestness of heart." Our prayer is transformed from words to an experience of God's presence in the center of our being that evokes our desire to "serve the Lord" with our whole being.

Intercessions

"In the third place there are intercessions, which we are accustomed to make for others when our spirits are fervent, beseeching on behalf of our dear ones and for the peace of the whole world."

Modern Christians usually think of prayer as "intercessions." We pray for something or someone. Abba Isaac reminds us that our intercessions take place in the context of meditation on biblical texts, awareness of our failings, and our desire to "serve the Lord with utter earnestness of heart." Our prayers for other people and the needs of the world can flow from an earnest relationship with God "when our spirits are fervent." In this way our "beseeching on behalf of our dear ones and for the peace of the whole world" will emerge from discernment and experience of what God desires and not be limited solely to our perspective. Intercession bonds us to those for whom we pray. It was an essential part of the desert elders' vocation to "love your neighbor." As Abba Evagrius said, they (and we) are "separated from all, yet united to all."

Thanksgivings

"Finally, in the fourth place there are thanksgivings, which the mind, whether recalling God's past benefits, contemplating his present ones, or foreseeing what great things God has prepared for those who love him, offers to the Lord in unspeakable ecstasies. And with this intensity, too, more copious prayers are sometimes made, when our spirit gazes with most pure eyes upon the rewards of the holy ones that are stored up for the future and is moved to pour out wordless thanks to God with a boundless joy."

It is significant that Abba Isaac saves his most passionate words to describe giving thanks. Thanksgiving is offered with "intensity" in "unspeakable ecstasies" both by the mind and the spirit. The mind by "recalling" present and past benefits and "foreseeing what great things God has prepared for those who love him" is led to gratefulness that transcends words. This is more than a thank-you note to God! It is total entrustment to the One who creates and sustains our lives with a heart overflowing with love and genuine hope. This intensity leads our spirits to embrace God's eternal love for us and give thanks with "boundless joy." This is fire!

An Experience beyond Words

"And so a still more sublime and exalted condition follows upon these kinds of prayer. It is fashioned by the contemplation of God alone and by fervent charity, by which the mind, having been dissolved and flung into love of him, speaks most familiarly and with particular devotion to God as to its own father."

Supplications, prayers, intercessions, and thanksgivings were a foundation for the desert elders' house of prayer. In later monasticism

they would evolve into a central feature of personal and corporate monastic life called "the work of God." Discipline and persistence were a
hallmark of this work. It required "devotion to God," even though it
was freely chosen. And yet there could be "a still more sublime and
exalted condition" evolving from these disciplines. They open a person
to "the contemplation of God alone," a formless experience of God
that transcends the mind's activities. Abba Isaac uses the relationship
of child and parent to describe this intense, yet intimate, wordless
experience of mutual love.

MARCH 25

God beyond Things

Abba Evagrius said, *"When you are praying do not fancy the
Divinity like some image formed within yourself. Avoid also allowing
your spirit to be impressed with the seal of some particular shape,
but rather, free from all matter, draw near the immaterial Being and
you will attain to understanding."*
Evagrius, like Isaac, is speaking of prayer without an agenda: "the
contemplation of God alone." He gives advice for going beyond the
limitations of words or thoughts that so often determine our expectations for prayer. We can avoid imagining "the Divinity like some
image" or "the seal of some particular shape." The challenge of im-
ageless contemplative prayer is to be "free from all matter" and trust
that there is a way of knowing God that does not depend on rational
and physical activity. Without denying the integrity of our bodies and
minds, we can release control of our prayer and "draw near the immaterial Being" and "attain to understanding." This is knowledge of
the heart based on relationship. It is resting in God. Evagrius was a
scholar who valued rational knowing and yet recognized that drawing
"near the immaterial Being" is also valid knowledge.

God within Things

Abba Evagrius also said, *"We seek after virtues for the sake of attaining to the inner meaning of created things. We pursue these latter, that is to say the inner meanings of what is created, for the sake of attaining to the Lord who has created them. It is in the state of prayer that he is accustomed to manifest himself."*

The path to "the contemplation of God alone" begins with what we can see, touch, and smell. Praxis gives us another way of seeing the world. Evagrius is practical in his understanding of prayer and creation. He begins "where we are" and moves to "the inner meaning of created things." The purpose of prayer is not to escape created things but to discern God's presence in them. Our experience of God in prayer helps us see that same presence in created things "for the sake of attaining to the Lord who has created them." The sacredness of creation becomes manifest because of the Creator's presence in it. This awareness of "the inner meanings of what is created" is prayer! It is a "mutual seeing." The heavens and the earth manifest the presence of God and lead us toward "the contemplation of God alone."

Desire and Persistence

Abba Evagrius said, *"If you long to pray then avoid all that is opposed to prayer. Then when God draws near he has only to go along with you."*

This is such great advice. It is so simple. Yet the path from "If you long to pray . . ." to a life of prayer is not easy. The catchphrase is "avoid all that is opposed to prayer." We may say, "I'm too busy." "There is never enough time." "My mind wanders." "I can't find a good place." "There are children all around and they need my attention." "I'm not sure what to do." "I don't like the silence." "I can't stay still." "My schedule changes all the time." "I don't want to change." What opposes your prayer? How can your longing for God be fulfilled? What decisions will you have to make to honor your longing? Even though there are many venues and methods for prayer, Evagrius's advice requires some action. "Showing up" is the hard part. Then, with a twinkle in his eye, Evagrius reminds us that whenever and however we pray, God is already waiting and desires "only to go along with you." Do not lose heart.

Fasting

"Abba Joseph asked Abba Poemen, 'How should one fast?' Abba Poemen said to him, 'For my part, I think it is better that one should eat every day, but only a little, so as not to be satisfied.' Abba Joseph said to him, 'When you were younger, did you not fast two days at a time, abba?' The old man said, 'Yes, even for three days and four and the whole week. The Fathers tried this all out as they were able and found it preferable to eat every day, but just a small amount. They have left us this royal way, which is light.'"

Food is a fundamental human need and a sacred gift. The desert elders wrestled with discerning the proper use of food in the process of their spiritual transformation. There was no single rule about eating or the limitation of food through fasting. Abba Poemen describes a "royal way" that is practical and yet acknowledges that abstinence is a positive virtue in a person's life of prayer. One should "eat every day, but only a little, so as not to be satisfied." Moderate denial develops a path leading toward what we truly need each day. One of the most difficult, yet essential, results of the desert elders' praxis was the development of easily satisfied needs. Fasting was one way to give thanks for what we need, yet avoid the desire to have more than we need.

Food for the Soul

Abba Moses was asked, *"'What is the good of the fasts and watchings which a man imposes on himself?' and he replied, 'They make the soul humble. For it is written, "Consider my affliction and my trouble, and forgive all my sins." (Ps. 25.18) So if the soul gives itself all this hardship, God will have mercy on it.'"*

"What is the good of the fasts . . . ?" is a fair question. Abba Moses' response points beyond the physical discipline of eating less. The physical praxis of limiting food for the *body* becomes nourishment for the *soul*. Abba Poemen's moderate "royal way" leads to self-knowledge and inner fasting from self-reliance. A humble soul knows its "affliction," "trouble," and "sins." The outward discipline of fasting leads toward an inward discipline of desiring God's "mercy." The "hardship" of "the fasts and watchings" opens a person's soul to desire the mercy of God's forgiving and healing presence. These austerities remind us to feed our soul as well as our body. The hardship of fasting trains our whole being to depend on God.

MARCH 30

Fasting Is a Faithful Teacher

Amma Syncletica said, *"Just as the most bitter medicine drives out poisonous creatures so prayer joined to fasting drives evil thoughts away."*

Amma Syncletica reminds us that fasting is not practiced in a vacuum. Limitation of food, linked with prayer, is a powerful discipline for total fasting from "evil thoughts" and a host of other distracting thoughts, temptations, and behaviors that will harm a person's soul. Like all praxis, the fundamental purpose of fasting is transformation of the heart. *"Abba Poemen heard of someone who had gone all week without eating and then had lost his temper. The old man said, 'He could do without food for six days, but he could not cast out anger.'"* Fasting is a discipline that helps place limits on thoughts, words, and actions that feed our self-interest at the expense of other people. At the same time we can temporarily fast from good things like speech, intellectual activity, making decisions, and productivity so that God can speak to and soften our hearts.

Gratefulness

Abba Evagrius said, *"When the soul desires to seek after a variety of foods then it is time to afflict it with bread and water that it may learn to be grateful for a mere morsel of bread. For satiety desires a variety of dishes but hunger thinks itself happy to get its full of nothing more than bread."*

Evagrius's advice to fellow monks sets fasting in the context of an already austere diet. The limitation of amounts and variety of foods was related to the monastic praxis of placing highest priority on being nourished by the word of God. *"Reading, vigils and prayer—these are the things that lend stability to the wandering mind."* Fasting keeps the mind centered and aware of God as the source of both physical health and spiritual transformation. "When the soul desires to seek after a variety of foods" and finds contentment in being well fed, the discipline of fasting will teach the soul "to be grateful for a mere morsel of bread." Voluntary limitation of food, possessions, and pleasures will help form an attitude of gratefulness that influences the stewardship of every aspect of our lives.

APRIL

Beginning and Sustaining an Ascetic Life

As we have seen, beginning in the late third century men and women left their usual patterns of life in family, society, and the church to withdraw into the deserts of Arabia, Egypt, Palestine, and Syria for solitude, silence, and experience of God. They were moving away from what they experienced as the futility of Roman society toward a life of single-minded devotion to prayer. But withdrawal was only the first step.

Once in the desert, they settled in cells where, in solitude, they came face-to-face with themselves. They learned that in order to experience the rebirth and transformation they desired, they must first come to terms with the life experiences they brought with them to the desert. Self-knowledge was a first step to seeking God without distraction. They built cells as places for inner discernment, experience of God, and transformation.

Gradually they developed disciplines of prayer that opened them to the transforming grace of the Holy Spirit. This austere ascetic life was not an end in itself, yet it helped them strip away the layers of self-centeredness, distracting thoughts, and unrestrained passions that led them away from what Amma Syncletica called the path to salvation. Their whole being—body, mind, and soul—was part of this process. The external disciplines and the cell itself were helping form an internal transformation whose goal was love of God and neighbor.

The men and women who entered the desert or who lived as monks in or near towns and cities came from every walk of life. Some came seeking God; others came because they were running away from something (taxes, crime, arranged marriages, failed relationships, or frustration with life in general), were curious, or were pilgrims seeking wisdom or discernment. In the midst of these very different lives and experiences patterns of ascetic life and praxis were gradually beginning to evolve. Older abbas and ammas shared different forms of praxis and wisdom that had formed their lives with novices and younger monks, but they were very clear that each person's life with God was unique and monks should avoid comparing themselves to each other. The elders learned that this manner of life was not easy and that it required patience, endurance, and trust in God. They discouraged novices, full of enthusiasm for progress, from moving too fast in their ascetic life. Therefore, older and wiser monks became mentors and formed small groups of disciples who lived in separate cells but met with their abbas and ammas for instruction and worship.

Entry into this new life could not be rushed. It required total dependence on God and a willingness to embrace an ascetic life freely. Therefore, the abbas, ammas, and monastic communities did not make life easy for newcomers. They made it "tough" because monastic life had to be experienced gradually and honestly. Each novice had to face the personal and emotional aspects of seeking God. It was easy to become discouraged during struggles with thoughts prompted from old memories of the life left behind; new temptations that could profane body, mind, and spirit; and emotional issues that could dissipate the new monk's resolve to continue. They had to learn not to depend on themselves and to balance enthusiasm for progress with patience.

This month we will reflect on sayings that focus on beginning and sustaining monastic life.

APRIL 1

First Things First

Amma Syncletica said, *"We ought not, therefore, make our treatment of the soul superficial, but we ought to put our soul in order throughout, paying particular attention to its depths. We have our hair cut off; at the same time let us remove also the 'lice' on our head, for by themselves these will cause us still more grief. Our 'hair,' you see, was the worldly element in life: honours, fame, possession of goods, splendid outfits of clothing, use of baths, enjoyment of foods.*

These we thought it wise to discard; but rather let us cast off the soul-devouring 'lice,' some of which are these: slander, perjury, avarice."

Most people do not choose Syncletica's austere monastic life. But all of us have a soul, the fundamental aspect of our true identity. The soul is "who we are." It is our "head" and, although a sacred gift, can be scattered and distorted from its life with God by "the worldly element in life." Yet, these "superficial" distractions can hide even deeper "soul-devouring" influences. Whether we are monks or not, it is wise "to put our soul in order throughout." The desert fathers and mothers often referred to the life they had chosen as "the monastic art." Becoming an artist of the soul took time. This month we will reflect on the art of caring for the soul.

APRIL 2

Where It All Begins and Ends

Amma Syncletica said, *"My children, all of us—male and female—know about being saved, but through our own negligence we stray from the path of salvation. First of all we must observe the precepts known through the grace of the Lord, and these are: 'You shall love the Lord your God with your whole soul, and your neighbor as yourself.' . . . Whatever people say by the grace of the Spirit, therefore, that is useful springs from love and ends in it. Salvation, then, is exactly this—the two-fold love of God and of our neighbor."*

As we have seen, the Great Commandment was at the center of the lives of the desert elders because it was at the center of the life of Jesus. It is the foundation of "the path of salvation." In Syncletica's day the Greek word for salvation carried the meaning of health and wholeness. She sees salvation as a present reality rooted and grounded in "the two-fold love of God and of our neighbor." It is not "pie in the sky after you die." Everything "that is useful springs from love and ends in it." Salvation is about love, here and now. But Syncletica is streetwise enough to know that we can "stray from the path of salvation." We must not ignore what leads us from "the path of salvation." This self-knowledge will help keep us on the path.

Born Again

Amma Syncletica said, *"Whatever we do or gain in this world, let us consider it insignificant in comparison to the eternal wealth that is to come. We are on this earth as if in a second maternal womb. In that inner recess we did not have a life such as we have here, for we did not have there the solid nourishment such as we enjoy now, nor were we able to be active, indeed, as we are here, and we in fact existed without the light of the sun and of any glimmer of light. . . . We have sampled the nourishment here; let us reach for the Divine! We have enjoyed the light in this world; let us long for the sun of righteousness."*

Like Jesus, Syncletica uses major events in the human life cycle to describe the development of our life with God. Jesus told the Pharisee Nicodemus that he must be born again to live in the realm of the Spirit. Syncletica points out that in our mother's womb "we did not have a life such as we have here," with "solid nourishment" and "the light of the sun." The transformation from prenatal life to birth is a foretaste of a second birth through which we "reach for the Divine" and "long for the sun of righteousness." Our first birth is incomplete without the second. The desert elders used the disciplines of praxis to "reach for the Divine." How will we respond to our longing for righteousness?

Our Second Childhood

Amma Syncletica said, *"Three times we are born to life. The first of these births is the passage from our mother's womb, when we are brought from earth to earth; the remaining two lead us from earth up to heaven. The first one of this second group is by grace which comes to us from holy baptism and this birth we rightly call 'being born again.' The third birth is granted to us as a result of our conversion and good works."*

A child has no choice about its natural birth or parents. Infancy and early childhood are periods of dependency when we receive the nurturing and attention we need for physical and emotional growth.

Syncletica uses this process to demonstrate essential elements in the movement from physical childhood to completion as a child of God. Perhaps she is thinking of the passage in Genesis where God breathes on the newly created, yet strictly physical, human being and the human becomes a "living being." Our journey to completion is first made possible by the gift of God's grace and the guidance of the church community (the second birth). We, then, must collaborate directly through openness to "conversion" and the "good works" of love and prayer.

God's Birth in Us

"Because humility is good and salutary, the Lord clothed himself in it while fulfilling the economy [of salvation] for humanity. For he says, 'Learn from me, for I am gentle and humble of heart.' Notice who it is who is speaking; learn his lesson perfectly. Let humility become for you the beginning and end of all virtues."

Syncletica saw a Christian's life after baptism as a gradual "conversion" to Christlike living. She told her monastic sisters that their primary calling is to *"put on Christ."* Although she believed this level of conversion was unique to monastic life, her bias was undoubtedly related to knowledge of the power of materialism and hedonism on persons living in the midst of late Roman society. Yet she echoes St. Paul's exhortation for all Christians to be clothed with Christ and is correct in asserting that the foundation of Christlike living is humility. "Let humility become for you the beginning and end of all virtues." This is not easy, but Syncletica will have practical advice for those who try.

Simple but Not Easy

Amma Syncletica said, *"For those who are making their way to God there is at first great struggle and effort, but then indescribable joy. For just as those who wish to kindle a fire are at first choked with smoke, suffer watery eyes, and in this way achieve their purpose (indeed Scripture says, 'Our God is a consuming fire'), so we too must kindle the divine fire within us with tears and effort."*

It is tempting to say, "The way to God should be simple; all the rules are unnecessary. Just have love in your heart." As a little girl Syncletica desired nothing more than loving God. Her desire and love were authentic, but as she matured she discovered how hard it is to let go of control of our lives. Our desires often lead us away from God and we become "choked with smoke." Awareness of sins will bring "watery eyes" as we learn that being a steward of our desires is a "great struggle." God's "consuming fire" can replace our self-centeredness with "the divine fire" of selfless love. Although the monastic art includes many exterior practices, its goal is kindling "the divine fire within us."

APRIL 7

A Single-Minded Purpose

Amma Syncletica continued, *"The Lord himself says, 'I came to cast fire on the earth.' Some, too, through their remissness, have endured the smoke, but have not kindled the fire because they did not have perseverance and, even more, because their attachment to the Divine was tenuous and uncertain."*

Each desert mother and father was called a "monakos," a monk, because of their single-minded devotion to one thing: their life with God. This passionate relationship was the source of love for their neighbor. Syncletica understood that everything on earth and in a person's life that inhibited this inner fire for God should be burned or cast away, not by literal fire but through "attachment to the Divine." There is no room for "tenuous and uncertain" commitment or lukewarm perseverance. This is not rigid legalism. Syncletica knows from experience that if we voluntarily "long for the sun of righteousness," we must constantly kindle the divine fire within. But will God help us?

Our Spiritual Birth Is Gradual

"Since, then, prayer is petition for the blessings given by the incarnate Logos, let us make him our teacher in prayer. And when we have contemplated the sense of each phrase as carefully as possible, let us confidently set it forth, for the Logos himself gives us, in the manner that is best for us, the capacity to understand what he says. 'Our Father, who art in heaven, hallowed be thy name; thy kingdom come' (Matthew 6:9-10). It is appropriate that at the outset the Lord should teach those who pray to start with theology [contemplation of God], and should initiate them into the mode of existence of him who is by essence the creative Cause of all things. For these opening words of prayer contain a revelation of the Father, and of the kingdom of the Father, so that from this beginning we may be taught to revere, invoke, and worship the Trinity in unity."

Although Maximus the Confessor was born just over a century after Syncletica's death, he too declares God's willingness "to be born spiritually in those who desire him." God "fashions himself" in us through our practice of ascetic virtues. Unlike Syncletica, he was a well-traveled monk and mystic who lived in cities and was a theologian, teacher, and bishop. Yet both Maximus and Syncletica knew that spiritual birth, although challenging, is not the same for every person and that God "recognizes the capacity and resources of those who desire to see him." We are never coerced by God. It is wise to have the same patience with ourselves and others as God bestows on us all.

God's Birth in Us Has No Temporal Limits

Amma Syncletica said, *"There are many who live in the mountains and behave as if they were in the town, and they are wasting their time. It is possible to be a solitary in one's mind while living in a crowd, and it is possible for one who is a solitary to live in the crowd of his own thoughts."*

As we have seen, Syncletica preferred the monastic manner of life as the highest form of Christian commitment. At the same time she acknowledged God's presence and grace in the lives of persons who lived "secular" lives, including marriage. But Syncletica insisted that neither way of life is an end in itself. She was aware that monks "who live in the mountains" can misuse their wilderness solitude by crowding their lives with holy thoughts and ascetic practices. At the same time a person "living in a crowd," whether in a city or monastery, layperson or monk, can make space "in one's mind" for the gradual process of being clothed with Christ.

Making Space for God's Presence

"The way of the Lord must be prepared within the heart; for great and spacious is the heart of man, as if it were the whole world. But see its greatness, not in bodily quantity, but in the power of the mind which enables it to encompass so great a knowledge of the truth. Prepare, therefore, in your hearts the way of the Lord, by a worthy manner of life. Keep straight the path of your life, so that the words of the Lord may enter in without hindrance."

Origen of Alexandria died about 120 years before the birth of Syncletica and was the head of Alexandria's Christian catechetical school, the Didaskaleion. Syncletica grew up in the shadow of this center of learning and perhaps Origen's sermons influenced her teaching about the "divine fire within." Origen locates the place of this fire as "within the heart." This is where "the path of your life" begins, yet its capacity is not "bodily quantity" but unlimited spaciousness for the knowledge and experience of Christ. Origen and Syncletica agree that "a worthy manner of life" prepares our heart for God's presence. Today we have great competition for what occupies our minds. How can we make room for "the way of the Lord"?

Obedience Is the Place to Begin

Amma Syncletica said, *"Just as one cannot build a ship unless one has some nails, so it is impossible to be saved without humility." She also said, "As long as we are in the monastery, obedience is preferable to asceticism. The one teaches pride, the other humility."*

Syncletica often uses sailing as a metaphor for the process of sanctification. Nails bind parts of a ship's hull together to make it sea worthy; "so it is impossible to be saved without humility." But what is humility and how does a person become humble? It is tempting to think of humility as something we can obtain through our own virtuous efforts. That was a primary "demon" for the desert monks: self-reliance and pride of accomplishment. But Syncletica learned that obedience teaches humility. Obedience is a stature of listening and openness to the presence of God in other persons in whom we place our trust. After Jesus spoke with the elders in the Jerusalem temple, "he went down with [Joseph and Mary] and came to Nazareth, and was obedient to them" (Luke 2:51).

What Does Humility Look Like?

"One day Abba Arsenius consulted an old Egyptian monk about his own thoughts. Someone noticed this and said to him, 'Abba Arsenius, how is it that you with such a good Latin and Greek education, ask this peasant about your thoughts?' He replied, 'I have indeed been taught Latin and Greek, but I do not know even the alphabet of this peasant.'"

Humility is honest self-knowledge and awareness of your place in life. Arsenius had not forgotten his education and former stature as tutor to the sons of the emperor Theodosius I and respected rhetorician. But now he was a monk in the desert seeking spiritual transformation. The tutor willingly became the student, obedient to the life experience and wisdom of "an old Egyptian monk" and a "peasant." Because both Arsenius and the older monk were single-minded in their desire for God, Arsenius knew his need to know "the alphabet of this peasant" to guide him in his new life as a monk. Each of us has knowledge and skills that help us live responsible and productive lives. But in our life with God we can learn from each other. Where are the "peasants" you and I need to consult?

Humility's Venue

Abba Poemen said, *"Life in the monastery demands three things: the first is humility, the next is obedience, and the third which sets them in motion and is like a goad is the work of the monastery."*

Humility is not acquired through desire or personal effort. It is not an achievement that a person applies to "life in the monastery" or any other community. Humility is set "in motion" in the context of our daily work and relationships. That is the hard part, the "goad." Humility is born in our willingness to see the needs of other people and the whole community as well as our own. The crucible of hard work, sharing resources, and interdependence draws us away from placing personal needs and satisfactions above the life of the community. Humility is not "about me" or the way I act. It is about what my behavior makes possible in the lives of other people. Humility is conceived in our hearts and is born in our words, actions, and relationships.

"Learn from Me"

Amma Syncletica said, *"Because humility is good and salutary, the Lord clothed himself in it while fulfilling the economy [of salvation] for humanity. For he says, 'Learn from me, for I am gentle and humble of heart' [Matt 11:29]. Notice who it is who is speaking; learn his lesson perfectly. Let humility become for you the beginning and end of virtues. He means a humble heart; he refers not to appearance alone, but to the inner person, for the outer person will also follow after the inner."*

Being "clothed in Christ" means openness to "learn his lesson perfectly." The desert elders looked to the risen Christ as the exemplar and source of energy for spiritual transformation. In this context, "perfectly" means completely and wholeheartedly. Syncletica, like her peers, knew that being a disciple means not simply "following" but "being with," and prayer was the primary way to "learn [Jesus'] lesson perfectly." She echoes Jesus in declaring that the foundation of our relationship with God and other people lies within our hearts. The grace of humility is an attitude that makes prayer and compassion possible. Our external behavior will "follow after the inner."

APRIL 15

Humility Is Given, Not Achieved

Abba John Cassian said, *"A humility of heart must be maintained which is genuine and which does not come from an affected humbleness of body and speech but from a deep humbleness of mind. It will glow with the clearest indication of patience precisely when a person does not boast to others about crimes of his that are not to be believed, but rather disregards what is insolently said against him by someone else and endures insults inflicted upon him with a gentle and placid heart. . . . True patience and humility are not acquired or held onto without profound humility of heart. If they proceed from this source they will stand in need of neither the benefit of a cell nor the refuge of solitude. For whatever is sustained from within by the virtue of humility, which is the begetter and guardian, does not require the protection of anything."*

Modern society is suspicious of humility. Some psychologists and philosophers interpret humility as weakness, false pride, passive-aggressive behavior, and claim it is a source of chronic guilt. Self-assertion is preferred. But Abba John knows the deep psychological power of authentic humility that cannot be affected or controlled. "It will glow." Perhaps Abba John was thinking of St. Paul's description of love in 1 Corinthians 13. A humble person has no need for boasting or protecting himself or herself from gossip or slander. Humility begins and "is sustained from within." It does not need protection from either the cell or solitude. Humility can neither be created nor taken away.

In the Company of Others

Abba Evagrius said, *"You know very well, my brother, that someone who wants to set out on a long journey will first of all examine himself, and then he will attach himself to other travelers with whom he is able and willing to keep up; otherwise he may get left behind by his companions on the journey and come to harm. It is exactly the same way with the person who wants to travel on the road to righteousness. First of all let him look into himself and see how strong he is, then let him choose a way of life that is appropriate to himself."*

Each person who freely chooses "the road to righteousness" is unique and begins his or her journey toward transformation at a different place. Each person should "first of all examine himself" or herself. We should not be afraid or avoid being honest about where we are in our life with God. There is a danger in setting our goals too high or wanting to be like someone we admire. It is best to see "how strong" we are, choose spiritual practices that are "appropriate," and seek "other travelers" who will guide us along the way with challenging but realistic advice and example. Mentors should avoid coercion and disciples should avoid emulation.

A Simple yet Challenging Beginning

"When someone comes to the door of the monastery, wishing to renounce the world and be added to the number of the brothers, he shall not be free to enter. First the father of the monastery shall be informed (of his coming.) He shall remain outside at the door a few days and be taught the Lord's prayer and as many psalms as he can learn. Carefully shall he make himself known. . . . If they see that he is ready for everything, then shall he be taught the rest of the monastic discipline: what he must do and whom he must serve, whether in the synaxis [assembly] of all the brothers or in the house to which he is assigned, as well as in the refectory [dining hall]. Perfectly instructed in every good work, let him be joined to the brothers."

Abba Pachomius did not "invent" monastic community life. His innovation was to gather men and women from existing, separate communities, small or large, as well as persons newly attracted to monastic life, and enable them to share a mutually accepted manner of life. Pachomian *koinonia* was a way to live a life of prayer with "fellow travelers." Entrance into a community began with waiting outside with just a taste of the inner life of the community. The decision to join was coupled with the community's decision to accept because it would become a mutual and interdependent experience. In the next few days we will reflect on this process.

APRIL 18

Don't Take Anything for Granted

"When someone comes to the door of the monastery, wishing to renounce the world and be added to the number of brothers, he shall not be free to enter. First the father of the monastery shall be informed (of his coming.) He shall remain outside at the door a few days and be taught the Lord's prayer and as many psalms as he can learn."

At first glance this sounds rude, harsh, and inhospitable. Surely the monks would be glad to include you in their community! You have let go of the futility of worldly things and answered a call to the monastic manner of life. Where are the welcoming arms? At "the door of the monastery" it becomes clear that monastic life is different from conventional communities. The waiting is related to discernment, patience, and preparation. The open arms are present but are not superficial. Love requires honest awareness of what this new life will be like and what the novice will bring to the community. This is true for male or female communities. So, he or she "shall remain outside at the door a few days." Whether a faith community is a monastery or modern congregation, it is wise to enter slowly and look beneath the surface of things.

Who Is Knocking?

"Carefully shall he make himself known: has he done anything wrong and, troubled by fear, suddenly run away? Or is he under someone's authority? Can he renounce his parents and spurn his own possessions?"

Men and women were drawn to desert monastic life for a variety of reasons. Some motives were naïve and self-serving and included persons evading taxes, military service, or fleeing the consequences of serious crimes. Others were tired of the superficiality of conventional society and wanted to be alone with God and headed for heaven. Many were attracted to monastic life or the life of a hermit because they had been influenced by holy men and women near their towns and cities. Most motives really did not matter, because the goal of monastic life is transformation. But it was essential for each person to know his or her motive and to carefully "make himself [or herself] known." They must be transparent to themselves and to the community. Fear was a motive that often blinded a person to the authentic desires of her or his heart. Renouncing parents and possessions was not denial of their worth but awareness that commitment to Christ must be single-minded and undivided. Knowing one's self was the beginning.

Self-Knowledge Leads beyond Yourself

"But you my beloved in the Lord, know yourselves, so that you may know this time, and 'be prepared to offer yourselves to God as a pleasing sacrifice' [Rom 12:1]. Truly, my beloved, I write to you as 'wise men' [1 Cor 10:15], who are able to know themselves. I know that he who knows himself knows God and his dispensations for his creatures."

Pachomius's exhortation for the person waiting at the door of the monastery to "make himself known" echoes the wisdom of Antony the Great in a letter to monks who sought his wisdom. "This time" refers to entrance into a monastic life of prayer when monks are to "be prepared" to offer themselves to God. The first step toward being "wise men" is to "know yourselves." This self-knowledge is fundamental because it leads to discernment of what is false and self-serving in a person's life. Through a discipline of prayer a person will confront and be led beyond his or her false self and discover the image of God within. The person who "knows God" in this way is on the path toward the "dispensations" of transformation.

Readiness for Discipline

"If they see that he is ready for everything, then shall he be taught the rest of the monastic discipline: what he must do and whom he must serve, whether in the synaxis [assembly] of all the brothers or in the house to which he is assigned, as well as in the refectory [dining hall]. Perfectly instructed in every good work, let him be joined to the brothers."

Entrance into a Pachomian *koinonia* required mutual acceptance and responsibility. When the community sees "that he is ready for everything," the candidate is "taught the rest of the monastic discipline." Both self-knowledge and awareness of unique responsibilities are preludes for embracing this manner of life. There will be specific tasks, the expectation of cooperation and obedience, and willingness to be "instructed in every good work." The wisdom of Pachomius is his firm desire for both individuality and communal life. The individual commits himself or herself to the life of the community and the community commits itself to accept and support each person. Both say yes to each other and both become responsible for each other as a faith community.

The Rest of Monastic Discipline

Abba John the Dwarf said, *"I think it best that a man should have a little of all the virtues. Therefore, get up very early every day and acquire the beginning of every virtue and every commandment of God.*

Use great patience, with fear and long-suffering, in the love of God, with all the fervor of your soul and body."

In the same way that Pachomius advises patience before entering the monastic community, John the Dwarf urges "great patience" in embracing the disciplines of monastic life. It is natural to want to "jump right in" and make progress. Every convert or new member of a faith community shares this initial excitement and enthusiasm. But it is not easy to "have a little of all the virtues," nor is it wise to be over confident. A steady and moderate pattern of disciplines will balance "the fervor of your soul and body" with humble awe and sometimes painful persistence. The important thing is to "get up very early every day" and realize that you are always a beginner and the goal is not efficient mastery of the life of prayer you have chosen. This is the first of all the virtues. More will follow.

A Tall Order

Abba John the Dwarf continues, *"Exercise great humility, bear with interior distress; be vigilant and pray often with reverence and groaning, with purity of speech and control of your eyes. When you are despised do not get angry; be at peace, and do not render evil for evil."*

As we have seen, the fundamental virtue of a monk is humility. A monk newly welcomed into the community legitimately wonders, what does humility look like? Abba John shows genuine love by being honest about what he or she may expect. There will be "interior distress." Do not deny what you are feeling. The beginning is hard, but remain open, knowing that the hardship is part of the path you have chosen. It is all right to express the hardship and "groaning" as long as your words come from a heart that is genuinely open to God's movement within you. Avoid dwelling on things that will scatter your vision of the path you have desired. You will be tempted to get angry when others lose patience with you, but do not let that anger define your relationship with members of your new community. If another monk tries to lead you away from your path because it is difficult, remain committed to your new manner of life.

Maintaining Perspective

Abba John continues advice for beginners: *"Do not pay attention to the faults of others, and do not try to compare yourself to others, knowing you are less than every created thing. Renounce everything material and that which is of the flesh."*

Abba John was a beginner once and knows the enthusiasm of a "new convert." We are eager to make progress and look at the world with new eyes. Things are different now and we tend to see and evaluate everyone and everything on the basis of our newly chosen life. All of a sudden we see others with a more critical and often impatient eye. But John learned that paying "attention to the faults of others" will shatter the peace God is calling us to embody. It's not our job. At the same time we, as conscientious beginners, are tempted to use others as a measure of our "progress." We can see ourselves as "worse" or "better" than others. If we are able to know that we "are less than every created thing," we will be open to see people and things as they really are rather than how we want them to be. We will "renounce" what is futile and of limited value. Our human relationships will not be based solely on pleasure and personal satisfaction.

Essential Provisions for the Journey

Abba John describes how to care for your soul: *"Live by the cross, in warfare, in poverty of spirit, in voluntary spiritual asceticism, in fasting, penitence and tears, in discernment, in purity of soul, taking hold of that which is good."*

This is quite a shopping list of spiritual practices. Some may say, "Get serious!" That is precisely what John is doing. At the heart of human transformation is living "by the cross." Jesus was willing to face the consequences of loving his neighbor. Abba John is telling us that our life with God is a matter of life and death and requires a completely open and dependent spirit. The desert elders depended totally on God. Their "voluntary spiritual asceticism" was a willingness to cooperate with God's grace and energy in their lives. "Fasting" helped keep their physical and emotional needs under control so they could direct their full energies toward God's desire for their lives. They did not always succeed, and "penitence and tears" helped them discern their failings and desire restoration to the "purity of soul" God saw in them. All of these "provisions," difficult as they were, helped them "tak[e] hold of" their life with God.

Perseverance Needed

Abba John continued, *"Do your work in peace. Persevere in keeping vigil, in hunger and thirst, in cold and nakedness, and in sufferings."*

Abba John knew the path to transformation must be single-minded but is not easy. The "work" is not an end in itself and we will have difficulty letting go of control of life and our false self. A decision to commit our lives to God does not automatically mean freedom from temptations or anxieties. We will be distracted from God's voice. The desert elders valued stillness because it helped them do their "work in peace." Their peace was not the absence of inner conflict. It was resting in an openness to God's grace. One example is "keeping vigil," a period, usually at night, where various postures of openness, combined with chanting psalms or expressions of a desire for God's presence, open the heart for God's presence. Fasts from food and water helped keep their focus on God rather than physical satisfactions. The desert nights were cold and their clothes were simple. The self-imposed hardships brought a variety of "sufferings" that would refine the soul's quest.

The Gift of Life's Limited Duration

Abba John finishes with an unusual exhortation: *"Shut yourself in a tomb as though you were already dead, so that at all times you will think death is near."*

Abba John has not lost his mind and is not recommending mental or physical suicide. He is not alone. Abba Antony said, *"And in order that we not become negligent [in our discipline], it is good to carefully consider the Apostle's statement: I die daily."* Abba Evagrius said, *"Sit in your cell, collecting your thoughts. Remember the day of your death."* This fundamental advice is a reminder that each day is lived in the presence of God, is a gift of God, and is totally sustained by God. Life is limited by time and space yet is a sacred gift. Paying attention to our mortality extends our vision of human life beyond what we can control or desire. If we "die daily," we are relieved from anxiety about time and personal progress in our life with God. Each day is an opportunity to share in the new life Christ offers and an opportunity to make Christ tangible in ours.

APRIL 28

The Unity of Birth and Death

"A nun asked Blessed Sarah: 'Tell me my lady, how can I be saved?' The saint said to her, 'Be as though you were dead: do not care about human dishonor; nor about worldly glory; in stillness, retreat into your cell; continually remember only God and death, and you will be saved.'"

Earlier this month Amma Syncletica said, "We are on this earth as if in a second maternal womb." She spoke of a third birth that "is granted to us as a result of our conversion and good works." Now blessed Sarah, along with Antony, Evagrius, and John the Dwarf, speaks of living this new life "as though you were dead." We have seen earlier this year that the cell is the place of human transformation. Sarah reminds her new sister to go to her cell and in its stillness let go of both "human dishonor" and "worldly glory." This acknowledges the deep psychological disease that shame, guilt, and vainglory impose on authentic human life. If a person can die to the power of these diseases, the power of God's love will give birth to wholeness.

Remembering Who We Are

Amma Sarah said, *"As long as the soul loves its body it cannot love God, because the Lord said, 'He that loveth his life shall lose it; and he that hateth his life in this world shall keep it until life eternal.' (Jn. 12:25)"*

Remembering our death each day also refers to dying, daily, to our control of life and valuing bodily desires more than God. In Amma Sarah's day, to "hate" one's life meant not to prefer it above something else. She echoes St. Paul's exhortation not to value something that has limited duration over our authentic life that is eternal. Sarah's focus is on Jesus' fundamental invitation to "take up your cross and follow me." Remembering our death is a matter of life and death, for as God said to Adam (the human made from dust of the earth), "for out of [the ground] you were taken; you are dust, and to dust you shall return" (Gen 3:19). It is tempting to seek mastery of the resources and pleasures of the earth and our bodies. But "as long as the soul loves its body it cannot love God." I am sure Sarah had these words of Jesus in mind too: "No one can serve two masters" (Matt 6:24). Amma Sarah is reminding her sisters, and us, that a "monk" is someone who lives an undivided life.

The Bottom Line

"Abba John the Dwarf said, 'A house is not built by beginning at the top and working down. You must begin with the foundations in order to reach the top.' They said to him, 'What does this saying mean?' He said, 'The foundation is our neighbour, whom we must win, and that is the place to begin. For all the commandments of Christ depend on this one.'"

This month John the Dwarf, Pachomius, Syncletica, and a few other elders have mentored us in "a little bit of all the virtues." It has been a rich but austere summary of the "foundations" of monastic life. In this context, a virtue is a core value, a deep root that feeds daily life. But what is the purpose of all this work? Is it spiritual progress? Is it to become a holier person? John is very clear that all this work is not an end in itself. These "foundations" support our relationships with other people. They are not directed toward self-reliance in our life with God. The foundation of our identity is rooted in "our neighbour, whom we must win." Winning our neighbor does not mean controlling others for our self-interest but fulfilling Christ's command to love others as ourselves. This commandment reminds us that love is the source of authentic relationships and the source of life-giving community.

MAY

The Mystery of Human Transformation

We have seen that the men and women who withdrew to the desert from the dominant Roman society were searching for a new way of life. Some of them believed it was the only way they could offer themselves completely to God. Many Christians had been put to death during Roman persecution and the sacrifice of their lives was considered the ultimate gift to God: red martyrdom. Fleeing to the desert for a life dedicated to prayer was a new form of martyrdom: white martyrdom. Although there were many motives for fleeing to the desert, eventually the desert monks learned that they could not give their lives totally to God until they were willing to let go of control of their lives. This became a process of self-knowledge and purification from the passions and desires of an unrestrained ego that had profaned their inner life and created a false self. This was not a denial of the sacredness of human life or human society. It was the awareness that, in the words of Abba Dorotheos of Gaza, their "original nature" had been abandoned through the desires of the ego to be in control of one's life. The transformation of this false self was not always a conscious desire but it lay behind a yearning for the kingdom of heaven. It was the desire for the abundant life Jesus offered.

The process of transformation was not the replacement of an evil ego with a "good" ego. It was the transformation and completion of the creation of an incomplete and misguided ego. The image of God remained within the false self but yearned to be released. The purpose of transformation was nothing less than fulfillment of the Great Commandment: to love God with one's entire being and love one's neighbor.

Transformation, as we shall see, was not a goal that could be achieved through human effort. It was a mystery that led monks toward the frontiers of genuine human life. Transformation is a gift of God and requires total dependence on God's grace. After decades as an austere hermit, Abba Arsenius cried, "Do not leave me, Lord, for I have not yet made a beginning." Yet all monks embraced life in their cells and communities as the venues for praxis. As we have seen, silence, solitude, prayers, meditation, vigils, chanting of psalms, manual labor, study, and care of one's neighbor demonstrated that the primary venue for transformation was the life of the monk, body, mind, and spirit. Praxis made collaboration with God's Spirit possible. Transformation was not a "leaving the world" even though there was the yearning for heaven. The desert elders had a sense of time that enabled them to be aware that embedded in their incomplete progress toward transformation was the "final" transformation in heaven.

During May we will reflect on this mystery of transformation and observe how honest the desert elders were about roadblocks, discouragements, and their weaknesses and failures. At the same time we will see their commitment to relying on God's power, not their own.

What Is Transformation?

Abba Matta El-Meskeen said, *"If honey, which is transient food, warms the human body, how much more will God enkindle a person's whole spiritual being, so that he or she feels a divine fire raging within, working for purification and remorse, for gladdening and comforting—at one time instilling in a person the earnest yearning for the kingdom of heaven, at another spurring him or her on to service and sacrifice for others. And so man receives during his or her prayers the inspirations of the will of God relevant to him or her."*

Abba Matta is a modern abba and until his death in 2006 was the spiritual leader of the Monastery of St. Macarius the Great in Scetis, Egypt. The modern monastery is on the same site where Macarius gathered a small group of disciples in 367 CE. This ancient tradition, with its common life and wisdom, has not changed its purpose in sixteen hundred years: human transformation. The modern monks of this ancient monastic community have withdrawn from the busy life of cities like Cairo and Alexandria to live an ancient ascetic life. Most of them are hermits, yet all are committed to love of God and neighbor. They receive thousands of short daytime visits a year from pilgrims. What draws them? For the next three days Abba Matta will help us understand the mystery and reality of how God can "enkindle a person's whole spiritual being."

The Whole Person

Abba Matta said, *"If honey, which is transient food, warms the human body, how much more will God enkindle a person's whole spiritual being, so that he or she feels a divine fire raging within."*

When God spoke to Moses on Mount Horeb, God promised to lead the Israelites from slavery in Egypt "to a good and broad land, a land flowing with milk and honey" (Exod 3:8). The Hebrews used honey to sweeten food, for medicinal purposes, and for gift giving. It was considered pure, without blemish, and the purity and righteousness of God's laws are described as "sweeter also than honey, and drippings of the honeycomb" (Ps 19:10). Abba Matta has all this in mind when he speaks of God's desire to "enkindle a person's whole spiritual being." Honey is valuable for our physical sustenance but is "transient food." God's desire is to transform and sustain our whole being. We are beings that include body, mind, and spirit, and the "divine fire raging within" will warm not only our bodies but also the fullness of our being.

Sanctification and Love

Abba Matta continues, *"Working for purification and remorse, for gladdening and comforting—at one time instilling in a person the earnest yearning for the kingdom of heaven, at another spurring him or her on to service and sacrifice for others."*

Abba Matta uses very few words to describe the gradual and balanced process of human transformation that takes place in our life of prayer. Part of our prayer is "working for purification." This takes place through honest "remorse" (awareness) of those aspects of our lives that are not congruent with God's desires. At the same time we experience "gladdening and comforting" as the burdens and futile consequences of our self-centeredness are lifted and we become more aware of God's love and desires for us. This holy praxis of prayer results in a firm "yearning" for intimacy with God and what God desires (the kingdom) and at the same time a genuine passion to share our lives with our neighbor. It is neither self-centered nor self-serving. Inner transformation becomes tangible in our way of life.

MAY 4

Remorse Is Not Self-Loathing

Abba John Climacus said, *"As I ponder the true nature of compunction [sorrow for sins], I find myself amazed by the way in which inward joy and gladness mingle with what we call mourning and grief, like honey in a comb. There must be a lesson here, and it surely is that compunction is properly a gift from God, so that there is a real pleasure in the soul, since God secretly brings consolation to those in their heart of hearts who are repentant."* He also said, *"God does not insist or desire we should mourn in agony of heart; rather, it is his wish that out of love for him we should rejoice with laughter in our soul. Take away sin, and tears become superfluous; where there is no bruise, no ointment is required."*

Abba John (575–649 CE) was a monk on Mount Sinai. He wrote about vices that threaten a person's transformation and virtues that lead to fullness of life. Abba Matta and Abba John agree that "remorse" and "compunction" are both "a gift from God" that leads toward "gladdening and comforting." In the same way a honeycomb holds its honey, "mourning and grief" for sins "mingle" with the mystery of God's forgiveness and love. This gives birth to encouragement and desire for transformation through "inward joy and gladness." Rather than being a morbid, "guilt-ridden" experience, sorrow for sins begins a turning toward God that helps us desire newness of life. Remorse may be painful, but the self-knowledge it brings will lead to "a real pleasure in the soul."

The Fullness of Prayer

Abba Matta El-Meskeen said, *"If honey, which is transient food, warms the human body, how much more will God enkindle a person's whole spiritual being, so that he or she feels a divine fire raging within, working for purification and remorse, for gladdening and comforting—at one time instilling in a person the earnest yearning for the kingdom of heaven, at another spurring him or her on to service and sacrifice for others. And so man receives during his or her prayers the inspirations of the will of God relevant to him or her."*

Abba Matta concludes this long saying that is repeated from May 1 with a remarkable statement: "And so a man receives during his or her prayers the inspirations of the will of God relevant to him or her."

It is tempting to think of prayer as requests or desires with a focus on fulfillment in the future, especially during the process of spiritual transformation. Abba Matta is clear that "a man receives *during* his or her prayers." He is clear that "inspirations of the will of God" are received during the flow of energy between God and a human being in the context of personal prayer. These inspirations are the movement of God's Spirit within the spirit of the person who "works for purification." A first step is openness to the movement of the Holy Spirit so that the desires of God for a person become the same desires that person wills for herself or himself. But this is a gradual process and Abba Matta knows that this will happen in a manner that is "relevant" and personal.

The Mystery of Tears

"A brother asked Abba Poemen what he should do about his sins. The old man said to him, 'He who wishes to purify his thoughts purifies them with tears and he who wishes to acquire virtues, acquires them with tears; for weeping is the way the Scriptures and our Fathers give us, when they say "Weep!" Truly, there is no other way than this.'"

Every person who desires transformation asks what he or she "should do about his sins." We carry the faults and failures that have harmed us and others to the process of purification and change. The desert elders experienced this deep psychic burden and knew that it must be acknowledged and released before we can begin to move toward what God desires for us. They knew, also, that it is not simply a matter of personal resolve. The Bible and the ammas and abbas discovered a "way." We must "weep!" Weeping is a response to our sins and "there is no other way than this." It is also the beginning of a new way of living. Some of the desert elders' eyes and cheeks were red from long periods of weeping. The external tears were a manifestation of an internal cleansing experience. What is the mysterious power of tears?

The Cleansing Waters of Tears

Abba Poemen said, *"For weeping is the way the Scriptures and our Fathers give us, when they say 'Weep!' Truly, there is no other way than this."*

When Abba Poemen refers to "our Fathers," he is speaking about the wisdom of the abbas who were most revered because their lives spoke louder than their words. Abba John the Dwarf speaks of tears in the context of a summary of the most fundamental virtues leading toward transformation. *"Live by the Cross, in warfare, in poverty of spirit, in voluntary spiritual asceticism, in fasting, in penitence and tears, in discernment, in purity of soul, taking hold of that which is good."* He links tears with penitence because tears are the bodily expression of sorrow for sins. They are the visible expression of the release of burdens that will inhibit and delay our openness to God. Tears are a natural and powerful psychological cleansing of a negative self-image that memory of sins imposes on us. They are the "way" to "purity of soul."

Inner Freedom

Abba Elias said, *"What can sin do when there is penitence? And of what use is love where there is pride?"* He also said, *"Men turn their minds either to their sins, or to Jesus, or to men."*

Abba Elias experienced the power of sin to control his external and internal life. He must have been familiar with St. Paul's dilemma: he realized he failed to do the good he desired and chose sinful behavior. How can a person be released from this prison and its impediments to wholeness of life? The focus of our minds and a penitent heart can release us from this self-imposed prison. The memory and personal consequences of sinful behavior will lose their power when we release them through genuine sorrow and tears. Elias declares, also, that we have a choice. We can keep our minds focused on sinful desires and memory of previous sins. We can direct all our energy to other persons. Or we can turn our minds toward Jesus. *"Where attention goes, energy flows."*

Penitence and Humility

Amma Sarah said, *"If I prayed God that all men should approve of my conduct, I should find myself a penitent at the door of each one, but I shall rather pray that my heart may be pure towards all."*

Penitence and tears will release inner burdens that inhibit our openness to God's grace. Amma Sarah learned that sorrow for sins will lead also to a renewed desire to love our neighbors. If we seek approval in each relationship, we shall find ourselves "penitent[s] at the door of each one." We are not the source of our love. Knowing her weakness, yet desiring loving relationships, Sarah "pray[s] that my heart may be pure towards all." Yes, she will still fail at times and be penitent, but she yearns for a heart that first seeks her neighbor's welfare above her own. She does not want to take control of every relationship. Yet, like Amma Syncletica she knows that in the beginning this requires *"many battles"* with ourselves. *"So we must kindle the divine fire in ourselves through tears and hard work."*

Tears Clear a Path to Salvation

"Abba Isaiah questioned Abba Macarius saying, 'Give me a word.' The old man said, 'Flee from men.' Abba Isaiah said, 'What does it mean to flee from men?' The old man said, 'It means to sit in your cell and weep for your sins.'"

"As he was dying, Abba Benjamin said to his sons, 'Be joyful at all times, pray without ceasing and give thanks for all things.'"

Abba Macarius describes fleeing from men as "sit[ting] in your cell" in order to "weep for your sins." Rather than antisocial behavior, this is voluntarily chosen solitude that includes tears and penitence. It is part of the "way toward salvation." But where does the "way" take us? After a lifetime of prayer, Abba Benjamin passes on the fruits of the transformation he experienced. "Be joyful at all times, pray without ceasing and give thanks for all things." Tears freed him to experience the joy of God's presence and gratefulness for life itself. There is a tendency today to want the joy without the tears. There is no guarantee that "tears" will eventually bring joy. But the psychological and spiritual wisdom of abbas Macarius and Benjamin reminds us to be honest with ourselves. We cannot manufacture joy by ignoring tears.

From Self-Interest toward Charity

Abba Matta El-Meskeen said, *"We are not to entreat God that our interests may thrive, or that our responsibilities and works may grow and flourish, thereby giving us earthly fame and glory, carnal peace and comfort. Rather, we should ask [God] to root out of all our affairs the spirit of selfishness, which glorifies the human ego, and to inspire in us uprightness of mind and heart that we may not use guile, deceit, covetousness, falsehood, theft or lying in our work."*

Tears and repentance free us to desire the hard work of transformation. They turn the attitude of our prayer away from "the spirit of selfishness, which glorifies the human ego," toward the work of the Holy Spirit in the roots of our being. The unrestrained human ego desires success, comfort, and personal peace. Our transformation is made possible when we ask God to help us place these desires behind and "to inspire in us uprightness of mind and heart." Notice that Abba Matta speaks of both the mind and the heart, our whole being. When mind and heart are bonded, there is no need for the satisfaction and false security of "earthly fame and glory, carnal peace and comfort." We are freed from using the weapons of "guile, deceit, covetousness, falsehood, theft or lying in our work." Transformation transcends the need for "our interests [to] thrive."

Binding Head and Heart

Pseudo-Macarius said, *"For the heart directs and governs all the other organs of the body. And when grace pastures the heart, it rules over all the members and the thoughts. For there, in the heart, the mind abides as well as all of the thoughts of the soul and all its hopes. This is how grace penetrates throughout all parts of the body."*

Pseudo-Macarius was a fourth-century Syrian monk. We know little about him except through his writing. Abba Matta, the spiritual father of the modern St. Macarius Monastery in Egypt, still heard his voice after sixteen hundred years. Macarius believed that the heart is an axial place where a person's spirit and the Spirit of God exist together. It is the seat of a person's desires and action "and governs all the other organs of the body." The mind, the seat of rational thought, is made complete when it abides in the heart and becomes enlightened by "all of the thoughts of the soul and all its hopes." Only then is the whole person filled with grace, the energy of God. The mind is an essential part of who we are, but it is only "at its best" when it is bonded with the heart. They are not separate, competing aspects of our lives.

Wonder Completes Knowledge

Abba Isaac of Nineveh said, *"What time is more holy and more appropriate for sanctification and for receiving of divine gifts than the time of prayer, when a person is speaking with God? It is then, when someone is engaged in supplicating and beseeching God, with every stirring and every thought forcibly concentrated, as he thinks on God alone, with his entire mind swallowed up in discourse with him, his heart filled with him. It is from this point onwards that the Holy Spirit, in accordance with a person's capacity and complementing what he is praying, sets in motion in him certain inaccessible insights, with the result that prayer is cut off from any movement by these very insights, and the intellect is swallowed up in wonder, forgetting the desired object of its supplication: instead its stirrings are submerged (or baptized) in a profound inebriation, and the person is no longer in this world."*

Experiencing God in one's heart enables the mind to see and experience life in a more complete way. Wonder is an essential aspect of knowledge. Abba Isaac paints a vivid picture of the flow of energy between a person and God in prayer. The mind and the heart are "swallowed up in discourse with him." Abba Isaac is telling us that rational discourse, as good as it is, has its limits. It is possible for a person to shift from personal control of discourse so that "the Holy Spirit, in accordance with a person's capacity and complementing what he is praying, set[s] in motion in him certain inaccessible insights." When "the intellect is swallowed up in wonder, forgetting the desired object of its supplication," it transcends the boundaries of rational thought. When Isaac says that "the person is no longer in this world," he means that he or she sees more than meets the eye.

MAY 14

When Temptations Take Over

Amma Syncletica said, *"Those who put out to sea at first sail with a favorable wind; then the sails spread, but later the winds become adverse. Then the ship is tossed by the waves and is no longer controlled by the rudder. But when in a little while there is a calm and the tempest dies down, then the ship sails on again. So it is with us, when we are driven by the spirits who are against us; we hold to the cross as our sail and so we can set a safe course."*

Every person, monk or not, begins a new spiritual discipline with enthusiasm. The decision fills us with determination for progress and the whole world seems transformed. Everything is new and our focus is positive. We have put the past aside and look to a new way of life. Then it hits without warning! Old temptations return and we become obsessive about not "giving in." We take on more austere discipline in hopes that we will prevail over our battle and not "fall back into the old patterns." Syncletica experienced this as well and encourages us not to lose heart. The desire to "sail with a favorable wind" is normal, yet we almost always seem surprised and disappointed when "later the winds become adverse." When that happens, the only "safe course" is to rely on the power of the risen Christ and not our own efforts.

Relying on God

In a letter to his disciples Abba Macarius the Great, like Syncletica, gives advice about the reality of recurring temptations. In the midst of temptations we learn to rely on God's power, not our own: *"It is God who gives [us] strength. The monk now truly understands how to give glory to God in the midst of total humiliation and from the depths of a broken heart as David says: 'the sacrifice God requires is a broken heart' (Ps 50:19). For it is from this difficult combat that humility, that broken heart, goodness and mercy issue forth."*

Any person beginning his or her journey toward transformation reaches a dilemma. If we truly experience sorrow and tears for our sins and failures, why do we continue to be hounded by continuing temptations? If we seek a new life, why are we burdened by thoughts and actions that were part of our "old life"? A battle begins in our mind; thoughts emerge trying to convince us that it is not worth it. Our former life was not so bad after all. The urge to leave the path to salvation is strong. Macarius reminds us that in this really "difficult combat" it is only "God who gives [us] strength." Humility will emerge from the "humiliation" of not being able to fix the situation ourselves. A "broken heart" is not a sad heart. It is a heart that relies totally on God so that "goodness and mercy issue forth."

Calling upon the Name of Christ

Abba Macarius the Great said, *"Concentrate on this name of our Lord Jesus Christ with a contrite heart, the words welling up from your lips and drawing you to them. And do not depict him with an image in your mind but concentrate on calling to him: 'Our Lord Jesus, have mercy on me.' Do these things in peace and you will see the peace of his divinity within you; he will run off the darkness of the passions that dwell within you and he will purify the inner person just as Adam was pure in paradise."*

What does Macarius mean when, in the midst of recurring temptations, he recommends saying "Jesus, have mercy on me"? He wants you to focus on what is happening within your heart. The saying of the *name* of Jesus will draw you to "the peace of his divinity within you" and "purify [your] inner person." The temptations are coming from "the darkness of the passions that dwell within you" and your invoking Christ will "run off the darkness." In the Middle East a person's name is more than identification. To invoke a person's name is to summon the energy and characteristics of the person. Abba Macarius knows that saying "Our Lord Jesus, have mercy on me" is to enter into a relationship with Jesus at that moment. It is not a prayer to someone far off, neither is it a physical image. It is the realization that Jesus can be present in the midst of these temptations so that "you will see the peace of his divinity within you."

Remaining Bound to Christ during Hardship along the Path

Abba Evagrius said, *"I visited Abba Macarius, distressed by my thoughts and passions of the body. I said to him, 'My father, tell me a word so I may live.' Abba Macarius said to me, 'Bind the ship's cable to the mooring anvil and through the grace of our Lord Jesus Christ the ship will pass through the diabolical waves and tumults of this murky sea and the deep darkness of this vain world.'"*

Temptations are like the flu; the extreme discomfort colors your whole experience and you believe it will go on forever. You feel helpless and discouraged. Abba Evagrius felt the same way about his "thoughts and passions of the body." They made his life of prayer seem like a "murky sea and the deep darkness of this vain world." Notice that in the midst of his "diabolical waves and tumults" he seeks the experience and support of someone he trusts. The desert elders knew the dangerous consequences of trying to "go it on your own." Macarius's word to Evagrius is simple and profound: remain connected to Christ and you will pass through this dark and difficult period. The "mooring anvil" is Christ's presence in personal prayer and in the experience of a fellow traveler.

MAY 18

Experiencing the Dark Side of Life

"One of the elders related that one night he had begun to pray in the inner desert, when he heard the very loud sound of a horn, like a call to battle. He was astonished, telling himself the desert was empty and no one was there. So where did the sound of a horn come from in such a desert? Would there be a war? Then the demon came face-to-face with him and said in a loud voice, 'Yes, monk, it's war. If you want, fight; if not, surrender to your enemies.'"

The desert was not empty. In the Hebrew worldview the desert and the depths of the oceans were the habitation of evil spirits. The desert was a fearsome place. Many elders believed it was the last and most powerful refuge of evil demons fleeing to a place they could call their own. The desert elders too fled to the desert for a place they could call their own and seek God in solitude. Some believed that the ensuing "call to battle" was a face-to-face confrontation with real and external demons. Others knew that the demons they experienced in the desert were the demons they brought with them within their own lives. The elder quoted above knew that "the very loud sound of a horn" represented his own need to confront the demonic influences in his life that could scatter and deflect his desire for God. Unless he came to terms with what the horn announced, he would have to surrender what he wanted the most.

Are Demons Real?

Athanasius's *Life of Antony* presents the struggles that Antony the Great had with demons and describes their psychological and physical presence: *"The assault and appearance of the evil ones, on the other hand, is something troubling, with crashing and noise and shouting—the sort of disturbance one might expect from tough youths and robbers. From this come immediately terror of the soul, confusion and disorder of thoughts, dejection, enmity toward ascetics, listlessness, grief, memory of relatives [a strong desire to 'go home'] and fear of death; and finally there is craving of evil, contempt for virtue, and instability of character."*

Not all monks believed that "the evil ones" were real. In fact, abbas Evagrius and John Cassian were not convinced that they had physical or even spiritual substance. Others thought they were "fallen angels" or nonhuman spirits whose purpose was to destroy a monk's intimacy with God. Creatures or not, their influence was real. There is no reason to doubt that Antony's experiences with demons were real, whether or not what he describes is personified. His list of demonic (scattering) symptoms is daunting and includes almost every psychological dysfunction produced by physical or spiritual stress: terror, confusion, dejection, alienation from peers, listlessness, grief for what is desired yet seems unattainable, fear of death, instability, and, finally, capitulation to evil. Antony's transformation was not easy!

Interior Warfare and Fear

Abba Antony experienced demons as a troubling invasion into his life of prayer. *"From this come immediately terror of the soul, confusion and disorder of thoughts, dejection, enmity toward ascetics, listlessness, grief, memory of relatives [a strong desire to 'go home'] and fear of death; and finally there is craving of evil, contempt for virtue, and instability of character."*

Antony experienced demons both internally and with physical sensory awareness of "crashing and noise and shouting." His descriptions of these consequences come from personal experience of years of solitude. Whatever was happening came in unexpected ways and brought "terror of the soul." The terror lay in not knowing what was happening and scattered, helpless thinking. The panic brought on a depressing sense of abandonment and anger that his austere life of prayer was not working. Why bother, if this is what happens? Where is God? Who is really in control? Should I go home? Perhaps I'm dying. Evil must be stronger than God. As uncomfortable as these experiences were, Antony could not deny their reality. He had to face them.

Away from Home and Vulnerable

"Among the brothers there was still another who set about asking our father Pachomius, 'If you do not allow me to go home and see my family, I will go home and become a secular again.'"

In the eastern Mediterranean world family is the central community that gives life and support to an individual. It is a person's primary loyalty. Nothing is more important. A home is not simply a domicile; it is a sanctuary. Jesus understood this when he exhorted followers to "hate" their family members if they wanted to be his disciples. (See Luke 14:26.) In Jesus' culture the word translated "hate" means to "prefer," not detest. He was calling for a radical change in loyalty that placed life with God above family and redirected the security of family life to placing one's life in God's hands. The desert elders had chosen a life with God, but their strong emotional ties with family often interfered with single-minded devotion to prayer. The security of family was replaced with vulnerability to demons.

A New Earthly Family

Abba Poemen said, *"It is written, 'As the hart longs for flowing streams, so longs my soul for Thee, O God.' (Ps. 42.1) For truly harts in the desert devour many reptiles and when their venom burns them, they try to come to the springs, to drink so as to assuage the venom's burning. It is the same for the monks: sitting in the desert they are burned by the venom of evil demons, and they long for Saturday and Sunday to come to be able to go to the springs of water, that is to say, the body and blood of the Lord, so as to be purified from the bitterness of the evil one."*

In the desert a monk was far from the security of his or her birth family. It could be a lonely and dangerous place, physically and spiritually. But even the remote hermits became part of a new and larger community of brothers and sisters, as well as spiritual fathers and mothers. They supported each other in prayer, shared wisdom, and worship. Abba Poemen gives a vivid description of the power of this new family to provide security, nurture, and healing. The weekly Eucharist (Holy Communion) was at the center of monastic life in the desert in the monasteries of Pachomius and in the small hesychastic communities in places like Scetis and Nitria. Poemen was not exaggerating the importance of receiving "the body and blood of the Lord, so as to be purified from the bitterness of the evil one" in the company of the brothers. Even Arsenius, who rarely had visitors, was once brought to the Eucharist on a bed because of illness.

MAY 23

A Heavenly Family

Abba Evagrius said, *"Do not wander off. His elect angels surround you, do not be dismayed; the ranks of the demons stand facing you, so do not grow lax."*

The desert elders lived at a time when wilderness areas were recognized as the domain of evil, filled with spirits that wanted to discourage and defeat a monk's desire for sanctification. The demons, whatever they were, tried every strategy to scatter a monk's resolve and fill him with fear. The greatest danger was not to "wander off" further in the physical wilderness but to stray from God's powerful presence and ignore God's "elect angels." Evagrius describes how a monk, beginning his prayer, saw the devil in the shape of a lion that *"sank his claws into the athlete's two cheeks"* and would not let go until the monk stopped his praying. The demons "stand facing you," but at the same time the extended spiritual family of angels offers help that will keep you from being discouraged and giving up, "so do not grow lax."

Malign Thoughts and Images

Abba Evagrius describes a pattern of interior distractions that often plagued a monk's prayer: *"It happens at times that the demons suggest some bad thoughts to you and again stir you up to pray against them, as is only proper, or to contradict them. Then they depart of their own choosing so as to deceive you into believing that you have conquered your thoughts of yourself and have cast fear into the demons."*

The desert elders called these distracting images and thoughts *logismois*. These demons are "bad thoughts" and they drain a person's energy because they "stir you up to pray against them." This is misplaced energy directed away from our desire for God and our true self. It can result in spiritual fatigue and will eventually lead to a lack of persistence in our prayer. But, as Evagrius points out, these *logismois* can also give us a false sense of accomplishment when they leave our consciousness. We are tempted to believe it is our own spiritual strength that has driven them away. This pride will deflect our dependence on God. Self-righteousness is an insidious danger lurking within the psyche. It is the source of another danger: self-reliance.

The Most Serious Demon of All

Abba Evagrius said, *"The demon of accedia—also called the noonday demon—is the one that causes the most serious trouble of all. . . . First of all he makes it seem that the sun barely moves, if at all, and that the day is fifty hours long. . . . Then, too, he instills in the heart of the monk a hatred for the place, a hatred for his very life itself, a hatred for manual labor . . . and brings before the mind's eye the toil of the ascetic struggle and, as the saying has it, leaves no leaf unturned to induce the monk to forsake his cell and drop out of the fight."*

In modern society results rule. We want progress and we want it now. When our efforts are not productive or seem unproductive, we want to change our strategy or the resources that are not working to our satisfaction. This is nothing new. Evagrius and the desert elders knew this firsthand, but Evagrius points to an even more serious consequence of impatience. The "mind's eye" begins to tire of strategies that are not working and "instills in the heart of the monk" distaste for the life he has chosen. Tiredness and lack of desire prompt us to ask, why bother? and give up. Evagrius's caricature of "accedia" is almost humorous, yet he is utterly serious about its consequences. The long desert days seem twice as long, the sun gets hotter, and the mind wants to leave such a "godforsaken place." Everything seems so much harder and eventually the monk asks, why bother? This is, indeed, "the most serious trouble of all."

MAY 26

Returning to the Center

Abba Moses the Robber had some practical advice for overcoming the scattering influence of demonic thoughts: *"But because we said it is impossible for the mind not to be approached by thoughts, you must not lay everything to the charge of the assault or to those spirits who strive to instill them in us. . . . For this purpose we employ frequent reading and continual meditation on the Scriptures to give us an opportunity for spiritual recollection. . . . We also use earnest vigils and fasts and prayers, that the mind may be brought low and not mind earthly things but contemplate things celestial."*

Abba Moses is streetwise and knows that "it is impossible for the mind not to be approached by thoughts." To confront the *accedia* that discourages and scatters the heart, Moses reaffirms the importance of staying with "frequent reading and continual meditation on the Scriptures to give us an opportunity for spiritual recollection." This will assist the mind and heart to return to their center in God. Moses demonstrates a very practical rationale for praxis. It helps distract the monk from distractions! Reading and meditation on Scriptures, vigils, fasts, and prayers restore the monk's center. Praxis, praxis, and more praxis is indispensible because it helps the monk respond to Jesus' exhortation, "Remain in my word."

Unexpected Grace

"When the holy Abba Anthony lived in the desert he was beset by accidie, and attacked by many sinful thoughts. He said to God, 'Lord, I want to be saved but these thoughts do not leave me alone; what shall I do in my affliction? How can I be saved?' A short while afterwards, when he got up to go out, Anthony saw a man like himself sitting at his work, getting up from his work to pray, then sitting down and plaiting a rope, then getting up again to pray. It was an angel of the Lord sent to correct and reassure him. He heard the angel saying to him, 'Do this and you will be saved.' At these words, Anthony was filled with joy and courage. He did this and was saved."

Antony was not a novice to monastic life and was already well known and revered as "the holy Abba Antony." Yet, he had not "mastered" the ascetic life and remained vulnerable to "accidie" and "many sinful thoughts." One could easily say that his prayer was not "working" and question the efficacy of this manner of life. Antony was equally frustrated and "got up to go out." Was he giving up? Perhaps. But a surprise was waiting for him. He "saw a man like himself sitting at his work, getting up from his work to pray, then sitting down and plaiting a rope, then getting up again to pray." Sometimes it is important to step back from ourselves and routines that seem mundane or hollow. Antony was not failing, but he needed to be reassured that his praxis was worthwhile. His vision had become too narrow. A second look brought "joy and courage."

An Angelic Mirror

The desert elders experienced a variety of "visions" in the desert. The simplicity of their lives and openness to God provided a different way of seeing reality. Antony's vision of an angel in the form of *"a man like himself sitting at his work, getting up from his work to pray, then sitting down and plaiting a rope, then getting up again to pray"* came at a time of confusion and frustration. Antony's prayer, *"Lord, I want to be saved but these thoughts do not leave me alone; what shall I do in my affliction?"* infers he had tried everything in his warfare against evil thoughts and was exhausted by his efforts to be "saved." In his helplessness and lack of resolve, from God came *"an angel of the Lord sent to correct and reassure him."* Antony wanted to be whole and to experience more progress in his desire for God. The angelic vision corrected his desire for something "better" than what he was doing. It reassured him to continue his pattern of constant integration of work and prayer, mundane as it was. The angel "became" a vision of what Antony was already doing and helped him see its integrity in a new way. His frustration had blinded him from the joy and courage already present in his life of prayer.

A Genuine Struggle

Abba Evagrius said, *"When an angel makes his presence felt by us, all disturbing thoughts immediately disappear. The spirit finds itself clothed in great tranquility. It prays purely. At other times, though, we are beset with the customary struggle and then the spirit joins the fight. It cannot so much as raise its eyes for it is overtaken by diverse passions. Yet if only the spirit goes on striving it will achieve its purpose. When it knocks at the door hard enough it will be opened."*

The "customary struggle" between angels and demons represents the difficulty of overcoming unhealthy psychological wounds in the lives of the desert elders. Angels personify the power of God's presence and their presence overcomes persistent "disturbing thoughts" so that the monk's "spirit finds itself clothed in great tranquility." Although monks were not obsessed with evil thoughts and passions, they did not ignore them. When the burdens of the "battle" were heavy, their eyes became heavy too. The body language Evagrius describes is graphic. Sometimes we dare not look up when we are discouraged. But the spirit has not left us! When struggles return, we can continue knocking at the door of God's presence and rely on a power greater than our own. Raising our eyes is a first step.

Angelic Reminder

"One day Abba Isaac went to a monastery. He saw a brother committing a sin and he condemned him. When he returned to the desert, an angel of the Lord came and stood in front of the door of his cell and said, 'I will not let you enter.' But he persisted saying, 'What is the matter?' and the angel replied, 'God has sent me to ask you where you want to throw the guilty brother whom you have condemned.' Immediately he repented and said, 'I have sinned, forgive me.' Then the angel said, 'Get up, God has forgiven you. But from now on, be careful not to judge someone before God has done so.'"

Angels often protected the monks from themselves as well as from external demons. Forgiveness was a fundamental monastic virtue. Impatient anger and judgment are serious threats to community and impeded a person's relationship with God. Isaac's condemnation was no less serious than his brother's fornication. The angel's question awakened Isaac to his own weakness and became an opportunity for repentance. He experienced the forgiveness he was unwilling to give his brother. The humor in this incident is unavoidable. A visit from an angel is a rare gift. But the gift was not what Isaac expected! Perhaps Isaac had a good laugh with himself once he got over the shock of being confronted with his self-righteousness. Perhaps he had a good laugh with the brother he had condemned too. Reconciliation follows repentance.

Discernment and Self-Knowledge

Abba Antony said, *"Once a very tall demon appeared in an apparition and had the daring to say, 'I am the power of God' and 'I am Providence; what do you wish that I would give you?' But then, especially, I puffed at him, and speaking the name of Christ I made an attempt to strike him. I seemed to have hit home, and at once, with the mention of the name of Christ, this giant figure vanished, along with all his demons."*

In their desire for transformation, the desert elders battled with desperation and pride. The burden of temptations and the battle with demons had the positive consequence of making them more dependent on God's assistance. The negative aspect of their desperation was that they could easily be deceived. A demon disguised as an angel was always willing to prey on a monk's desire for help. On the other hand, some monks, filled with a sense of accomplishment in their ascetic disciplines, could easily be vulnerable to a demon's offer of God's grace or reward. When a person's heart has little room for God, it is easy to convince one's self that a harmful desire or action is not so bad. Antony's encounter seems to mirror Jesus' confrontation with the devil in the wilderness. Experienced monks, like Antony, retained their focus on Christ for guidance. Just as the devil eventually left Jesus, "this giant figure vanished" from Antony.

JUNE

The Art of Monastic Life

Monastic art was learned like all art: by being an apprentice to an experienced person who was committed to that form of art. Although all monks shared the goal of transformation in Christ, each person's path was unique and each abba or amma shared the art in his or her own way. Monks taught by personal example more than words because this process was not simply a matter of "mastering" praxis or knowledge. It always remained an art. It was not simply "going through the motions." There were exceptions. Some elders over-emphasized austerity and were striving to be more competent in the art than others. They criticized peers who were different. But these monks were corrected by wiser elders like Isidore: *"If you fast regularly, do not be inflated with pride, but if you think highly of yourself because of it, then you had better eat meat. It is better for a man to eat meat than to be inflated with pride and to glorify himself."*

Eager young monks and novices were discouraged from making rapid progress. One of the elders suggested that when an abba discerns that a novice wants to climb directly to heaven and avoid all the work of praxis, he should grab the novice firmly by the feet and pull him back to earth. The path to transformation requires patience and a willingness to depend on the advice and experience of others. These mentors, themselves, should be patient with their disciples and avoid harming them with too much austerity too soon. Amma Theodora exhorts elders to be "lovers of souls," above all.

Like all art, praxis had to be learned gradually. Abba John the Dwarf recommended that a monk try a little bit of all the virtues, rather than jumping in and mastering a single virtue all at once. Checking off items from lists for spiritual progress is not helpful. On the other hand, both a novice and master potter will make mistakes and failure will promote discouragement. Distractions will take one's eyes off the task at hand and the clay, earthy or human, will get off center. Abba Evagrius emphasizes keeping track of thoughts, temptations, and other activities of the mind and giving them, along with lack of progress, to Christ who will help the monk move on. Self-knowledge and dependence on Christ permeate every aspect of monastic art.

Monastic art is really stewardship of one's soul. It is entering into unfamiliar territory where the self cannot be in control. It is risky. The desert elders developed strong and faithful relationships with their disciples. Both abba/amma and disciple had to practice obedience, the art of listening in the context of trust. This did not mean that the elders made it "easy" for novices. On the contrary, they challenged their novices, not for the sake of control per se but to lure them into the frontiers of human transformation so that they would not look back.

JUNE 1

The Art of Monastic Life

Abba Evagrius said, *"If there is any monk who wishes to take the measure of the more fierce demons so as to gain experience in his monastic art, then let him keep careful watch over his thoughts. Let him observe their intensity, their periods of decline, and follow them as they rise and fall. Let him know well the complexity of his thoughts, their periodicity, the demons which cause them, with the order of successions and the nature of their associations. Then let him ask from Christ the explanations of these data he has observed."*

We ended last month with a focus on the desert elders' struggle with temptations and evil thoughts, prompted by internal and external demons. However they are defined, the demons represent an authentic psychological dimension of a person's spiritual journey toward transformation. Evagrius describes a disciplined way of responding to these troubling thoughts and desires. He points to two aspects of self-knowledge. The first is "keep[ing] careful watch over [our] thoughts" and then "ask[ing] from Christ the explanations of these data." Releasing control of our thoughts to Christ will help us accept their reality, learn from them, and seek assistance from Christ in our life of prayer. This process is part of the daily practice of "monastic art."

Artistic Balance

In the late fourth century seven monks from Palestine visited eleven monastic sites in Egypt. Their journey provides rich details about the "monastic art" in Egypt. Here is an account of a visit with Abba Or. *"When the father saw us, he was filled with joy, and embraced us, and offered a prayer for us. Then, after washing our feet with his own hands, he turned to spiritual teaching. For he was very well versed in the Scriptures, having received this charism from God. He expounded many key passages in the Scriptures for us, and having taught us the orthodox faith, invited us to participate in the Eucharist. For it is a custom among the great ascetics not to give food to the flesh before providing spiritual nourishment for the soul, that is, the Communion of Christ."*

Life becomes a work of art when it includes joy-filled hospitality, caring for one's neighbor, study, teaching, and eucharistic worship. It provides care and nourishment for body and soul. Abba Or gives a brief outline of the monastic art. His genuine joy-filled embrace of visitors demonstrates that such "interruptions" are actually part of his ascetic practice; every opportunity to love one's neighbor makes Christ tangible. Or's embrace of visitors is followed by tending to their spiritual and physical needs. After an initial prayer, he washes the desert sand from their tired, sweaty feet. Only then does Or give them his personal spiritual gift of teaching Scriptures. He shares what the Spirit has given him. Finally he invites them to share the spiritual food of the Eucharist, followed by some nourishment for their bodies.

Art Requires Passion

Abba Lot went to Abba Joseph of Panephysis and said to him, *"Abba, as far as I can I say my little office, I fast a little, I pray and meditate, I live in peace and as far as I can, I purify my thoughts. What else can I do? Then the old man stood up and stretched his hands towards heaven. His fingers became like ten lamps of fire and he said to him, 'If you will, you can become all flame.'"*

Abba Lot gives a concise summary of "monastic art." It includes ritual prayer, fasting, personal prayer and meditation, resisting evil thoughts, and seeking peace in his relationships. Yet, he sensed something was missing. He went to his abba for advice, who reminded him that all his monastic discipline, as good as it is, is not an end in itself. The art of monastic life is more than "doing." Abba Lot was, perhaps, too conscientious. His focus was on competence. He wanted to make sure he was not leaving out something important. He was. But it was not what he expected. Abba Joseph, with an eye of love and a gentle word, tells him that "you can become all flame." Lot's disciplines without passion are incomplete.

JUNE 4

Being an Apprentice

Abba Dorotheos said, *"In the Book of Proverbs it says, 'Those who have no guidance fall like leaves but there is safety in much counsel.' Take a good look at this saying, brothers. Look at what Scripture is teaching us. It assures us that we should not set ourselves up as guideposts, that we should not consider ourselves sagacious, that we should not believe we can direct ourselves. We need assistance, we need guidance in addition to God's grace."*

Every experienced potter knows that it takes time to learn how to center the clay on the wheel. There is no room in the process for clever shortcuts. Every apprentice must first observe an experienced potter and then commit himself or herself to trial, error, and continuing advice. A failed "throw" can be reworked, but there are no shortcuts. The desert elders had little sympathy for novices who, either in excitement for the new life they had chosen or in prideful self-confidence, took control of their progress. They were clear that "there is safety in much counsel" as well as God's grace. An essential part of monastic art is observing, learning from, and following the lives of elders. The abbas and ammas did not emphasize "content," although they had much wisdom to share. Their greatest gift was the way they lived in the presence of novices. They stressed the importance of walking with another on the path to transformation.

Listening to the Master Artist

Abba Isaac the Syrian said, *"Love silence above all things, because it brings you close to fruit that the tongue cannot express. Let us force ourselves to be silent and then, from out of this silence is born something that leads to silence itself [i.e. inner silence]. God grant you may perceive some part of that which is born of silence! If you begin with this discipline, I know not how much light will dawn on you from it."*

Abba Isaac learned more about the art of monastic life from the lives of his abbas than from their words. Their inner silence bore "fruit that the tongue cannot express." His first lesson was to "love silence above all things" because silence is where the apprentice monk listens to the master. The only way to "perceive some part of that which is born of silence" is to "force ourselves to be silent." This is difficult because we would rather pursue more tangible progress. But if we seek the fruits of the Spirit, we must spend time with God. The light we cannot perceive on our own will dawn on us through the inner silence of God's presence. The elders took these words of Jesus seriously: "For from exuberance of heart one's mouth speaks."

A Little Bit at a Time

Abba John the Dwarf said, *"I think it best that a [person] should have a little bit of all the virtues. Therefore, get up early every day and acquire the beginning of every virtue and every commandment of God. Use great patience, with fear and long-suffering, in the love of God, with all the fervor of your soul and body."*

The list of monastic virtues is long. As we have seen, it includes fasting, penitence and tears, vigils, meditation, control of anger, purity of speech, humility, and many more. Even mature monks could become discouraged under the austere weight of these disciplines. It is tempting to concentrate on just one or two and really master them. But mastery is not the point. Abba John has learned that these virtues form a portrait rather than a checklist. He advises looking at the forest rather than each tree and to "acquire the beginning of every virtue and every commandment of God." He speaks of patient daily experience of "a little bit of all the virtues." What is most important is an attitude of "love of God," not perfection. Faithfulness in small things will lead to other possibilities when the time is right. Don't rush sanctification!

JUNE 7

Being Patient with One's Self

"It was said of Antony that one day he was relaxing with the brothers outside the cell when a hunter came by and rebuked him. Antony said, 'Bend your bow and shoot an arrow,' and he did so. 'Bend it again and shoot another,' and he did—and again and again. The hunter said, 'Father, if I keep my bow always stretched it will break.' 'And so it is with the monk,' replied Antony; 'if we push ourselves beyond measure we will break; it is right for us from time to time to relax our efforts.'"

The abbas and ammas often spoke about "long-suffering." It meant being present with another or one's self, in the midst of difficulty, pain, failure, or sinful behavior. Abba John the Dwarf spoke of using "great patience, with fear and long-suffering." Long-suffering did not mean ignoring a difficult situation. It meant recognizing one's limitations without judgment rather than losing patience and intensifying our discipline. Antony learned that "it is right for us from time to time to relax our efforts." Antony knew also that pride lurks behind unnecessary austerity. Self-knowledge coupled with patience will help us discern a proper balance between moving forward and relaxing in our life of prayer.

JUNE 8

No Turning Back

Abba Antony said, *"Having therefore made a beginning, and set out already on the way to virtue, let us press forward to what lies ahead. And let none turn back as Lot's wife did, especially since the*

Lord said, 'No one who puts his hand to the plow and turns back is fit for the Kingdom of heaven.' Now 'turning back' is nothing except feeling regret and once more thinking about things of the world. But do not be afraid to hear about virtue, and do not be a stranger to the term. For it is not distant from us, nor does it stand external to us, but its realization lies in us, and the task is easy if only we shall will it."

Antony points to a real tension "on the way to virtue." As we "press forward to what lies ahead," the transformation we desire already "lies within us." The energy and excitement of our "beginning" must become a daily conversion to the life we have chosen. The only things that will inhibit us are regretting the initial decision, preferring material pleasures, and a lack of will. When we direct our eyes and energy to learning the virtues that are "not distant from us," the Spirit will liberate their power. Antony learned that forward vision is essential in the monastic art. Self-knowledge is not dwelling in the past. It is naming our failures, regrets, and temptations and releasing them to God. Once released, our vision can be directed to "hear[ing] about virtue." We can move forward.

A Preliminary Virtue

Amma Syncletica said, *"As long as we are in the monastery, obedience is preferable to asceticism. The one teaches pride, the other humility."*

Abba Antony described the need for persistence in pursuing the "monastic art." "Having therefore made a beginning, and set out already on the way to virtue, let us press forward to what lies ahead." Amma Syncletica sets a context for "what lies ahead." Like Antony, she has learned that ascetic disciplines are not ends in themselves. As we press forward and experience a little of all the virtues, it is tempting to take credit for "our" progress. Ascetic disciplines are essential in the process of transformation, but their power is diluted and scattered by personal pride. Our attention must not be self-centered and our efforts must not reflect self-reliance. This is why the desert elders valued the relationship between mentor and disciple. As we shall see in the next few days, obedience to an amma or abba was an *attitude* opening a path to collaboration with God's wisdom and grace. It inhibited personal control of "what lies ahead."

JUNE 10

Beyond Words

Abba Poemen heard that someone asked Abba Paësius, *"'What should I do about my soul, because it is insensitive and does not fear God?' He said to him, 'Go, and join a man who fears God, and live near him, he will teach you, too, to fear God.'"*

Paësius describes a relationship that warrants obedience. A person is genuinely concerned about the welfare of his soul. He is advised to "Go, and join a man who fears God, and live near him." The man's obedience begins with awareness that he cannot help himself. That initiative is followed by seeking advice. The opportunity to learn to "fear God" will take place by agreeing to "join a man who fears God, and liv[ing] near him." Learning is more than words. By living near his teacher, this person will submit himself to a relationship with a person whose life is lived in the fear of God. Paësius could have said, "Find someone who can tell you what you need to know." But words alone would not have satisfied the yearning of the man's soul; he wanted to change his life, not seek more information.

JUNE 11

Extending One's Family

"Abba Ammonas was asked, 'What is "the narrow and hard way?"' (Matt. 7.14) He replied, 'The "narrow and hard way" is this, to control your thoughts, and to strip yourself of your own will, for the sake of God. This is also the meaning of the sentence, "Lo, we have left everything and followed you."' (Matt. 19.27)"

The role and authority of a monastic "abba" or "amma" is related to the value of family life in Middle Eastern cultures. Most of the desert monks came from these cultures where a person's attachment to his or her family was a primary source of identity and support. The bonds of family were a person's primary loyalty. Although a father had authority for the well-being of the family, both fathers and mothers provided unique influences and guidance for their children. The word "abb-a" may signify "my father," as familial father, as well as any respected person with authority (such as a teacher/rabbi). In both cases the word is used in the context of a valued relationship. It was not easy to leave one's family of birth and learn to depend on another abba or amma and a new family.

JUNE 12

Looking beyond Ourselves

Abba Rufus said, *"He who remains sitting at the feet of his spiritual father receives a greater reward than he who lives alone in the desert."*

What does it mean to remain "sitting at the feet of [a] spiritual father" or mother? Rufus declares that the "reward" will be greater than relying solely on ourselves. Letting go of self-created rewards does not mean giving up our individuality or submitting to an arbitrary and hierarchical relationship. Learning to walk in the steps of a spiritual father or mother widens the horizons of our pathway and lures us beyond the limits of goals or disciplines we set for ourselves. We commit ourselves to one who has more experience and, through obedience to their guidance, listen to their wisdom, observe their life of prayer, and follow their example. They commit themselves to us as one who listens, mentors our movement toward transformation, and shares the presence of God in their lives with us. We enter a relationship of mutual obedience. In Greek the words for listen and obey share the same root.

JUNE 13

The Purpose Is Love, Not Control

"The same amma [Theodora] said that a teacher ought to be a stranger to the desire for domination, vain-glory, and pride; one

should not be able to fool him by flattery, nor bind him by gifts, nor conquer him by the stomach, nor dominate him by anger, but he should be patient, gentle and humble as far as possible; he must be tested and without partisanship, full of concern, and a lover of souls."

Amma Theodora is clear about the expectations of a spiritual "teacher." Patience, gentleness, and humility are essential "as far as possible." She understands from awareness of her own weaknesses that any spiritual guide can make mistakes in judgment and lose patience. But there is no room for imposition of ideology or enforcement of preferred styles of praxis. Concern for the disciple's personal and spiritual health is the fundamental test of whether or not an amma or abba is a lover of souls. Love, not control, is the context for the sometimes rigorous testing of a disciple's willingness to embrace guidance, self-knowledge, and commitment to a praxis of prayer. The art of being an abba or amma is a combination of sharing in humility and knowing one's disciple well enough, "without partisanship," to be "a lover of souls." It is a sacred partnership.

Discerning a Relationship

"It was said of Abba John the Dwarf that he withdrew and lived in the desert at Scetis with an old man of Thebes. His abba, taking a piece of dry wood, planted it and said to him, 'Water it every day with a bottle of water until it bears fruit.' Now the water was so far away that he had to leave in the evening and return the following morning. At the end of three years the wood came to life and bore fruit. Then the old man took some of the fruit and carried it to the church saying to the brethren, 'Take and eat of the fruit of obedience.'"

This story is told also of John of Lycopolis. But after only one year of watering, the dry wood was still lifeless and John's abba pulled it from the ground and left it in the desert. Whether or not the narratives happened as narrated, they speak of "the fruit of obedience" and illustrate the need to discern whether a disciple is willing to trust his abba's guidance. Without this attitude of openness, a disciple will waste opportunities to learn and scatter his or her energy away from single-minded attention to the process of transformation. The abba does not automatically become the teacher; otherwise the emphasis is on content. The relationship must be built on obedience and trust. Obedience requires listening and trust is placing one's life into the hands of the one who speaks. Both stories show that a relationship of obedience and trust takes time.

It Works Both Ways

"There was an old man who had a good disciple. One day he was annoyed and drove the disciple out. Yet the disciple sat down outside of the cell and waited. When the old man opened the door, he found him sitting there, and repented before him, saying, 'You are my abba, for your humility and patience have overcome my narrow-mindedness. Come inside! From now on you are the old man and the father, for sure, and I am the young one and the disciple. For your good works have surpassed my old age.'"

The abba "was annoyed and drove the disciple out." In his frustration and anger he did not fulfill his obedience as spiritual guide to the young man. We do not know the details, but the old man, in the heat of a difficult situation, lost his trust in the zeal of his disciple. He assumed it was the disciple's fault. Yet the young man did not let anger cloud his trust in the integrity of his spiritual guide. He accepted his mentor's weakness and waited for reconciliation. His humble response taught the old man that we are always beginners. There is an underlying humor in this incident because the roles of abba and disciple are reversed. This insight demonstrates that the abba and disciple will learn from each other. Each has an indispensible role to play in the relationship. It is give and take.

The Context for Obedience

The seven monks who visited Egypt in the late fourth century describe the life of Abba Apollo and his disciples as a relationship formed by word, shared praxis, and personal example. *"Those who*

*live with him do not take any food themselves until they have assisted
at the Eucharist and received Holy Communion. They do this daily
at the ninth hour. Then, after having eaten, they sit and listen to the
father's teaching on all the commandments until the first watch of the
night. At this point some of them go out into the desert and recite the
Scriptures by heart throughout the night. The rest remain where they
are and worship God with ceaseless hymnody until daybreak. . . .
For nobody among them was gloomy or downcast. If anyone did appear a little downcast, Father Apollo at once asked him the reason,
and told each one what was in the secret recesses of his heart. . . .
But how can one describe the grace of his speech and all his other
virtues, which so amazed us that we fell silent whenever we heard
him teach or listened to the others speaking about him?"*

Abba Apollo placed the daily Eucharist at the heart of his relationship with his disciples. Each day they were united in Christ. Then, after
a meal, they listened to their abba's wisdom on the road to salvation.
Only then did they begin their personal praxis of recitation of and
meditation on Scripture or chanting psalms and singing hymns. This
daily food of worship, teaching, and praxis bonded the abba and his
disciples so well that "if anyone did appear a little downcast, Father
Apollo at once asked him the reason, and told each one what was
in the secret recesses of his heart." It is no wonder that the visitors
from Egypt "fell silent whenever we heard him teach or listened to
the others speaking about him."

JUNE 17

The Greatest Vision

*"Abba Psenthaisius, Abba Surus and Abba Psoius used to agree
in saying this, 'Whenever we listened to the words of our Father,
Abba Pachomius, we were greatly helped and spurred on with zeal
for good works; we saw how, even when he kept silence, he taught
us by his actions.'"*

We have seen that obedience is directly related to becoming rooted
in specific ascetical disciplines that form the "monastic art." The spiritual father or mother challenges the beginner to build her or his life as
if it were a work of art. But the artist is never self-made. Repetition of
active participation in prayer, recitation of the psalms, manual work

for self-support, giving of alms, and hospitality give birth to monastic life. Obedience to this pattern of behavior gradually forms the beginner into an artist. The abba or amma is the visible manifestation of what the novice seeks. Pachomius's disciples discovered that his example gave life to his words, because "even when he kept silence, he taught us by his actions." His life gave authenticity to his teaching and guidance, even when he had nothing to say!

Roots Come First

Around 323 CE Pachomius began to develop a pattern of monastic life based on a common rule. But his vision for monastic community was the fruit of seven years of formation with an old monk named Palamon. His apprenticeship began with zeal: *"Then, moved by the love of God, he sought to become a monk. When he was told of an anchorite called Palamon, he went to him to share his anchoritic life. When he arrived, he knocked on the door. The old man looked down from above and said, 'What do you want?'—for he was abrupt in speech. He replied, 'I ask you, father, make me a monk.' He said to him, 'You cannot. This work of God is not so simple; for many have come but have not persevered.' Pachomius said, 'Put me to the test at it and see.'"* Palamon agreed and after a trial period, *"They practiced the ascesis together and gave time to prayers. . . . In their work [spinning] they toiled not for themselves but they remembered the poor, as the Apostle says."*

Pachomius's roots were in Palamon's life. It was a small community, abba and disciple, but it was enough. It is tempting when "moved by the love of God" to strike out on our own. As we have seen, the desert elders knew that one must have guides along the way, especially in the beginning. Part of God's love that moved Pachomius was to lead him to Palamon and give him the willingness to be "tested." This was not "jumping through institutional hoops." It was confirming his desire to be a monk by beginning to live the life he desired. It was being tested by reality. Eventually Pachomius left Palamon to found monasteries of his own. He took what he learned from Palamon with him. Monks in monasteries who wanted to live a solitary life were required to learn to live in community before they left to be on their own.

The Value of Community

"One day Abba Longinus questioned Abba Lucius about three thoughts saying first, 'I want to go into exile.' The old man said to him, 'If you cannot control your tongue, you will not be an exile anywhere. Therefore control your tongue here, and you will be an exile.' Next he said to him, 'I wish to fast.' The old man replied, 'Isaiah said, "If you bend your neck like a rope or a bulrush that is not the fast I will accept; but rather control your evil thoughts."' He said to him the third time, 'I wish to flee from men.' The old man replied, 'If you have not first of all lived rightly with men, you will not be able to live rightly in solitude.'"

Many monks of the desert wanted to become hermits. Some wanted to be independent in their life of prayer and withdraw from the responsibilities or distractions of community life. Other monks were called to solitude from the very beginning. In both cases the desert elders learned that a person's inner life must first be formed and strengthened by the disciplines of community. Independence is the child of obedience to mutual needs, experience, and wisdom. Isolation from other people, by itself, would not help Longinus control his tongue, fast, or control his evil thoughts. These weaknesses lay within him and would be carried wherever he went. His task was to learn to live "rightly with men" in order to "live rightly in solitude."

An Obedient Abba

"It was related of a brother who had committed a fault that when he went to see Abba Lot, he was troubled and hesitated, going in and coming out, unable to sit down. Abba Lot said to him, 'What is the matter, brother?' He said, 'I have committed a great fault and I cannot acknowledge it to the Fathers.' The old man said to him, 'Confess it to me and I will carry it.' Then he said to him, 'I have fallen into fornication, and in order to do it, I have sacrificed to idols.' The old man said to him, 'Have confidence; repentance is possible. Go sit in your cave, eat only once in two days and I will carry half of your

fault with you.' After three weeks, the old man had the certainty that God had accepted the brother's repentance. Then the latter remained in submission to the old man until his death."

Genuine sorrow and fear of judgment placed an unbearable burden on the younger monk. He literally did not know what to do until Abba Lot noticed his troubling behavior. He discerned pain and disorientation in the monk's body language and opened the door for conversation. Lot expresses his concern by asking, "What is the matter, brother?" In this case it is not the disciple who is called to listen; it is the abba. Not only does he listen but he also offers the opportunity for the monk to let go of his dilemma by saying, "Have confidence; repentance is possible." Then Lot offers a path to repentance that was not easy or patronizing. The next two daily reflections will look more closely at this path.

A Shared Journey

"Abba Lot said to him, 'What is the matter, brother?' He said, 'I have committed a great fault and I cannot acknowledge it to the Fathers.' The old man said to him, 'Confess it to me, and I will carry it.' Then he said to him, 'I have fallen into fornication, and in order to do it, I have sacrificed to idols.' The old man said to him, 'Have confidence, repentance is possible.'"

Abba Lot's nonjudgmental question frees the younger monk to tell him what he was afraid to tell other abbas. His "great fault" had imprisoned him in a house of fear and may have given him reason to question his monastic vocation. He could see nothing but the negative consequences of his weakness. Abba Lot offers an opportunity to move forward by entering into the monk's dilemma. "Confess it to me, and I will carry it." Lot is willing to hear the monk describe his sinful behavior and "carry it" with him. The abba's compassion is not given as one who is greater but as one who is willing to enter into the monk's experience. Then, without minimizing the seriousness of the sinful behavior, Lot offers the confidence of repentance.

A Committed Relationship

"The old man said to him, 'Have confidence; repentance is possible. Go, sit in your cave, eat only once in two days and I will carry half of your fault with you.' After three weeks, the old man had the certainty that God had accepted the brother's repentance. Then the latter remained in submission to the old man until his death."

Without ignoring the seriousness of the younger monk's "great fault," Abba Lot invited him to move from his sorrow and fear to confidence that new life was possible. The acknowledgment of sin and disappointment in his weakness could lead to renewal of his life with God. But he would have to turn to God and wait, in solitude and fasting, for the power of God's Spirit to release him from his faults and redirect his desires. "Go, sit in your cave, eat only once in two days and I will carry half of your fault with you." Lot knew healing requires letting go of both the sinful behavior and the sorrow. Only then would the gift of new sight be possible. But Lot offered more than instruction; he offered to share the burden. It is no wonder that the monk "remained in submission to the old man until his death."

Two Kinds of Sight

"A brother at Scetis committed a fault. A council was called to which Abba Moses was invited, but he refused to go to it. Then the priest sent someone to say to him, 'Come, for everyone is waiting for you!' He took a leaking jug, filled it with water and carried it with him. The others came out to meet him and said to him, 'What is this, Father?' The old man said to them, 'My sins run out behind me, and I do not see them, and today I am coming to judge the errors of another.' When they heard that they said no more to the brother but forgave him."

There is no doubt that abbas could misuse their responsibility and personal power as spiritual guides. This incident helps us understand why the brother who went to Abba Lot was afraid to go to "the Fathers." It must have been a daunting experience to be called before the council and confronted with your fault. But Moses, like Lot, could see through the fault into the life of the sinful brother as well as the lives of his fellow fathers. Abba Moses becomes an abba to his fellow abbas in their weakness. Love requires honesty and must acknowledge that all of us fail and therefore temper judgment with perspective. At the same time love's responsibility is to expect more from a person and guide him or her beyond the failure to forgiveness and renewal.

Seeing What Others Cannot See

"It was said of Abba Isidore, priest of Scetis, that when anyone had a brother who was sick, or careless or irritable, and wanted to send him away, he said, 'Bring him here to me.' Then he took charge of him and by his long-suffering he cured him."

Isidore was not naïve or looking for hardship. When other abbas gave up on a person, "he took charge of him." What gave him the patience to heal troubled lives? *"The same Abba Isidore said, 'It is the wisdom of the saints to recognize the will of God. Indeed, in obeying the truth, man surpasses everything else, for he is the image and likeness of God. Of all evil suggestions, the most terrible is that of following one's own heart, that is to say, one's own thought, and not the law of God. A man who does this will be afflicted later on, because he has not recognized the mystery, and has not found the way of the saints in order to work in it. For now is the time to labour for the Lord, for salvation is found in the day of affliction: for it is written: "By your endurance you will gain your lives."' (Luke 21.19)"*

Isidore's "calling" was to help others discover "the image and likeness of God" in themselves. Sometimes that takes a lot of patience.

A Constant Reminder

"A brother asked Abba Poemen, 'Some brothers live with me, do you want me to be in charge of them?' The old man said to him, 'No,

just work first and foremost, and if they want to live like you, they will see to it themselves.' The brother said to him, 'But it is they, themselves, Father, who want me to be in charge of them.' The old man said to him, 'No, be their example, not their legislator.'"

Poemen is a common Egyptian name and the collection of sayings attributed to "Poemen the Shepherd" reflects the wisdom of several persons and forms a portrait of Egyptian monastic teaching. Therefore this advice about spiritual guidance is fundamental. A brother has attracted disciples who want him to be their abba. Should he take charge of their lives? "No, just work first and foremost, and if they want to live like you, they will see to it themselves." An abba must teach and guide by his working example. Yet, the disciples want an easier method. They want to be told what to do! They must learn also that monastic art must be experienced rather than enforced. "No, be their example, not their legislator." Love is not efficient.

JUNE 26

Looking in the Wrong Direction

"It was said of Abba Ammoes that when he went to church, he did not allow his disciple to walk beside him but only at a certain distance; and if the latter came to ask him about his thoughts, he would move away from him as soon as he had replied, saying to him, 'It is for fear that, after edifying words, irrelevant conversation should slip in, that I do not keep you with me.'"

Ammoes's reply to his disciple may seem insensitive, even anti-social. What harm is there in talking to your abba returning from church to your cell? The issue, from Ammoes's point of view, is the need to remain centered on "edifying words." At this point in his formation the young monk may not be able to discriminate between edifying thoughts and "irrelevant conversation." He wants to discuss what is on his mind, rather than patiently focus on the teaching of his abba. Ammoes's response is a sharp call to remain centered on the life the disciple has freely chosen. Random thoughts may be interesting, but they will limit deeper experience of the reality the young monk is seeking. Lack of focus will inhibit the soul's formation.

Whom Will You Serve?

"A brother who followed the life of stillness in the monastery of the cave of Abba Saba came to Abba Elias and said to him, 'Abba, give me a way of life.' The old man said to the brother, 'In the days of our predecessors they took great care about these three virtues: poverty, obedience and fasting. But among the monks nowadays avarice, self-confidence and great greed have taken charge. Choose whichever you want most.'"

The need for obedience and the austere virtues of the desert elders were based on a desire to be "born from above," as Jesus had exhorted the Pharisee, Nicodemus (see John 3:7). They saw the polarity between Roman society and their own way of life as a struggle between darkness and light. It was a matter of life and death, and the virtue of obedience was rooted in their preferring light, rather than darkness. It was a difficult struggle and Elias points to the reality that many monks slipped back into the darkness. Elias reminds the brother that he stands in the tradition of predecessors who "took great care about these three virtues: poverty, obedience and fasting." Although the brother wants Elias to give him "a way of life," the abba says he must make the choice himself.

An Internal Dwelling

Amma Syncletica said, *"It is dangerous for anyone to teach who has first not been trained in the 'practical' life. For if someone who owns a ruined house receives guests there, he does them harm because of the dilapidation of the building. It is the same in the case of someone who has not first built an interior dwelling; he causes loss to those who come. By words one may convert them to salvation, but by evil behavior, one injures them."*

A spiritual guide and her or his disciple must practice obedience. It is a mutual obligation. An authentic spiritual guide is worthy of the disciple's obedience only when he or she has "first built an interior dwelling." That inner dwelling is an attitude of submission to the will and transformative power of God. The inner dwelling is "built" both by attitude and being "trained in the 'practical' life." Without this experience, the guide can do harm to others. The disciple's obedience is to the inner dwelling of obedience present in the words and life of the amma or abba. The disciple will follow the direction of his or her guide because the guide manifests what the disciple seeks. Words without authentic inner formation are dangerous.

A Heavenly Dwelling

"Another time [Silvanus's] disciple Zacharius entered and found him in ecstasy with his hands stretched towards heaven. Closing the door, he went away. Coming at the sixth and ninth hours he found him in the same state. At the tenth hour he knocked, entered, and found him at peace and said to him, 'What has happened today, Father?' The latter replied, 'I was ill today, my child.' But the disciple seized his feet and said to him, 'I will not let you go until you have told me what you have seen.' The old man said, 'I was taken up to heaven and I saw the glory of God and I stayed there till now and now I have been sent away.'"

This narrative shows the mutual intimacy and respect that Silvanus and Zacharius shared. The disciple did not want to intrude on his abba's ecstasy and the abba, like his peers, was reluctant to share a deeply personal experience of God. He did not want to seem "above" Zacharius nor make the disciple feel inferior. Yet, in humorous intimacy, the disciple grasps his abba's feet and demands to know what Silvanus has seen. Zacharius's grasping is not an effort to vicariously possess the ecstasy of his abba. There is no way to conjure an ecstatic experience. Zacharius was not asking for technique. His passion was prompted by what he saw happening to his abba. As always, the abba shares wisdom through experience more than words. "I was taken up to heaven and I saw the glory of God." He did not add, "Therefore . . . " He simply told where he had been taken in his prayer and that now he was "back." That was enough.

Learning the Art of Patience

When he appointed Theodore as master of the monastery's guest-house where men were coming to become monks, Abba Pachomius said, *"It is a mighty thing when you see someone of your house negligent of his salvation if you do not busy yourself with him and if you forbear to instruct him for his reform and his soul's salvation. If once he gets angry, be patient with him, waiting for him to be touched by the Lord. It is just as when someone wants to extract a thorn from somebody's foot. If he draws out the thorn and it causes bleeding, the man has relief. On the other hand, if he does not succeed in removing it but it goes in deeper, he applies some salve; and thus, with some patience on the man's part, the thorn comes out gently by itself and the man is healed."*

Patience must be the heart of Theodore's relationship with each novice. He should avoid imposing progress and wait "for him to be touched by the Lord." When the novice fails or is frustrated, he will learn patience and be healed by the example of his guide. Progress, especially rapid or "efficient" progress, is not the purpose of the monastic art, and the temptation to constantly "move forward" can plague mentor as well as novice. Pachomius is wise to point out that an emphasis on results can become a thorn causing pain rather than healing. Although it seems like an oxymoron, transformation through disciplined praxis should be a gentle process. Next month we will focus on patience.

JULY

Patience

"May you be made strong with all the strength that comes from his glorious power, and may you be prepared to endure everything with patience, while joyfully giving thanks to the Father, who has enabled you to share in the inheritance of the saints in the light" (Col 1:11-12).

We have seen that the monastic art could not be rushed. But the desert elders learned that patience is more than waiting for something to happen or putting up with something that is difficult. Patience is remaining in the company of God in the midst of frustration over a perceived lack of progress in ascetic life. It is natural to desire progress, but when a monk decides what progress should look like, he or she is taking control of the process of transformation rather than depending on God. The result is frustration, despondency, and often a desire to let go of monastic life and return to conventional society.

One of the greatest consequences of lack of progress was called *accidie*. It was a listless feeling that distorted the monk's sense of reality. It sapped resolve and replaced it with laziness and cynicism about the integrity of monastic life. It turned the monk's timetable back and made any steps forward unbearably heavy.

But accidie did not have to be the end of the path to salvation. Older ammas and abbas learned from their own experience and reminded younger monks and novices that they did not need extraordinary efforts or forms of praxis to continue on the path. The simple forms of "basic training" could last for the whole journey, especially when accidie seemed to take over. These basic forms of praxis were being aware of what is happening (self-knowledge), seeking help from an amma or abba, remaining in the cell, working, meditating on the Bible, and reciting or chanting the psalms. There was nothing magic in this list. It was a very practical way of taking attention away from the self and directing one's energy toward God.

During July we will reflect on the grace and power of patience.

Joyful Patience

Saint Paul describes what the desert elders longed to inherit: "May you be made strong with all the strength that comes from his glorious power, and may you be prepared to endure everything with patience, while joyfully giving thanks to the Father, who has enabled you to share in the inheritance of the saints in the light. He has rescued us from the power of darkness and transferred us into the kingdom of his beloved Son, in whom we have redemption, the forgiveness of sins" (Col 1:11-14).

The men and women who went to the desert were turning *from* dark influences in a society that profaned human life. They desired a "share in the inheritance of the saints in the light." They were turning their lives *toward* a different kingdom where they would have to depend on the "glorious power" of God. Paul spent years in the desert right after his powerful conversion and was confronted with his need for forgiveness. The desert taught him that the path toward redemption required him "to endure everything with patience, while joyfully giving thanks to the Father." His entrance into the realm of the risen Christ was just beginning. It was a journey toward the restoration of his true self and it could not be rushed.

Remaining in the Company of God

Abba Antony said, *"Whatever you find in your heart to do in following God, that do, and remain within yourself in Him."*

Sharing in the inheritance of the saints of God will take time. Desire and persistence are the only prerequisites. But the persistence is not simply in the "doing," in the praxis. It is "remain[ing] within yourself in Him." An ancient prayer from the desert fathers and mothers sums up this wisdom of Antony: "Bind my head and my heart in you, Holy One, and may I remain in your company this day." When our head and heart are united, the desire of our whole being is placed before God. This desire is expressed by doing what we can to follow God in our life of prayer and love of neighbor. But the consummation of that desire begins with patient waiting. Following the desire of our hearts will include doing what we can each day without rushing toward or controlling the outcome, yet the bonding of our desire with God's desire is in the waiting. We must learn the stature of waiting.

A New Experience of Time

"An old man said, 'For nine years a brother was tempted in thought to the point of despairing of his salvation, and being scrupulous he condemned himself, saying "I have lost my soul, and since I am lost I shall go back to the world." But while he was on the way, a voice came to him on the road, which said, "These nine years which you have been tempted have been crowns for you, go back to your place, and I will allay these thoughts." Understand that it is not good for someone to despair of himself because of his temptations; rather, temptations procure crowns for us if we use them well.'"

The causes of the brother's despair were self-reliance, self-condemnation, passage of time without "progress," and fear. These are symptoms of a lack of patience. He believed his nine years of scrupulous praxis would eliminate his temptations. When the brother perceived time as "duration," he "despair[ed] of his salvation" because he could not fit what he wanted to accomplish into a span of time acceptable to him. His focus was on personal effort and the passage of time. In lieu of results he assumed, "I have lost my soul, and since I am lost I shall go back to the world." Frustration with time caused panic, lack of awareness about self-knowledge embedded in the temptations, and loss of hope in God's grace. He could not see the "crowns."

The End Is Present in the Beginning

"'These nine years which you have been tempted have been crowns for you, go back to your place, and I will allay these thoughts.' Understand that it is not good for someone to despair of himself because of his temptations; rather, temptations procure crowns for us if we use them well."

How could nine years of temptations bring blessing and a sense of personal integrity? For some, one year would be too much waiting, especially when a person is trying so hard. The answer is in patient acceptance of weakness, persistence in one's life of prayer, and depending on God for the outcome. The monastic virtue of patience opens the door for a different experience of "time." Conventional time is related to the mind and body's need to find solutions and facilitate progress. Monastic time is detachment from purely temporal needs and "active responses" so that our whole being begins to see ourselves as God sees us. Our weaknesses are real but will not obstruct our eternal communion with God "if we use them well." Patience is making room for who we already are.

Impatience Clouds Reality

"An affliction befell some brothers in the place where they were living, and wishing to abandon it they went to find Abba Ammonas. And it happened that the elder was coming by boat down the river. And when he saw them walking along the bank of the river, he said to the boatman, 'Put me ashore.' And calling to the brothers he said to them, 'I am Ammonas, whom you wish to visit.' And having encouraged them, he made them return to the place from which they had come. For the matter was connected not with spiritual damage, but with human affliction."

An unnamed "human affliction" caused serious anxiety in this small community of brothers. The stress created fears for survival of the community and clouded their discernment of a solution. They wanted to leave the affliction behind! But Ammonas encourages the brothers to stay where they are by pointing out that the problem would not cause "spiritual damage." Since their souls were not endangered, persistence in their asceticism would help them face the problem. It is easy to think that a change of venue will solve problems. Often that option is a temptation to avoid the true nature of a dysfunctional situation. Ammonas was aware of the need to discern whether or not the deeper issue of "spiritual damage" was present.

The Power of Tranquility

"Abba Ammonas once went to cross the river and found the ferry untended and seated himself nearby it. Just then another boat arrived at that place and embarked the people waiting there in order to take them across. And they said to him, 'You come, too, Abba, and cross over with us.' But he said, 'I will only board the public ferry.' He had a bundle of palm leaves and sat plaiting a rope and then unfolding it until the ferry was made ready. And so he went across. Then the brothers bowed low before him and said, 'Why did you do this?' And the elder said to them, 'That I may not always be dwelling on my thought.' And this is also an example that we may walk the path of God in tranquility."

Ammonas was not "making work" while he was waiting for the public ferry. He was making space for "the path of God in tranquility." Since his work plaiting a rope and his prayer were united, he did not want to fill that time with thought about a more efficient way to cross the Nile. Tranquility is more essential than efficiency, even though efficiency has its place. Without an inner peace that is not rushed to "fit" life, we can stray from the path of God. Ammonas shows that tranquility is not simply the absence of activity; it is to "not always be dwelling on my thought." Dwelling on the solution to the fastest way across the Nile would have replaced his patient focus on the path to salvation he had chosen. Ammonas shows an example of what the desert elders experienced as "resting in the Lord." It was a state of being, not an activity.

Wisdom Cannot Be Rushed

Abba John of Lycopolis said, *"There are some who seem to have renounced this age but have no concern for purity of heart, nor do they take care to cut the vices and passions out of their souls and build up character. They only take pains to see certain of the fathers and listen to some words from them which they can relate to others, in order to glorify themselves by having heard this or that father; and if by sheer chance either by listening or learning they discover a little knowledge, at once they want to become teachers and teach not that which they have experienced but that which they have heard or seen, and they look down on others."*

John's stern words point to the need for humility and long-term commitment in a life of prayer. Transformation of one's ego is not simply a matter of getting information. The desert elders emphasized experience over words and insisted on gradual, hard work "to cut the vices and passions out of their souls and build up character." False "progress" will produce vainglory and judgmental attitudes. Wisdom is not a possession or a weapon. John's advice mirrors the advice of Amma Syncletica, who said, "It is dangerous for anyone to teach who has first not been trained in the 'practical' life." Amma Theodora adds that a teacher should be "patient, gentle and humble; he must be tested and without partisanship, full of concern, and a lover of souls."

A Silent Companion

"A hermit had persevered for thirty years. One day he said to himself, 'I have now spent so many years here and I have had no vision and performed no miracle as did the Fathers who were monks before me.' And he was tempted to go back to the world. Then he was told, 'What miracle do you want to perform that would be more extraordinary than the patience and courage God has given you and which allowed you to persevere for so long?'"

There is danger in using the duration of time and experiences of other people as criteria for discerning one's spiritual maturity. It is natural to desire tangible signs of God's presence and power, but this desire can mask the constant presence of God in the little things of life. This hermit had been faithful to his life of prayer for three decades and, by comparing himself to "the Fathers who were monks before me," was not able to trust "the patience and courage" of his own life as a monk. Patience is the author of hope and provides space to listen for God's presence when God's voice is not heard. It is tempting to think of miracles as extraordinary supernatural interventions when they are most always simple gifts of God embedded in daily life.

JULY 9

Slow but Sure

"The disciple of a great old man was once attacked by lust. The old man, seeing it in his prayer, said to him, 'Do you want me to ask God to relieve you of this battle?' The other said, 'Abba, I see that I am afflicted, but I see that this affliction is producing fruit in me; therefore ask God to give me endurance to bear it.' And his abba said, 'Today, I know that you surpass me in perfection.'"

This narrative has multiple layers of wisdom. The steady relationship between the abba and disciple enabled the abba to discern his disciple's affliction, "in his prayer." This bonding of spirits does not happen overnight. The abba's desire "to ask God to relieve you of this battle" demonstrates his awareness of the depth of the disciple's struggle and is an expression of loving concern. Normally, he would say that such attacks are opportunities to learn dependence on God's grace. But the disciple has already learned this truth and "see[s] that this affliction is producing fruit in me." Rather than freedom from affliction, he asks for "endurance to bear it." He and his abba are learning together.

An Environment of Grace

Abba Stephen of Thebes said, *"Sitting in your cell, do not act like it is a tomb but rather behave like it is a banquet room filled with gold that has guards protecting it night and day. The 'guards' are the powers of God that protect your spirit, that is, knowledge and faith and patience and abstinence, sincerity and innocence, purity and chastity, love, concord, and truth."*

Patience is not an end in itself. It is a disposition of openness to God's presence and grace. The power of patience is that "it is a banquet room filled with gold," whose spaciousness makes room for "the powers of God that protect your spirit." Although patience may require the passage of chronological time, the temporal space is filled and transformed by the timelessness of God's protecting Spirit. Patience is withdrawal from self-assertion and self-reliance that will provide access to essential virtues that Stephen has learned will "guard" and protect a person's spirit. We are not lost in the process. The desert banquet makes us whole with the rich food of "knowledge and faith and patience and abstinence, sincerity and innocence, purity and chastity, love, concord, and truth."

A Stable Environment

Amma Syncletica said, *"If you find yourself in a monastery do not go to another place, for that will harm you a great deal. Just as the bird who abandons the eggs she was sitting on prevents them from hatching, so the monk or nun grows cold and their faith dies, when they go from one place to another."*

Progress is often associated with a specific place or inner disposition. Syncletica was aware of monks and nuns who changed the venue of their monastic life in order to suit their personal timetable of "progress" in the spiritual life. They were unwilling to become rooted in one place in hopes that they would find another place, spiritual mentor, or pattern of monastic praxis that was most satisfying. This pattern "will harm you a great deal" because, by taking control of your spiritual life, you abandon the patience and obedience that make room for the inner working of the Holy Spirit. You also limit the possibilities and challenge of embracing new frontiers of human experience. Constantly looking for a better nest gives little chance for trust and inner passion to develop.

Remaining in Jesus

Abba Paul said, *"Keep close to Jesus."*

"It was said of Abba Paul that he spent the whole of Lent eating only one measure of lentils, drinking one small jug of water, and working at one single basket, weaving it and unweaving it, living alone until the feast."

Like his peers, Abba Paul's behavior was more important than his words. What does it mean to "keep close to Jesus"? Paul's method is his personal experience of "synaxis," a pattern of constant prayer in the midst of ordinary work. Synaxis refers to being focused on a specific action; it can also mean a gathering of persons for a mutual purpose. Most desert monks gathered daily for synaxis, a combination of meditation on the Bible, prayers, and manual labor, usually weaving. Paul lives alone during Lent, like many of the elders, and his "working at one single basket, weaving it and unweaving it" is not "making work" to pass the time. What seems like a senseless repetition of labor is a description of his constant prayer, his keeping close to Jesus. His "work" is a timeless action that places him in the company of Jesus as he prepares for the feast of the Resurrection.

Staying on the Path

"Someone said to Abba Arsenius, 'My thoughts trouble me, say-ing,' "You can neither fast nor work; at least go and visit the sick, for that also is charity." But the old man, recognizing the suggestions of the demons, said to him, 'Go eat, drink, sleep, do no work, only do

not leave your cell.' For he knew that steadfastness in the cell keeps a monk in the right way."

Frustration, loss of energy, and impatience can cause a person to lose direction in his or her life with God. The monk who came to Arsenius was having continual difficulty with prayer (work) and fasting. He was tempted to leave the solitude and discipline of his cell to visit the sick. Surely, this act of charity would be an acceptable alternative to his tiredness and boredom. In his state of mind he could not make a decision and sought Arsenius's advice. Arsenius recognizes the "demon" of accidie and tells the monk to remain in his cell so that he will not be distracted from "the right way." Accidie was known as the "midday demon" and could easily result in laziness, loss of initiative, or depression. It was sometimes caused by illness or repeated frustration with a person's ascetic discipline. Sometimes it was pure laziness. Healing would come through "steadfastness in the cell."

JULY 14

A Common, yet Serious, Danger

Amma Theodora said, *"It is good to live in peace, for the wise man practices perpetual prayer. It is truly a great thing for a virgin or monk to live in peace, especially for the younger ones. However, you should realize that as soon as you intend to live in peace, at once evil comes and weighs down your soul through accidie, faintheartedness, and evil thoughts. It also attacks your body through sickness, debility, weakening of the knees, and all the members. It dissipates the strength of soul and body, so that one believes one is ill and is no longer able to pray."*

The desert elders sought transformation of their whole being: body, mind, and soul. Their desire to "live in peace" followed a path of listening to God through solitude and silence, "keeping watchful for God's Spirit" through constant vigils (day and night), and "feeding on God's Word" by limiting their diet and fasting. The peace they sought was called *purity of heart*, a state of complete openness to God's will, unattachment to material possessions, easily satisfied needs, and letting go of control of their life with God. This resting in God was the source of true charity and compassion. But it was not easy. Amma Theodora describes how purity of heart is endangered by faintheartedness of spirit and bodily weaknesses that the desert elders called accidie. It had to be faced honestly and with patience.

Trapped in a Barren Land

Abba Simon described his accidie to Abba John Cassian: *"I am on fire with innumerable and various wanderings of soul and shiftiness of heart and cannot collect my scattered thoughts. I cannot even pour forth my prayer without interruption from useless images and memories of conversations and actions. I feel myself tied down by such dryness and barrenness that I cannot give birth to any spiritual ideas."*

One goal of the monastic art is to live an undivided life with both mind and body centered on God through spiritual disciplines. Jesus said, "If your eye is single, your whole body will be filled with light." But Simon's mind's eye was scattered, his soul was wandering, and his heart was shifty. We do not know the content of his endless thoughts, but he describes their crippling effect. "I cannot even pour forth my prayer without interruption." The inner fire of God's Spirit was replaced by a burning and barren desert that evaporated his ability to "give birth to any spiritual ideas." No one is free from thoughts and influences that scatter our vision and experience of God. Like Simon, we must acknowledge them before we can escape their bondage. How will that happen?

Remaining in the Company of God

Amma Syncletica said, *"There is grief that is useful, and there is grief that is destructive. The first sort consists in weeping over one's own faults and weeping over the weakness of one's neighbors, in order not to destroy one's purpose, and attach oneself to the perfect good. But there is also a grief that comes from the enemy, full of mockery, which some call accidie. This spirit must be cast out, mainly by prayer and psalmody."*

Syncletica makes a distinction between the awareness and burden of one's sins and faults and a destructive frustration with the routine of one's life of prayer. The first "grief" will lead to renewed life and the second leads to loss of energy and "mockery" of the monastic art. If a person consciously continues in a state of accidie, he or she will focus on a spirit that debilitates the soul and blocks the path to transformation. "This spirit must be cast out, mainly by prayer and psalmody." One's mind and body, the whole person, must replace the malign spirit with a conscious and determined effort to remain in the company of God. "Prayer" means turning one's whole being toward God, in trustful expectation. Recitation of the psalms will return one's thoughts and images to "the perfect good."

JULY 17

Acknowledging the Problem

"When the holy Abba Anthony lived in the desert he was beset by accidie, and was attacked by many sinful thoughts. He said to God, 'Lord I want to be saved but these thoughts do not leave me alone, what shall I do in my affliction? How can I be saved?' A short while afterwards, when he got up to go out, Anthony saw a man like himself sitting at his work, getting up from his work to pray, then sitting down and plaiting a rope, then getting up to pray. It was an angel of the Lord sent to correct and reassure him. He heard the angel saying, 'Do this and you will be saved.' At these words Anthony was filled with joy and courage. He did this, and he was saved."

Antony's affliction was hopelessness caused by accidie. His personal expectation to rid himself of "sinful thoughts" had become the primary measure for "progress" in his spiritual life. Unable to move ahead, he saw his desire for salvation slipping away. He was aware of his problem but did not know what to do. In his helplessness he appealed to God: "what shall I do in my affliction?" God's response was to help Antony see himself being faithful to his daily praxis of prayer and work. When Antony was able to see himself through God's eyes, he was reassured that the way out of accidie is something he *already knows*: the simple yet constant integration of prayer and work. This simple form of self-knowledge brought him "joy and courage" and he moved on. Like Syncletica, he learned he must return to prayer, psalmody, and work.

The Fruit of Patience and Steadfastness

Abba Evagrius joins Antony, Arsenius, Theodora, Simon, and Syncletica in describing the deep psychological effects of accidie and at the same time gives hope by reminding us of the fruits of the struggle: *"[Accidie] instills in the heart of the monk a hatred for the place, a hatred for his very life itself, a hatred for manual labor . . . [accidie] depicts life stretching out for a long period of time, and brings before the mind's eye the toil of the ascetic struggle and, as the saying has it, leaves no leaf unturned to induce the monk to forsake his cell and drop out of the fight. No other demon follows close upon the heels of this one (when he is defeated) but only a state of deep peace and inexpressible joy arise out of this struggle [i.e., apatheia]."*

Whether one is a monk or not, accidie is a dangerous part of life. It "instills in the heart" an unreal and pessimistic way of looking at illness, challenges in daily work, difficulties in attaining personal goals, faulty relationships, and sinful behavior. It creates a "why bother?" mentality that will sap energy and resolve. We lose the ability to know and desire what is real. Evagrius reminds us that if we persist in the struggle, "a state of deep peace" will follow. That sounds great, but when we are in the midst of despondency, it is hard to believe that there is light at the end of the tunnel. The only place we want to be is somewhere else. Is Evagrius naïve to suggest that this struggle will result in "inexpressible joy"? What does he mean?

Purity of Heart

Abba Evagrius is emphatic: *"No other demon follows close upon the heels of [accidie] (when he is defeated) but only a state of deep peace and inexpressible joy arise out of this struggle [i.e., apatheia]."*

If a person returns to and is steadfast in his or her daily praxis of prayer and work, the struggle with accidie will lead to a heart that is open to God's healing grace. The praxis becomes a way of letting go of attachment to a solution to the struggle. When this happens, the ego is freed from the despondency caused by its lack of power to reach "salvation." This freedom becomes the source of "deep peace and inexpressible joy." By remaining in the physical cell (the place of praxis), our "inner cell," the place where our spirit and God's presence are joined, is renewed. The disciplines of our praxis centered our attention and desire, once again, on God. This return to our center will gradually disarm the distracting power of malign thoughts and lack of will. Gradually peace will return and we let go of the control our thoughts and self-centered will impose on us. This restores stewardship of the whole person and our authentic self emerges bonded with God's desires for us.

JULY 20

Becoming Rooted in the Psalms

Amma Syncletica said, *"But there is also a grief that comes from the enemy, full of mockery, which some call accidie. This spirit must be cast out, mainly by prayer and psalmody."*

Syncletica's advice about overcoming accidie points to the fundamental role of the Psalter in the lives and prayer of the desert elders. They depended on a twofold manifestation of God's voice: the lives and words of their ammas and abbas and the Bible. The life of Jesus and the wisdom of his Hebrew heritage formed the rich soil that nourished their spiritual roots. The unique power of reciting psalms lies in their poetic portrait of the spectrum of human life, from the depths of self-pity and petty triumphalism to sincere gratitude for life and the sincere yearning of the soul for experience of God. "As a deer longs for flowing streams, so my soul longs for you, O God" (Ps 42:1). The psalms are honest about the sacredness and darkness of human living. "For I know my transgressions, and my sin is ever before me" (Ps 51:3). There is a place in the psalms for every person and almost every human emotion, failure, and challenge. This is why the desert elders constantly recited and chanted the Psalter.

Beyond Words

On a visit to an Egyptian village Abba Serapion visited a prostitute and arranged to spend the night with her. As he entered her room he said, *"'Wait a bit, for we have a rule of prayer and I must fulfill that first.' So the old man began his prayers. He took the psalter and at each psalm he said a prayer for the courtesan, begging God that she might be converted and saved, and God heard him. The woman stood trembling and praying beside the man. When he had completed the whole psalter the woman fell to the ground. Then the old man, beginning the Epistle, read a great deal from the apostle and completed his prayers. The woman was filled with compunction [genuine sorrow] and understood that he had not come to see her to commit sin, but to save her soul and she fell at his feet saying, 'Abba, do me this kindness and take me where I can please God.'"*

The power of the psalms is not in their words but in what they make possible. The act of oral recitation and chanting join the person or group to the presence of God in the words. The psalms are both a conversation and an openness that makes the conversation possible. It is a mutual presence. The hearing becomes an experience of God that has the power to nourish, heal, and transform. But this power will not become manifest if the words are not recited, chanted, or heard. This is why reciting or chanting the psalms became a daily discipline of the desert elders. Even though Serapion was away from his cell, he knew his "rule of prayer" would fill the cell of the prostitute. God's presence in the words transformed the woman's life.

The Fruit of Discipline

"It was said of the same Abba John [the Dwarf] that when he returned from the harvest or when he had been with some of the old men, he gave himself to prayer, meditation, and psalmody until his thoughts were re-established in their previous order."

The psalms were an integral part of Abba John's life. When he combined recitation of the psalms with prayer (openness to the Spirit) and meditation (repetitive recitation of Scripture and reflection), "his thoughts were re-established in their previous order." The Psalter was a daily focus on his relationship with God in the midst of work and relationships with his neighbors. This constant pattern gave order to his life. When Abba Serapion prayed for the conversion of the village courtesan, he told her, "Wait a bit, for we have a rule of prayer and I must fulfill that first." He was not using the psalms as a tool to convince her to change her life. He was sharing, in her presence, an authentic pattern of praying the psalms that was already a rich and necessary pattern of his life. She became aware of the presence of God in his recitation and through that experience of God realized, with genuine sorrow, that her life was futile. The same voice that Serapion knew so well spoke words of life to her.

The Battle Within

Abba Theodore of Enaton said, *"If God reproaches us for carelessness in our prayers and infidelities in our psalmody, we cannot be saved."*

Theodore echoes his peers with this firm insistence on faithfulness in prayer and recitation of the psalms. But he is more direct in describing the consequences of "carelessness in our prayers and infidelities in our psalmody." Openness to God and psalmody become a pathway leading to the salvation we desire. Theodore is not talking about the future! Like St. Paul, he knows that salvation—wholeness of being—can be a present reality. But our ego's resistance to letting go of control of life and our battle with temptations and accidie stand in the way of what God desires for us. The "reproach" of God is a firm, but loving, reminder that salvation begins within. The desert elders learned that responsibility for turning toward ourselves (evil) or turning toward God (salvation) does not lie outside us in the realm of the demons or the devil. The responsibility for turning toward evil or goodness lies *within* each human life. Faithfulness in prayer and psalmody are essential and trustworthy companions in this struggle.

Beyond Duty

"Another old man came to see one of the Fathers, who cooked a few lentils and said to him, 'Let us say a few prayers,' and the first completed the whole psalter, and the brother recited the two great prophets by heart. When morning came, the visitor went away, and they forgot the food."

Visits from pilgrims and monks were not an interruption to solitude and silence. Abba Antony the Great taught that such visits were opportunities to fulfill Christ's exhortation to love one's neighbor. Hospitality was a core monastic value, even when it was inconvenient. Many monks grew small amounts of vegetables and kept dried fruit and vegetables to feed visitors. Their hospitality included sharing opportunities of food for the body and the soul. The narrative above describes an abba visiting another father who immediately offers his guest two simple but cherished gifts. While the lentil soup is cooking, "let us say a few prayers." The prayers (openness to God through recitation of the Bible) are expressions of sheer delight, not fulfillment of duty. The joy they experience extends through the night and they forget their soup. The humor here underlines how the psalms and prophets had become essential parts of their lives.

Opening the Door of the Heart

The Syrian monk Pseudo-Macarius said, *"As near as the body is to the soul . . . so much nearer is God present, to come and open the locked door of our heart and to fill us with heavenly riches. . . . [God's] promises cannot deceive, provided we only persevere to the end."*

Pseudo-Macarius learned that God is always present, but we are not always receptive. Our patience and persistence are needed to "open the locked door of our heart." Abba Evagrius said, "Let us make provisions for protecting this power of our soul by praying to Christ in our nightly vigils." The regular pattern of recitation of biblical verses, especially the psalms, was a threshold between the presence of God and the monk's heart. Here is a vivid description of these vigils. "Then, after having eaten, they sit and listen to the father's teaching on all the commandments until the first watch of the night. At this point some of them go out into the desert and recite the Scriptures by heart throughout the night. The rest remain where they are and worship God with ceaseless hymnody [recitation of the psalms] until daybreak."

JULY 26

A Daily Companion

Abba Isidore said, *"When I was young and stayed in my cell, I had no way of keeping track of the divine offices; both night and day were for me times for the offices."* Abba Arsenius contrasts his life in the palace of the emperor with his simple life as a desert hermit. In the morning, *"instead of music and lyres, I say the twelve psalms and the same at night; instead of the sins I used to commit I now say my rule of prayer."* Palladius describes an afternoon routine of psalmody in the desert of Nitria: *"All these men work with their hands at linen-manufacture, so that all are self-supporting. And indeed, at the ninth hour it is possible to stand and hear how the strains of psalmody rise from each habitation so that one believes that one is high above the world in Paradise."*

It is uncertain when this twice daily pattern of recitation of twelve psalms evolved into the later monastic "offices" of Lauds and Vespers. Yet the rhythm and repetition of the psalms in morning and early evening renewed awareness of God's constant presence. It created an integration of prayer and work so that a person's life was undivided. The work provided a venue for and supported their life of prayer, including their offerings to the poor. The prayer acknowledged the sacred dimension of their work. Prayer and work are not two separate sectors of life. They are a seamless part of daily life.

More than Recitation

Abba Isaac the Syrian said, *"Do you wish to take delight in the psalmody of your liturgy and to understand the oracles of the Spirit which you recite? Then disregard completely the quantity of verses, and set at naught your skill in giving rhythm to the verses, so that you may speak them in the manner of a prayer. . . . And when your mind is made steadfast in these meditations, then confusion will give place and depart from you. Peace of thought is not to be found in slavish activity; nor in the freedom of the children of God is there found the confusion and turmoil."*

Like other forms of praxis, reciting the psalms either in the liturgy or in personal nightly vigils is not an end in itself. The goal is not in the number of verses or the beauty of the chanting. Too much emphasis on words and the meaning of words will take the mind away from "the oracles of the Spirit" and bring confusion or the turmoil of discerning the meaning of what the words describe. Recitation of the psalms offers an opportunity to be free of controlling prayer and following the letter of the discipline. The result will be delight in the freedom to hear the Spirit speak without conscious thought determining what the message should be. This does not detract from the beauty of the psalms; their beauty is present regardless of how they are recited or chanted. It is their inner beauty that will speak to the human heart in a mysterious way. This cannot be explained. It will become real through experience.

A Window into Ourselves

Abba John Cassian learned the inner wisdom of the psalms from Abba Isaac: *"For divine Scripture is clearer and its inmost organs, so to speak, are revealed to us when our own experience not only perceives but even anticipates its thought, and the meanings of the words are disclosed to us not by exegesis but by proof. When we have the same disposition in our heart with which each psalm was sung or written down, then we shall become like its author, grasping its significance beforehand rather than afterward. That is, we first take in the power of what is said, rather than the knowledge of it, recalling what has taken place or what does take place in us in daily assaults whenever we reflect on them. When we repeat [the psalms] we call to mind what our negligence has begotten in us or our diligence has obtained for us or divine providence has bestowed upon us or the enemy's suggestion has deprived us of or slippery and subtle forgetfulness has taken away from us or human weakness has brought upon us or heedless ignorance has concealed from us."*

Cassian shows how in the psalms we encounter our own mind, our most fundamental needs, and hear ourselves speaking about life. The psalms narrate almost every aspect of human emotional experience, human pain and weakness, human hope and desire, and human self-centeredness under stress or persecution. They express awareness of and thanksgiving for God's central place in life as creator and sustainer. Some psalms express frustration and anger at God for the unfairness of life, yet point toward the righteousness of God's judgment and compassion for the helpless. Many psalms are hymns used at liturgical feasts and others are very personal expressions of personal prayer. Abba Cassian describes how not only can we see ourselves in the lives of the authors of the psalms but we can also become like them before God. He learned that the power of the psalms transcends time and becomes tangible in our own hearts.

JULY 29

Being Set Ablaze with God's Presence

Abba John Cassian continues to share the powerful spiritual experiences a person may have through encountering God's presence in the psalms: *"Having been instructed [by praying the psalms] in this way, with our dispositions for our teachers, we shall grasp this as something seen rather than heard, and from the inner disposition of the heart we shall bring forth not what has been committed to memory but what is inborn in the very nature of things. Thus we shall penetrate its meaning not through the written text but with experience leading the way. . . . Rather, once the mind's attentiveness has been set ablaze, it is called forth in an unspeakable ecstasy of heart and with an insatiable gladness of spirit, and the mind, having transcended all feelings and visible matter, pours it out to God with unutterable groans and sighs."*

The psalms lead us from mere words to "something seen rather than heard." Learning words "by heart" leads beyond recitation to a transformation of "the inner disposition of the heart" so that we can experience "the very nature of things." When our mind becomes aware of what is happening, it lets go of "all feelings and visible matter" and our whole being pours itself out to the presence of God and has nothing more "to say." Rather than search for meaning, we are able to listen to the meaning given to us. The "mind's attentiveness [is] set ablaze" and is led beyond its own limitations to discover "an unspeakable ecstasy of heart and with an insatiable gladness of spirit." As it listens to the Spirit, it is able to respond without words. Human conversation is transformed.

JULY 30

A Cloud of Witnesses

"Eyes see only light, ears hear only sound, but a listening heart perceives meaning."

Amma Syncletica's advice about overcoming the demon of accidie was clear: "This spirit must be cast out by prayer and psalmody." We have seen that Abba Evagrius, Abba Antony, Abba Arsenius, Amma Theodora, Abba Simon, Abba Serapion, Abba John the Dwarf, Abba Theodore, Abba Pseudo-Macarius, Abba Isidore, Abba Isaac the Syrian, and Abba John Cassian all agree on the fundamental importance of psalmody. They represent a consensus of both practice and the wisdom that is the fruit of that experience. But they insist that the psalms are not an end in themselves. As beautiful as that poetic language may be, its purpose is to lead us to recognize ourselves in the many moods and situations reflected in the psalms and to be embraced there by God's faithful presence and grace. The meaning of the psalms is not in the words but in the placeless place the words embody. The demonic spirit of accidie wants to take us away from that place and scatter our spirit with the burdens of boredom, fatigue, and losing heart. A modern abba, David Steindl-Rast, reminds us not to stray from our heart and what our heart knows to be true.

"Eyes see only light, ears hear only sound, but a listening heart perceives meaning."

Patience Manifests Humility

"The same monk [possibly Abba Arsenius] used to say that there was a certain old man who had a good disciple. Through narrow-mindedness he drove him outside with his sheepskin. The brother remained sitting outside. When the old man opened the door, he found him sitting, and he repented saying, 'O Father, the humility of your patience has overcome my narrow-mindedness. Come inside and from now on you are the old man and the father, and I am the younger and the disciple.'"

Perhaps the old man was impatient with his disciple because he questioned something about his abba's teaching or was reluctant to follow his advice. The old man's mind was closed and there was no room for the additional listening. His lack of patience was the cause of rejection: "he drove him outside with his sheepskin." But the rejection was met by a patient spirit, not argument or defiance. Although the disciple could have left his abba forever, he loved him well enough to "stick around" and let the old man's hot temper cool off. The disciple valued the relationship enough to be patient about resolution of the conflict. "The brother remained sitting outside." Tension over words was going to be resolved without words. In showing respect for the old man by not leaving, the disciple emphasized what their relationship meant to him. When the old man opened the door of the cell, he suddenly realized that his disciple was practicing his teaching better than he. The disciple's waiting gave the abba an opportunity to discover his narrow-mindedness and he realized that he had endangered their relationship. This enabled him to say, "Come inside . . ." and to honor the integrity of his disciple's role in their relationship. "Come inside and from now on you are the old man and the father, and I am the younger and the disciple." Wisdom proceeds from experience if we are willing to wait rather than leap.

AUGUST

Persistence in Prayer and Work

Last month we reflected on the need for patience in pursuing the monastic art. This month our focus is on persistence. Is persistence different from patience? The lives of the desert mothers and fathers demonstrate a need for both virtues. They are different but complementary. Patience is a state of being. It is a willingness to "stay with the process" and not rush along the path to salvation. Patience is not the servant of chronological time and enables a monk to make room for God's guidance and grace. While patience is not passivity or simply letting time "pass," it is one form of letting go of personal control of and remaining faithful to a freely chosen vocation, even in the midst of discouragement and perceived "lack of progress."

How is patience related to persistence? It may be helpful to think of patience as a noun that must become an adjective describing what kind of a person the monk is on the path to transformation. The monk is called to be a patient person. Persistence, on the other hand, is a noun that must become a verb. It describes an active and single-minded commitment to praxis and the work of the monastery. The monk is persistent in prayer and work, even when accidie and distractions make them difficult. How did the desert elders understand and practice persistence? How did they balance prayer and work?

We have seen that accidie was the most serious danger to monastic life, other than depending on one's self. Patience was the willingness to "stay on course" and continue to listen to God. Persistence was the tangible faithfulness to continuing the praxis and work that made "staying on course" possible. Syncletica begins this month by saying that the spirit of accidie *"must be cast out by prayer and psalmody."*

147

Very practical advice. Its wisdom is that prayer and psalmody are activities that are *already* integral parts of the monk's life. Staying on course demands being faithful to fundamental forms of praxis. Don't look around for something new.

But persistence is not an end in itself. Evagrius will show that persistence in praxis helps the monk look beyond himself or herself. At the same time, continuing the patterns of daily work and caring for others will keep the monk from dwelling on personal disappointment in her or his pace of progress. *"An old man was asked, 'What is it necessary to do to be saved?' He was making rope, and without looking up from the work, he replied, 'You are looking at it.'"*

In the midst of dissipation of energy for continuing in monastic life, continued praxis and work sustained each monk by deflecting consciousness away from these negative influences. This was not activity for activity's sake. The monastic art was filled with opportunities for care of the soul and love of neighbor. During August we will reflect on how the desert elders remained rooted in God's presence and power through prayer and work.

Taking Refuge in Prayer

Amma Syncletica said, *"But there is also a grief that comes from the enemy, full of mockery, which some call accidie. This spirit must be cast out by prayer and psalmody."*

In July we focused on patience as a virtue leading toward transformation of self. Many abbas and ammas realized from experience that this is easier said than done. The greatest danger is accidie, an inner weakness of resolve and energy, both physical and spiritual, that will discourage us from what our heart desires. Amma Syncletica summarized the danger of accidie as "a grief that comes from the enemy, full of mockery, which some call accidie." She and so many other elders encouraged their disciples to take refuge from accidie in prayer and psalmody. We have seen how the psalms offer a place to see ourselves honestly as well as a venue for experiencing the transformational experience of God. In August we will look at ways prayer can "cast out" the seductive power of accidie. Tomorrow we begin several days of listening to Abba Evagrius, who said, *"Prayer that does not have mingled into it the thought of God and interior vision is a weariness of the flesh."* What does he mean?

Don't Focus on Yourself

"And when you want to get up to pray during the night and your body is feeling sluggish, ponder these things and recall how many others are standing in prayer on their feet, or are bowed, or kneeling; how many are weeping and gasping amid groans, how many are lamenting at the body's sluggishness, how many are drunk with love and have forgotten their own natures, how many are singing in their hearts to the Lord."

Abba Evagrius learned that the demon in accidie is self-centeredness. We can be so obsessed with wanting progress in our spiritual journey that we take over the process and then get upset when we do not achieve the goals we expect. On the other hand, we can "leave things up to God" and become impatient with God's timetable or blind to the inner changes that must precede more visible results. In both cases it is easy to become more and more turned in on ourselves and lose energy and resolve. "Nothing is working." "Why bother?" Syncletica, Evagrius, and the other elders remind us that the power of prayer begins by realizing that we are not alone or unique. When everything seems like a chore, remember that others are standing, bowing, and kneeling too. Some are burdened, like you, but others are filled with joy.

Change Will Not Be Easy

"If you think about all this, then you will find relief from all your sluggishness and weariness, and you will offer up your prayer eagerly and with many tears. Then recollect how many are awake and at their work, how many are traveling on journeys, are ploughing, or carrying out various crafts; remember the shepherds, the night

watchmen, those guarding their treasures. If all these take trouble over things that are transient, how much more should I take trouble over my Lord."

Evagrius knows from experience that looking beyond ourselves will help us "find relief." But widening our horizons is not a magical cure, nor will it happen overnight. It will take effort and in the process release "many tears" and emotions that have blocked our vision and confined or limited our voice and the freedom to be who we are. By looking beyond ourselves, but not ignoring our condition, we will see that the world and people all around us are alive with activity that sustains life. The "relief" Evagrius mentions will come from gaining new perspective on our condition. My condition will not be permanent if I "take trouble over my Lord" with renewed effort at the same time that I, like others around me, tend to the necessary but transient tasks of daily life.

AUGUST 4

A More Transparent Struggle

Abba Moses the Robber said, *"The man who flees and lives in solitude is like a bunch of grapes ripened by the sun, but he who remains among men is like an unripe grape."*

As we seek the meaning of Abba Evagrius's advice, it is legitimate to ask, If the desert monks were seeking God with simplicity of life, why were they plagued by accidie and so many demonic thoughts and temptations? As we have seen, it was revealed to Abba Antony that there was a physician in the city whose life was just as holy as Antony's life as a hermit. So why all the fuss about fleeing to the desert? Is this "spiritual masochism"? The elders learned that by withdrawing to the desert (or a monastic cell in or near a city), he or she was also withdrawing from the busyness and superficial aspects of conventional society that can so easily hide or sublimate a person's inner struggles with temptations and prideful control of his or her life. A person who chooses to flee from these futile influences, whether lay or monastic, becomes naked and faces more clearly the realities of his or her inauthentic life. When temptations, failures, and pride are openly faced, the struggle is more difficult, even if the goal is simple.

With Mind, Heart, and Body

Abba Evagrius continues, *"When you stand up for prayer, do not begin with a slovenly way, lest you perform all your prayer in a slack or slovenly and wearied way. Rather, when you stand up, sign yourself with the sign of the cross, gather together your thoughts, be in a state of recollection and readiness, gaze upon him to whom you are praying, and then commence. Force yourself, so that right at the beginning of your prayer tears may flow and you feel suffering in yourself, so that your whole prayer may prove beneficial."*

As we have seen, accidie may affect the whole being of a person. Evagrius says we must gather everything we are, without ambiguity or hesitation, and "gaze upon him to whom you are praying." It takes courage and real effort to avoid a "slack or slovenly and wearied way." A powerful beginning, using our body in prayer, is to center ourselves in God's presence with the sign of the cross. It marks us as God's own person, regardless of our weakness. It turns us away from our lack of power toward the "beneficial" grace of God. Evagrius knows from experience that if we surrender to God in this way, thoughts, temptations, fears, and suffering will flow in the form of tears that will, like rain, make seeds grow. This is not easy and we may have to force ourselves to begin. This is not coercion but a first step in crossing a necessary threshold.

A Little Bit at a Time

"When you do not have thoughts which hinder you, it is not necessary to make space between one group of psalms and the next. But if your thoughts are in turmoil, you should spend more time in prayers and tears, than in the recitation of psalms. Drive the thoughts away by whatever means you have tested out, whether by varying the words or by some other means. Take in what I am telling you. If you should then have some beneficial thought, let it take the place of the psalms for you; do not push away from yourself what is the gift of God just in order to fulfill your prescribed portion of the psalms.

Prayer that does not have mingled into it the thought of God and interior vision is a weariness of the flesh."

Evagrius confirms the need for both psalms and prayer in the midst of accidie. Yet he affirms the need for balance in their use; neither is an end in itself. If the psalms do not relieve internal turmoil, more attention should be given to prayers and the unloading of burdensome emotions through tears. But even then it is important not to "overdo" for the sake of prescriptive discipline. A "beneficial thought" should be accepted as a "gift of God." Follow that "interior vision," however small it may seem, and do not dwell on quantity of effort. Evagrius, the pastor, is speaking here. The person is more important than the prescribed form of praxis; otherwise the result is "a weariness of the flesh." Even in weaker moments we can trust that God is present and at work within us.

Learning to Wait

Abba Pseudo-Macarius said, *"As near as the body is to the soul . . . so much nearer is God present, to come and open the locked doors of our heart and to fill us with heavenly riches. . . . [God's] promises cannot deceive, provided we only persevere to the end. . . . Glory be to the compassionate mercies of [God] forever! Amen."*

Moving away from the grip of accidie or any other physical, emotional, or psychological burden can put stress on our patience. However, Abba Macarius (this time from Syria, not Scetis in Egypt) points out that perseverance is not simply "staying with the program." It is God's presence and power that will bring health and renewed energy, not simply the passage of time and prayerful discipline. Dwelling on what holds us back or overemphasis on praxis can hide awareness of God's presence. The desert elders constantly said, "I am nothing" to remind themselves to depend solely on God and trust that God's "promises cannot deceive." This is a form of patience that is unrelated to the passage of time. It is turning toward God who is *already* with us even when the "doors of our heart," for whatever reasons, are still locked. We can trust the "compassionate mercies" of God even when those riches seem far off.

Look for Treasure in the Right Place

"Someone asked Abba Agathon, 'Which is better, bodily asceticism or interior vigilance?' The old man replied, 'Man is like a tree, bodily asceticism is the foliage, interior vigilance the fruit. According to that which is written, "Every tree that bringeth not forth good fruit shall be cut down and cast into the fire" (Matt. 3.10) it is clear that our care should be directed towards the fruit, that is to say, guard of the spirit; but it needs the protection and embellishment of the foliage, which is bodily asceticism.'"

An authentic and whole person needs both the spiritual and physical aspects of his or her life. The monk who came to Agathon assumed that one of these should have a higher priority. But his abba shows him that one cannot do without the other. The real issue is "that our care should be directed towards the fruit." The purpose of bodily asceticism, especially when we are weakened by accidie, is to be good stewards of "interior vigilance." Recitation of the psalms and prayer will direct the focus of our life to what lies within the "tree" of life. Abba Pachomius said, *"For I have seen the treasure of God hidden in human vessels."* What we can see and do leads us to invisible treasure. The gift in "bodily asceticism" is that it leads to the discovery of that treasure. It is a way of seeing beyond the surface of life.

Going to the Source

Abba Pseudo-Macarius said, *"For the heart directs and governs all the other organs of the body. And when grace pastures the heart, it rules over all the members and the thoughts. For there, in the heart, the mind abides as well as all the thoughts of the soul and all its hopes. This is how grace penetrates throughout all parts of the body."*

The desert elders insisted that a person's whole being is the venue for transformation. Bodily and mental disciplines are essential, but they are incomplete without the realm of the heart. When the efforts of our physical and contemplative disciplines are impaired by illness, despondency, and impatience or by too much austerity of praxis, we should turn to the silent language of the heart. This placeless center of our being is filled with the energy (grace) of God's Spirit and, like our physical cardiovascular system, is the source of health that "directs and governs all the other organs of the body." Rather than being a separate part of our being, it is the source that empowers "all the other organs of the body." Pseudo-Macarius exhorts us to look inward for hope and strength, especially when we feel weak or when our mind takes over our life with God. The heart enlightens the mind.

Self-Giving Heals and Restores

Abba Pseudo-Macarius said, *"If there are those who because of their spiritual immaturity cannot yet commit themselves entirely to the work of prayer, they should fulfill obedience in other matters, serving as they are able. They should work gladly, serving diligently with joy, not out of reward or honor, nor for human glory nor thanks of men. Let them shun negligence or sluggishness. . . . Therefore, no one who sincerely seeks salvation will lack power to do good."*

Although this is advice for newer monks, it is relevant for us all. We assume that prayer should always be our highest priority. But when we get bogged down in "the work of prayer," we often turn inward and depend on ourselves or focus on unfulfilled personal needs. What can we do when prayer is not "working" or it has become a burden? Pseudo-Macarius recommends that when this happens, the best thing is to look at the needs of others, not for our sake, but for their sakes. Sometimes it is best to leave things unresolved and turn our focus to other people. Even if it takes effort, we can "shun negligence or sluggishness" because no person "who sincerely seeks salvation will lack power to do good." It is not for reward. By doing what we can, we bring grace to another person. This transforms mundane work into prayer.

Prayer and Work Are Colleagues

"They said of Abba Silvanus that his disciple Zacharius went out without him and, taking some brothers with him, moved the garden fence back to make it larger. When he knew this, the old man took his sheepskin, went out and said to the brothers, 'Pray for me.' When they saw what he was doing they threw themselves at his feet saying, 'Tell us what is the matter, Father.' He said to them, 'I shall not go back inside, nor take off my sheepskin until you have put the fence back where it was at the first.' So they moved the fence once again and put it back as it was. So the old man returned to his cell."

Silvanus was not a grumpy old man who wanted everything to be to his liking. Zacharius and his confreres saw an opportunity to increase the productivity of the hermitage garden. It would provide more food for pilgrims, more income for their needs, and greater offerings for the poor. This made good sense to them. But their abba acted firmly, wanting to show by his leaving that this increase in daily labor beyond their basic needs would destroy the balance between their prayer and work. The focus of their common life was openness to God and love of their neighbor. An overemphasis on manual labor, even for good purposes, would leave less room for prayer.

The Goad of Prayer

Abba Poemen said, *"Life in the monastery demands three things: the first is humility, the next is obedience, and the third which sets them in motion and is like a goad is the work of the monastery."*

Humility and obedience lead a monk along the path to transformation. They are also core virtues for leading a compassionate life. Poemen reminds his disciples that these inner aspects of a monk's life enable them to contribute to the life of their monastic community. But they do not exist in a vacuum. They must be set in motion and embodied in the daily life and work of the monastery. Humility and obedience are not rungs on a ladder leading up to spiritual perfection or divine approval. They are manifestations of an open and flexible heart that become embodied in the mundane and very specific tasks and relationships of daily life in any community. The challenge of every monk is to make his or her inner life with God tangible in "work of the monastery." Obedience will help a person listen to the needs of others and humility places the needs of others ahead of our own. These two "goads" make prayer and work an undivided way of life.

The Venue for Virtue

"Someone said to blessed Arsenius, 'How is it that we, with all our education and our wide knowledge get no-where, while these Egyptian peasants acquire so many virtues?' Abba Arsenius said to him, 'We indeed get nothing from our secular education, but these Egyptian peasants acquire the virtues by hard work.'"

The desert elders did not speak about holiness, but they recognized holiness as it was manifested in what they called "virtues." Abbas Evagrius, Paul of Tamma, and Stephen of Thebes speak of virtues such as patience, abstinence, sincerity, innocence, purity, chastity, love, humility, gentleness, and many more. Yet these are not personal characteristics that can be acquired through abstract knowledge or personal skill training. Virtues are embodied in specific encounters with other persons and in the mundane activities of daily life. Abba Arsenius is saying that we cannot learn about virtuous living in a vacuum. He learned about virtuous living by observing the Egyptian peasants in their relationships and work. The desert elders put more trust in behavior than words. They could see holiness in a person's actions, but this state of being came from the hard work of prayer embodied in life's labor.

When Work Becomes Prayer

"It was also said of him [Agathon] that, coming to the town one day to sell his wares, he encountered a sick traveller lying in the public place without anyone to look after him. The old man rented

a cell and lived with him there, working with his hands to pay the rent and spending the rest of his money on the sick man's needs. He stayed there four months till the sick man was restored to health. Then he returned in peace to his cell."

Every day the monks of the desert spent long hours at work with their hands during their prayer and psalmody. Many, like Agathon, would sell their work to buy personal supplies and make offerings for the poor. In the city Agathon found this ill and helpless old man and used his earnings to bring the man back to health. Knowing this would require a long time, Agathon rented a place to use for his cell. He made a compassionate commitment to the old man in a way that will enable him to maintain a personal commitment to his monastic discipline. Although he will eventually return to his cell in the desert, his "cell" of praxis is flexible enough to care for his neighbor. Although his four months in the city were different from his life in the desert, he maintained his prayer by caring for the old man in addition to his vigils and psalmody.

AUGUST 15

Becoming What Happens in Prayer

"One day Abba Daniel and Abba Ammoes went on a journey together. Abba Ammoes said, 'When shall we, too, settle down in a cell, Father?' Abba Daniel replied, 'Who shall separate us henceforth from God? God is in the cell, and, on the other hand, he is outside also.'"

Yesterday we learned from Abba Agathon that he could temporarily move his desert cell to the city to aid an ill old man. In caring for his neighbor, Agathon incarnated in the city what he had experienced in his desert cell. His contemplative experience of God in his desert cell became tangible in his care for the old man. His experience of God in his cell taught him not to ignore the needs of his neighbor, not out of duty, but through genuine love.

Abba Ammoes's question, "When shall we, too, settle down in a cell, Father?" expresses his desire to experience God in the solitude and silence of a cell. But Abba Daniel reminds him that "God is in the cell, and, on the other hand, he is outside also." Daniel has learned that God's presence has no limits and may be integrated in every aspect of our lives.

Tending to the Whole Person

"It was said of Abba John the Dwarf, that one day he said to his elder brother, 'I should like to be free of all care, like the angels, who do not work, but ceaselessly offer worship to God.' So he took off his cloak and went away into the desert. After a week he came back to his brother. When he knocked on the door, he heard his brother say, before he opened it, 'Who are you?' And he said, 'I am John, your brother.' But he replied, 'John has become an angel, and henceforth he is no longer among men.' Then the other begged him, saying, 'It is I.' However, his brother did not let him in, but left him there in distress until morning. Then, opening the door, he said to him, 'You are a man and you must once again work in order to eat.' Then John made a prostration before him, saying, 'Forgive me.'"

We have seen this story before and its wisdom and humor are worth repeating. John's enthusiasm for his new way of life and love of God is so typical. He wants to live like an angel, beyond the limitations of the human condition. But we are not like that. Work and prayer are integral parts of our lives. These dimensions are not in competition. In fact, they complete who we are. Prayer without work denigrates our humanity. Work roots our prayer in the integrity of serving our neighbor. But there is more wisdom here. Abba John's elder brother had learned that as great as heaven will be, the place for human transformation is here on earth. The desert elders took the incarnation of God's presence in Jesus seriously. The "path to salvation" is not a denial of the goodness of human life. Human transformation is not an escape from human life; it takes place right here "among men."

Work Is More than Getting a Job Done

"In the district of Arsinoë we also visited a priest named Sarapion, the father of many hermitages and the superior of an enormous community numbering about ten thousand monks. Thanks to the labours of the community he successfully administered a considerable rural economy, for at harvest time all of them came as a body and brought

him their own produce, which each had obtained at his harvest wage,
filling each year twelve artabas [about 400 bushels]. . . . Through
Sarapion they provided this grain for the relief of the poor, so that
there was nobody in that district who was destitute any longer. In-
deed, grain was even sent to the poor of Alexandria. "

These monks linked their prayer with "their own produce, which
each had obtained at his harvest wage." The monks from Palestine
who visited the district of Arsinoë went on to say that it *"was rare*
for anyone in need to be found living near these monasteries." Agri-
cultural work was woven into the monks' daily pattern of prayer to
form a seamless process of self-offering. Because their work sustained
their way of life and the lives of their neighbors, it was not selfish,
nor accomplished at the expense of others. In this way their labor was
more than earning a living. Arsinoë was over two hundred miles by
river from Alexandria and yet Serapion and thousands of monks in
this fertile area shared their fertile lives of prayer and work with the
poor as far as the great Mediterranean port city. Their separation from
conventional society to live a monastic life did not mean they were
disconnected from the lives of other people.

AUGUST 18

Threads of the Same Tapestry

Amma Melania records these words from a young hermit named
Alexandra who lived in a tomb near Alexandria, Egypt. *"From early*
morn until the ninth hour I pray hour by hour, spinning the flax all
the while. During the remaining hours I meditate on the holy patri-
archs and prophets and apostles and martyrs. And having eaten my
bread I remain in patience for the other hours, waiting for my end
with cheerful hope."

Although a hermit, Alexandra's work is similar to the pattern of
morning recitation of psalms and Bible verses in the "houses" of
Pachomian monastic communities. The monks continued to weave
palm fronds into rope, hats, and mats as they listened to Scripture.
Their work and prayer were threads of the same tapestry. Even though
she was alone physically, Alexandra was in the constant company of
"holy patriarchs and prophets and apostles and martyrs." Prayer is a
constant sharing of energy that has no spatial boundaries. When we

are at work, we do not leave God's company or the presence of our faith community. Work is never done in a vacuum, no matter how mundane. All our efforts have their place in God's continuing creation of the world.

The Fullness of Poverty

"They said of Abba Megethius, that if he left his cell and it occurred to him to leave the place where he was leaving he would go without returning to his cell. He owned nothing in this world, except a knife with which he cut reeds and every day he made three small baskets, which was all he needed for his food."

Megethius would be the first to say that the specific pattern of his simple life of prayer and work should not be seen as a model for anyone else. Yet the simplicity of his poverty is a message about poverty itself and its significance for monks and laypersons alike. He was a mendicant and needed both the freedom to move, when led by the Spirit, as well as his "knife with which he cut reeds and every day he made three small baskets, which was all he needed for his food." In addition to his knife, all he needed were his clothing, a sack to carry reeds, his sleeping pad, a water jug, and some bread. These possessions provided everything to sustain the life he had chosen. He saw no need for additional wealth or possessions. In this way his labor was an environment of grace supporting his life of prayer. Poverty is not being without any possessions. It is having easily satisfied needs. In the desert, poverty was not a problem; it was a virtue.

Unceasing Prayer

Abba Lucius was confronted by some monks who claimed that prayer was more necessary for salvation than manual labor. They were committed to the biblical injunction to "pray without ceasing." Abba Lucius responded in this way: *"'What is your manual work?'*

They said, 'We do not touch manual work but as the Apostle says, we pray without ceasing.' The old man asked them if they did not eat and they replied they did. So he said to them, 'When you are eating, who prays for you then?' Again he asked them if they did not sleep and they replied they did. And he said to them, 'When you are asleep, who prays for you then?' They could not find any answer to give him. He said to them, 'Forgive me, but you do not act as you speak. I will show you how, while doing my manual work, I pray without interruption. I sit down with God, soaking my reeds and plaiting my ropes, and I say, "God, have mercy on me; according to your great goodness, . . . save me from my sins."' So he asked them if this were not prayer and they replied it was. Then he said to them, 'So when I have spent the whole day working and praying, making thirteen pieces of money more or less, I put two pieces of money outside the door and I pay for my food with the rest of the money. He who takes the two pieces of money prays for me when I am eating and when I am sleeping; so, by the grace of God, I fulfil the precept to pray without ceasing.'"

The wisdom in Lucius's response is relevant to all persons who work and devote themselves to God. Prayer and work are part of an undivided life, and work, like prayer, is the venue for the flow of God's energy in daily life. We care for our neighbor through our work "so, by the grace of God," it is prayer. Lucius understood that his life with God was a seamless experience. His critics separated life into two sectors. Conventional wisdom today comes to a similar conclusion. The "secular" and "sacred" aspects of life are separate and people move from one to the other. Some prefer sacred as highest priority, others the secular. And many believe they should not mix. But Abba Lucius reminds us that all life is sacred and that "praying with heart and mouth" and weaving are both loving responses to God's desires for the world.

Making Space for Prayer and Work

Two desert abbas asked God to reveal to them how far they had advanced in their monastic life. They received an unexpected response. *"In a certain village in Egypt there is a man called Eucharistus and his wife who is called Mary. You have not yet reached their degree of virtue."* The two abbas reached the village and asked Eucharistus about the life he and his wife were living. *"At these words, Eucharistus was afraid and said, 'Here are these sheep; we received them from our parents, and if, by God's help we make a little profit, we divide it into three parts: one for the poor, the second for hospitality, and the third for our personal needs. Since I married my wife, we have not had intercourse with one another, for she is a virgin; we each live alone. At night we wear hair shirts and our ordinary clothes by day. No-one has known of this until now.' At these words the abbas were filled with admiration and went away giving glory to God."*

Like Abba Lucius, Eucharistus and his wife Mary have woven prayer and work into a seamless garment. Although they have chosen to be celibate within their marriage, they are a model for all "seculars." Through faithful stewardship of their "little profit," their generosity to others leaves room for their own needs and time for disciplined personal prayer. Their simple devotion to work, care of the poor, and prayer taught the visiting monks a valuable lesson. This incident mirrors a revelation to Abba Antony that there was a doctor in the city "who was his equal" and who gave "whatever he had beyond his needs . . . to the poor, and every day he sang the Sanctus with the angels." The lesson in both cases is that living according to the Great Commandment is the common vocation of every person who seeks God. The purpose is not "advancement" but faithfulness to love of God and neighbor.

AUGUST 22

Prayer and Busy Days Are Compatible

"It was revealed to Abba Anthony in his desert that there was one who was his equal in the city. He was a doctor by profession and whatever he had beyond his needs he gave to the poor, and every day he sang the Sanctus with the angels."

You and I do not have to be monks, especially hermits, to have a life of prayer that is authentic and full. A doctor, with his busy and unpredictable days, found time for both his patients' needs and his personal prayer. The pattern of monastic life is a reminder that authentic human life must include disciplined attention to both prayer and work. Antony and the physician lived very different lives, but they were equal. But where do we city or town dwellers find time for prayer? We have jobs, families, faith communities, and community responsibilities that demand our time and energy. Yet, this doctor found time. His secret was that "whatever he had beyond his needs he gave to the poor." He was committed to working only to provide care to his patients and to make enough money to satisfy his needs, not to gain wealth. This is a goal for all vocations. Easily satisfied needs will give us plenty of time for both work, caring for others, and prayer.

AUGUST 23

Work and Prayer Collaborate for Salvation

"An old man was asked, 'What is it necessary to do to be saved?' He was making rope, and without looking up from the work, he replied, 'You are looking at it.'"

A pilgrim or young novice walked into the desert, found an abba, and asked a most fundamental question. He or she wanted to get right to the point of life itself. "What is it necessary to do to be saved?" A rich young ruler asked Jesus the same question. Both questions assume it is necessary to "do something," something special, a unique spiritual discipline. But the abba, like Jesus, offers an unexpected response. "You are looking at it." He declares that living a very ordinary life of work is all that is needed. The abba's answer assumes that the questioner already knows that the abba weaves work and prayer into his rope, shares his income with the poor, and keeps only what he needs for himself. The venue for salvation (wholeness, health of being) is here and now. It is not something we work to obtain in the future. The rich young ruler left Jesus because Jesus asked him to share his wealth, rather than follow more rules.

When Work Dominates a Life

"While still living in the palace, Abba Arsenius prayed to God in these words, 'Lord lead me in the way of salvation.' And a voice came saying to him, 'Arsenius, flee men and you will be saved.'"

As we have seen, Arsenius's life was filled with work in Constantinople, where he held senatorial rank and was the tutor to the sons of the emperor, Theodosius I. He was a scholar of Greek and Latin and one of the finest rhetoricians of his day. He was a person of great influence in an empire dominated by political, social, and economic intrigues. His life was rich with expensive clothes and influential colleagues. His place in society was secure until he reached a point, "while still living in the palace," when he knew that something fundamental was missing. At the age of forty he realized the need for "salvation," not so much in the future, but in the present. He asked God to "lead [him] in the way of salvation." God's response was to lead him away from his busy, influential life in Roman society. He would need to make a break from his constant activities to discover a fundamental aspect of his life that he had overlooked. His work had become his life, but that was no longer satisfying. What was missing?

Being Silent Is Not Running Away

"Having withdrawn to the solitary life he made the same prayer again and he heard a voice saying to him, 'Arsenius, flee, be silent, pray always, for these are the sources of sinlessness.'"

Arsenius's life had been so full of people and activities that he needed to make a complete break from society. There is nothing wrong with politics, education, the classics, or public debate. Yet, these "possessions" had become tools Arsenius used to create his identity, his ego. They had become the "voices" he listened to and obeyed. Their weight and constant demands were burying him and he longed for breathing room. His prayer for "salvation" (in Greek, literally, abundant health) was genuine, but perhaps he had no idea it would lead to the desert of Egypt. Once there, he said the same prayer and was exhorted to flee further, be silent, and pray, "for these are the sources of sinlessness." Arsenius was being led to a place for solitude and silence. By listening to himself and God's Spirit in prayerful vigilance, he would shed the weight of his former life and make space for something new. His inner awareness that work in the palace was not congruent with "who he really was" was leading him on a path toward salvation.

Letting Go of a Life Defined by Work

Arsenius found solitude and silence in the remote hermitages of Scetis, Egypt. *"It happened that when Arsenius was sitting in his cell that he was harassed by demons. His servants, on their return, stood outside his cell and heard him praying to God in these words, 'O God, do not leave me. I have done nothing good in your sight, but according to your goodness, let me now make a beginning of good.'"*
When Arsenius found solitude, things did not change overnight. He was harassed by memories, temptations, and the perquisites of the power he had exercised in Constantinople. His work as tutor, rhetorician, scholar, and politician was still dominating his thoughts and desires. He felt helpless and unworthy and cried out, "O God, do not leave me. I have done nothing good in your sight." Arsenius's "new life" began with tension between the continuing lure of his old life and his powerlessness to change to something new. He realized his former personal power had no influence in his desert cell. He wanted to do "good," but as Jesus had recognized, "there is only one who is good." In his silence, the emptiness of his personal power led him to pray: "according to your goodness, let me now make a beginning of good."

Letting Go of the Desire for Privilege and Domination

"It was said of [Arsenius] that, just as none in the palace had worn more splendid garments than he when he lived there, so no-one in the Church wore such poor clothing."

"It was said of the same Abba Arsenius that he only changed the water for his palm-leaves once a year; the rest of the time he simply added to it. One old man implored him in these words, 'Why do you not change the water for these palm-leaves when it smells bad?' He said to him, 'Instead of the perfumes and aromatics which I used in the world I must bear this bad smell.'"

We have already seen that when Arsenius, with his Latin and Greek education, was criticized for listening to a peasant monk, he replied, *"I have indeed been taught Latin and Greek, but I do not know even the alphabet of this peasant."* Arsenius was beginning a new life, but he was not sure how he could make a "beginning of good." He wanted to "die" to the privileges of his former life and, at the same time, learn from persons who were living the life he now desired. He was having a hard time learning to let go of privilege and power. It is obvious that he brought memories of "splendid garments" and "perfumes and aromatics" with him to the desert. His rancid water for softening palms took his mind off what he had left behind. Enduring a foul smell year after year seems like an unorthodox form of praxis, but it helped him turn his focus away from the past and persist in attention to prayer.

A New Experience of Life and Work

"Abba Mark said to Abba Arsenius, 'Why do you avoid us?' The old man said to him, 'God knows that I love you, but I cannot live with God and with men. The thousands and ten thousands of the heavenly hosts have but one will, while men have many. So I cannot leave God to be with men.'"

"A brother questioned Abba Arsenius to hear a word of him and the old man said to him, 'Strive with all your might to bring your

interior activity into accord with God, and you will overcome exterior passions.'"

"He also said, 'If we seek God, he will show himself to us, and if we keep him, he will remain close to us.'"

In the palace, Arsenius did not leave room for the spiritual dimension of life. His work drained his spirit so dangerously that he was moved to pray for salvation. The change he sought was not a new venue for work but "a new way of life and a new experience of work." His new work was austere prayer and sharing his experience of God and wisdom with others. Weaving mats and rope earned him enough money for his basic needs and offerings for the poor. The healing of soul that he prayed for in Constantinople became manifest in this simple integration of prayer and work.

AUGUST 29

Healing of the Soul

"Abba Daniel used to tell how when Abba Arsenius learned all the varieties of fruit were ripe he would say, 'Bring me some.' He would taste very little of each, just once, giving thanks to God."

"It was also said of him that on Saturday evenings, preparing for the glory of Sunday, he would turn his back on the sun and stretch out his hands in prayer towards the heavens, till once again the sun shone on his face. Then he would sit down."

"A brother came to the cell of Abba Arsenius at Scetis. Waiting outside the door he saw the old man entirely like a flame. (The brother was worthy of this sight.) When he knocked, the old man came out and saw the brother marveling. He said to him, 'Have you been knocking long? Did you see anything here?' The other answered, 'No.' So then he talked with him and sent him away."

In the desert Arsenius found healing and transformation. His soul was now filled with gratitude rather than acquisition. His heart was open and turned toward God. And his work was sharing the inner fire of his soul with others. He had exchanged fancy clothes and costly perfumes for simple gratitude for an occasional taste of fresh fruit. The "big things" and important people of a palace were replaced by the small pleasures and ordinary people of desert monastic life. Standing alone in prayer all night on the vigil of Sunday replaced his expert rhetoric in public places. In the palace he did not know who he was. His life was aimless and he prayed for "salvation." In the desert he found himself and was afire with life.

Each Person Must Follow His or Her Own Path to the Way of Truth

"Another time the Blessed Archbishop [Theophilus], intending to come to see [Arsenius], sent someone to see if the old man would receive him. Arsenius told him, 'If you come, I shall receive you; but if I receive you, I receive everyone and therefore I shall no longer live here.' Hearing that, the archbishop said, 'If I drive him away by going to him, I shall not go any more.'"

"Abba Mark asked Abba Arsenius, 'Is it a good to have nothing extra in the cell? I know a brother who had some vegetables and he pulled them up.' Abba Arsenius replied, 'Undoubtedly that is good but it must be done according to a man's capacity. For if he does not have the strength for such a practice he will soon plant others.'"

It is tempting to become romantic about Arsenius's monastic life and wisdom. The truth is that he wanted to be alone and his primary work was his prayer. He did not want visitors to interrupt his solitude or scatter his vigilance because it was this disciplined, silent prayer that was his gift to the very people who sought his company. He was strict. He could be grumpy. Once he said that a monk who only needs an hour of sleep each night is a "good fighter." He followed his own path, yet he knew every person must find his or her own calling. Arsenius learned that persistence in the monastic art is different for each person. He insisted on his solitude and made no exceptions, even for an archbishop. Yet in his reply to Abba Mark he teaches that the monastic life "must be [lived] according to a man's capacity."

Following the Way of Truth, rather than Comfort

"Once when [Arsenius] was ill at Scetis, the priest came to take him to church and put him on a bed with a small pillow under his head. Now behold an old man who was coming to see him, saw him lying on a bed with a little pillow under his head and he was shocked and said, 'Is this really Abba Arsenius, this man lying down like this?' Then the priest took him aside and said to him, 'In the village where you lived, what was your trade?' 'I was a shepherd,' he replied. 'And how did you live?' 'I had a very hard life.' Then the priest said, 'And how do you live in your cell now?' The other replied, 'I am more comfortable.' Then he said to him, 'Do you see this Abba Arsenius? When he was in the world he was the father of the emperor, surrounded by thousands of slaves with golden girdles, all wearing collars of gold and garments of silk. Beneath him were spread rich coverings. While you were in the world as a shepherd you did not enjoy even the comforts you now have but he no longer enjoys the delicate life he led in the world. So you are comforted, while he is afflicted.' At these words the old man was filled with compunction and prostrated himself saying, 'Father, forgive me, for I have sinned. Truly the way this man follows is the way of truth, for it leads to humility, while mine leads to comfort.' So the old man withdrew, edified."

The old shepherd looked at Arsenius in church on a bed with a pillow under his head and made a false judgment. He was looking at Arsenius through the lenses of his own situation as a monk and his assumptions about Arsenius's past life. He saw preferential treatment rather than a weak and sickly old man, nearing the end of his life, wanting to worship with his brothers. The priest gave the old shepherd an opportunity to see the situation in a different light. Without judging the shepherd he pointed out the reality of the situation and this led the shepherd to realize his sin. But it was more than acknowledging sin. "'Father, forgive me, for I have sinned. Truly the way this man follows is the way of truth, for it leads to humility, while mine leads to comfort.' So the old man withdrew, edified." Next month we will focus on humility.

SEPTEMBER

Humility

"At that time the disciples came to Jesus and asked, 'Who is the greatest in the kingdom of heaven?' He called a child, whom he put among them, and said, 'Truly I tell you, unless you change and become like children, you will never enter the kingdom of heaven. Whoever becomes humble like this child is the greatest in the kingdom of heaven. Whoever welcomes one such child in my name welcomes me'" (Matt 18:1-5).

Amma Syncletica said, *"Because humility is good and salutary, the Lord clothed himself in it while fulfilling the economy [of salvation] for humanity. For he says, 'Learn from me, for I am gentle and humble of heart' [Matt 11:29]. Notice who it is who is speaking; learn his lesson perfectly. Let humility become for you the beginning and the end of virtues. He means a humble heart; he refers not to appearance alone, but to the inner person, for the outer person will also follow after the inner."*

Abba Dorotheos of Gaza said, *"Among the seniors it used to be told how a brother asked one of the elders, 'What is humility?' And the elder replied, 'Humility is a great and divine work and the road to humility is labor, bodily labor, while seeking to know oneself and to put oneself below everyone else and praying to God about everything: this is the road to humility, but humility itself is something divine and incomprehensible.'"*

The desert elders took Jesus' words about humility seriously. But more than his words, they saw humility present in his daily life. At the same time, they learned that humility is a mystery. It is the central virtue of Christian life, yet it cannot be acquired by personal effort.

170

It is the most powerful aspect of human transformation, but it can never be "mastered."

During September we will reflect on humility.

The Central Virtue

"Abba Anthony said, 'I saw the snares that the enemy spreads out over the world and I said groaning, "What can get through from such snares?" Then I heard a voice saying to me, "Humility."'"

We ended last month reflecting on Arsenius's transformation. Like Antony, he wanted to move through "the snares that the enemy spreads out over the world." He discovered that the "enemy" in his life in the palace of Theodosius lay embedded in his attachment to the earthly values of scholarship, influence, and public esteem. He withdrew from this public spotlight because these futile manifestations of the darker possibilities of human life were choking him. After decades in the subdued light of his desert cell, Arsenius emptied himself of the old influences that called attention to him. His ascetic "work" and openness to God's grace led to relinquishment of these self-assertive veneers. Gradually his life began to radiate the light of God's presence. Although alone, this was his self-offering to us. Rather than a name in a history of the empire, Arsenius's legacy is an example of the power of humility. His cell was the palace where he learned to be a temple of the Holy Spirit.

What Is Humility?

Abba Dorotheos of Gaza said, *"Among the seniors it used to be told how a brother asked one of the elders, 'What is humility?' And the elder replied, 'Humility is a great and divine work and the road to humility is labor, bodily labor, while seeking to know oneself and to put oneself below everyone else and praying to God about everything: this is the road to humility, but humility itself is something divine and incomprehensible.'"*

The desert elders were careful not to define humility. That would limit it to a concept and infer that humility can be mastered through training. When the brother asked, "What is humility?" the old man made it clear that humility is God's activity in a human life, rather than something a person accomplishes on his or her own. From our point of view humility is a gift, "something divine and incomprehensible." But there is a "road to humility" and it winds through the tangible labors of daily life. Along the road we begin to see ourselves with more clarity and honesty and learn to value those who walk alongside. We learn to trust that God will provide everything we need for the journey.

Experience Is the Best Teacher

Abba Dorotheos said, *"The first kind of humility is to hold my brother [or sister] to be wiser than myself, and in all things to rate him [or her] higher than myself, and simply, as that holy man said, to put oneself below everyone. The second kind is to attribute to God all virtuous actions. . . . So every single one of the saints, as I have said, acquired this humility from the fulfillment of the Commandments. No one can explain how this comes about, how humility is generated in the soul. Unless a man [or woman] learns this by experience, he [or she] cannot learn it by verbal teaching."*

Modern cosmologists tell us that there is no center of the universe. Wherever you travel in space, from your point of view, you will always perceive that you are at the center. Human conflict usually begins when a person acts as though he or she is the center of the universe. I value my knowledge, behavior, and competence more than yours. I am self-reliant. I trust my wisdom, power, and decisions. I have confidence in the path I chart for myself. The desert elders challenge me to change my perspective on life. What does it mean to "put oneself below everyone"? If I am willing, how do I learn to do that? What is the benefit? And if I succeed, why should God get all the credit?

An Example to Ponder

Amma Syncletica said, *"Because humility is good and salutary, the Lord clothed himself in it while fulfilling the economy [of salvation] for humanity. For he says, 'Learn from me, for I am gentle and humble of heart' [Matt 11:29]. Notice who it is who is speaking; learn his lesson perfectly. Let humility become for you the beginning and the end of virtues. He means a humble heart; he refers not to appearance alone, but to the inner person, for the outer person will also follow after the inner."*

The desert elders looked to Jesus as their exemplar. More than anyone else, his life demonstrated authentic human living. His intimate relationship with God was tangible in the way he lived. In the words of the Second Letter of Peter, Jesus, by his manner of life, shows us how to "become participants of the divine nature" (2 Pet 1:4). In Jesus' life, as St. Paul declares, the likeness of God was present in human form. Syncletica invites her sisters to wear Jesus' clothing of gentleness and meekness because without these attitudes of heart, all the other virtues are hollow. Like Dorotheos, she knows that humility is not a veneer applied to behavior. It begins in the inside of life.

The Demon of Self-Assertion

"An Elder said: 'If one gives an order to a brother in humility and the fear of God it will incline the brother to submit and do what is demanded of him. If, on the other hand, giving orders to a brother without fear of God and in a spirit of domination with an idea of exerting authority, God, who knows the secrets of the heart, will not inspire that brother to hear and submit. In fact, that which is done according to God is easily recognizable just as in an order done in an authoritarian way and through one's own will. That which is asked according to God is asked in humility and through prayer; that which is ordered with a spirit of domination reflects anger and disturbance coming from the Evil One.'"

The desert elders had plenty of opportunities to impose their will and authority on each other, especially their disciples. But they learned that self-assertion inhibits a person's ability to see a situation clearly and to listen to one's neighbor. Letting go of self-assertion is not weakness or loss of identity. It does not eliminate initiative but begins with knowing what is "according to God," through prayer, and avoids "a spirit of domination." Authoritarian self-assertion is dangerous because it begins with the assumption that another person should "submit and do what is demanded of him." Unlike compassion, it leaves no room for mutual perspective and cooperation. It is no wonder that it "will not inspire that brother to hear and submit." It creates a two-way lack of respect rather than an opportunity to act on what "is asked according to God."

SEPTEMBER 6

The Danger of Insisting on Control

"A brother whom another brother had wronged came to see Abba Sisoes and said to him, 'My brother has hurt me and I want to avenge myself.' The old man pleaded with him saying, 'No, my child, leave vengeance to God.' He said to him, 'I shall not rest until I have avenged myself.' The old man said, 'Brother, let us pray.' Then the old man stood up and said, 'God, we no longer need you to care for us, since we do justice for ourselves.' Hearing these words, the brother fell at the old man's feet, saying, 'I will no longer seek justice from my brother; forgive me, abba.'"

The disciple of Sisoes insisted on controlling the consequence of his brother's wrongdoing. He asserted his need to punish his brother and define a just response. Even though he sensed the need for his abba's advice, his unrestrained anger prevented him from accepting Sisoes's word. At the root of his malevolent response was his attitude of superiority over his brother. This limited possibilities for forgiveness and reconciliation. Sisoes's prayer, with gentle humor and directness, reminded his disciple that he too is in need of forgiveness. He has been unwilling to depend on what God desires for both him and his brother. Self-assertion narrowed the options for a just resolution of the wrongdoing.

Practical Implications of Restraint

"A brother asked Abba Poemen: 'How ought we to act in the place where we dwell?' 'Show discretion towards a stranger; show respect to the Elders; do not impose your own point of view; then, you will live in peace.'"

Does restraining from self-assertion mean you have to be a wimp and not hold firm convictions? "How *ought* we to act in the place where we dwell?" The young brother was confused. He wanted to live humbly, but he was not sure how to balance self-restraint and active engagement in his community and with strangers. Abba Poemen holds firmly to the primacy of humility and at the same time points to the wisdom of using self-restraint. He advises sensitivity and prudence in relationships with strangers. He affirms listening to the experience of elders. But in both cases he tells the brother, "do not impose your own point of view." He assumes the brother *does* have convictions and opinions but warns against forcing them on others. Humility affirms that in all relationships and actions there must be room for discretion, mutual respect, and sharing. Rather than being "wimpish," these aspects of humility are strong building blocks for living in peace.

Solidarity rather than Competition

"A brother asked Abba Tithoes, 'Which way leads to humility?' The old man said, 'The way of humility is this: self-control, prayer, and thinking yourself inferior to all creatures.'"

Tithoes, like Dorotheos, speaks of a "way" or road to humility. Self-control and prayer are easier to accept than "thinking yourself inferior to all creatures." Is it psychologically healthy to think of yourself as inferior? But the desert elders are not using "inferior" in a hierarchical context where one person is more or less important than another. Neither do they refer to a moral distinction that declares one person is better or worse than someone else. Like St. Paul, they realized the danger of comparing oneself with a neighbor or leader. The wisdom in "thinking yourself inferior" lies in awareness that we are walking the path of humility *together* and each person has unique gifts to offer. In like manner, we all have weaknesses and make mistakes. When "thinking yourself inferior" is understood as not desiring to be "in first place" in relation to another person, it becomes an attitude of solidarity, rather than competition or judgment. We can be present to another person as he or she is, not in reference to ourselves.

Knowing Our Limits

"A brother questioned Abba Motius, saying, 'If I go to dwell somewhere, how do you want me to live?' The old man said to him, 'If you live somewhere, do not seek to be known for anything special; do not say, for example, I do not go to the synaxis [prayer of the community]; or perhaps, I do not eat at the agape [a fellowship meal]. For these things make an empty reputation and later you will be troubled because of this. For men rush there where they find these practices.' The brother said to him, 'What shall I do then?' The old man said, 'Wherever you live, follow the same manner as everyone else and if you see devout men, whom you trust doing something, do the same and you will be at peace. For this is humility: to see yourself to be the same as the rest. When men see you do not go beyond the limits; they will consider you to be the same as everyone else and no-one will trouble you.'"

Abba Motius has learned what it takes to become part of a community. It is not easy to trust that our talents speak for themselves and, with God's grace, eventually will contribute to the good of a community. In like manner, if we assert special recognition for ourselves, we inhibit the community's ability to contribute to our formation. Everyone has unique gifts to offer. If we "go beyond the limits" with our own, we disrupt the life of the community. By focusing on sharing our talents, even with a good motive, we narrow our ability to recognize and be influenced by others. Motius suggests we wait and "follow the same manner as everyone else." By "fitting in" to what the community offers, we will eventually discover "devout" persons and learn to trust their way of life. They will show us the richness of what the community offers. The "sameness" of its way of life enriches every member.

A Humble Mind

"One day some old men came to see Abba Anthony. In the midst of them was Abba Joseph. Wanting to test them, the old man suggested a text from the Scriptures, and, beginning with the youngest, he asked them what it meant. Each gave his opinion as he was able. But to each one the old man said, 'You have not understood it.' Last of all he said to Abba Joseph, 'How would you explain this saying?' and he replied, 'I do not know.' Then Abba Anthony said, 'Indeed, Abba Joseph has found the way, for he has said: "I do not know."'"

The Bible was at the heart of the spiritual lives of the desert elders. We have seen the variety of ways they meditated on passages of Scripture, especially the psalms. Learning the meaning of biblical texts was essential, but just as the monks listened to God in the silence of their cells, they were diligent in listening to that same voice in Scripture. Study and sharing wisdom was important. But Abba Joseph "found the way" to learn from Scripture by listening, rather than filling his mind with ideas. Rather than searching Scripture with his mind, he was willing to let Scripture speak to him. He refrained from asserting himself into the passage of Scripture in order to be enlightened by the passage itself. His attitude of "I do not know" was a threshold to wisdom.

Relying on More than Words

"Abba Ammoun of Raithou asked Abba Sisoes, 'When I read the Scriptures, my mind is wholly concentrated on the words so that I may have something to say if I am asked.' The old man said to him, 'That is not necessary; it is better to enrich yourself through purity of spirit and to be without anxiety and then to speak.'"

Abba Ammoun was genuinely interested in having "something to say if I am asked" because he wanted to share the Scriptures with other people. But Abba Sisoes realized that Ammoun was more focused on his ability to master and share information than on letting the Scriptures speak for themselves. His approach was "concentrated on the words" and he was relying on his mind and excluding the openness of his spirit to God's voice in Scripture. Sisoes learned that overdependence on information will produce anxiety because it limits what we can say to our own knowledge. If we have an open spirit, we can hear more than words and speak in ways that transcend our personal knowledge. Purity of spirit is a riverbed that, in humility, makes space for the living water of God's Spirit to flow through us to others.

The Teacher as Lover of Souls

"The same amma [Theodora] said that a teacher ought to be a stranger for domination, vain-glory, and pride; one should not be able to fool him by flattery, nor blind him by gifts, nor conquer him by the stomach, nor dominate him by anger; but he should be patient, gentle and humble as far as possible; he must be tested and without partisanship, full of concern, and a lover of souls."

We have reflected on this saying earlier in the year, yet its power to embody the nature of humility warrants repetition. Even though Theodora is referring to monastic teachers, we are all teachers in some way. Our words, actions, characteristics, and demeanors let others know what our "window" is on what is fundamental in life. According to Theodora, this sharing of experience and wisdom is based on the foundation of genuine love for others. That is our motive, rather than "domination, vain-glory, and pride." We teach for the sake of others. Although we may value expertise, sharing what we know and value is never about us. Theodora gives a cameo of the fruit of "getting ourselves out of the way" when she describes a teacher as "patient, gentle and humble as far as possible." Teaching is a form of selfless love.

Mastery of Knowledge Is Not the Goal

A revered abba came a long distance to meet Abba Poemen, who greeted him with joy. The visitor began to speak about the Bible and spiritual wisdom, but Poemen would not respond. A disciple of Poemen said to him, *"Abba, this great man who has so great a reputation in his own country has come here because of you. Why did you not speak to him?"* Poemen replied, *"He is great and speaks of heavenly things and I am lowly and speak of earthly things. If he had spoken of the passions of the soul, I should have replied, but he speaks to me of spiritual things and I know nothing about that."* The disciple went to the visitor and said, *"The old man does not readily speak of the Scriptures, but if anyone consults him about the passions of the soul, he replies."* When the visitor realized his intention in the visit was to demonstrate and enlarge his knowledge by listening to Poemen, he saw that he was missing an opportunity to reflect on the genuine difficulties and temptations of monastic life. He said to Poemen, *"What should I do, abba, for the passions of the soul master me?"* Now it was possible to have an honest conversation about overcoming personal weaknesses and strengthening each other's life of prayer.

It is easy to mask our weaknesses by focusing on our strengths. The revered abba had genuine gifts to share with others and hoped a visit with Abba Poemen would enhance his reputation. Abba Poemen was very streetwise about himself and the visiting abba. When he offered to share struggles, he and the proud visiting abba were on common ground and could learn from each other's experience.

SEPTEMBER 14

A Humble Spirit Knows a Person's Limits

Speaking to her sisters, Amma Syncletica said, *"For further illustration, let us examine how the experienced farmer will water more often the plant that is weak and small. He exercises greater care towards that plant so that it might improve. If he observes that the plant has put forth shoots prematurely, he will prune it to prevent further withering. The same case exists when a physician will encourage certain patients to increase their intake of food and to exercise more, whereas to others, the physician will order a fast. This same type of care is to be used by physicians of souls. It is plain that humility is the summit of the virtues, and difficult for one to obtain."*

Humility is an attitude of trusting restraint. Syncletica, as a wise and experienced mentor, is guiding sisters who may push themselves, or others, too fast or hold back unnecessarily. Just as farmers and physicians discern what is best for the growth and health of plants and human beings, so "physicians of souls" should restrain themselves from forcing what those under their care need. Perhaps Syncletica had a passage from the prophet Isaiah in mind as she spoke to her sisters. Isaiah is speaking about God's servant who will bring justice to the nations. "He will not cry or lift up his voice, or make it heard in the street; a bruised reed he will not break, and a dimly burning wick he will not quench; he will faithfully bring forth justice" (Isa 42:2-3).

Not Getting in Our Own Way

Amma Syncletica gives practical advice about being a good physician of one's, or someone else's, soul. *"Another example is a sharp cutting knife which is easily blunted by stone. The same may be said for sharp asceticism, which is readily dulled by pride. Thus, a person must defend the soul from every position. Consequently, the soul that is consumed by flammable pride, when considering her own asceticism, must be brought down and humbled by the grace of God. In a timely manner, she must curtail that which is excessive and unbounded, thus strengthening the root of virtue that she may branch forth fruit more abundantly."*

Overly aggressive asceticism, one form of rigid self-assertion, is like a sharp knife used so carelessly that it hits a stone and becomes dull. We have already seen how the "sharp asceticism" of some monks, young or old, aimed at either rapid personal progress in prayer or the desire to surpass the progress of others, resulted only in "flammable pride." The only remedy is a grace-filled "fall" that will, over time, help the person "curtail that which is excessive and unbounded." Otherwise the person's pride will eventually cut him or her from the root that is the only source of the fruits of the Spirit. Pruning is a powerful image in the Bible used to demonstrate God's desire to cut away influences that sap a person's life with God. "Curtail[ing] that which is excessive and unbounded" may be painful, but it leads to spiritual health.

Knowing Our Place

Using an example from the plant world, Amma Syncletica also said, *"However, the coenobitic life is not suited for everyone. Each must examine herself in this matter as to which will be more spiritually profitable: the community life or to live alone. Study the plant world and thou shalt observe that some bloom in a moist environment, while others thrive in dryer conditions. It is the same with people: some flourish in the mountains while others in the desert. The monk or nun should dwell in that place which is to their benefit. There are some who dwell in the middle, that is, in cities, and find salvation, because they abide virtuously as though they were in the wilderness. It is possible for a mindful monastic to dwell among many and yet abide alone. Similarly, the lax monastic, dwelling alone, may abide with many in mind and thought."*

Self-knowledge is at the heart of a humble spirit. It is futile to pretend that we can be anyone other than who we are. Syncletica exhorts her sisters to choose a monastic manner of life that "will be more spiritually profitable." This requires honest discernment and will mean letting go of places and lifestyles that are not congruent with our true self. Only then will we "find salvation" and "abide virtuously." On the other hand, she points out that a monk or nun can deceive himself or herself by thinking that either community life or hermit life will automatically be the place to "find salvation." Self-knowledge will lead the way.

A Key to Forgiveness

"A brother at Scetis committed a fault. A council was called to which Abba Moses was invited but he refused to go to it. Then the priest sent someone to say to him, 'Come, for everyone is waiting for you.' So he got up and went. He took a leaking jug, filled it with water and carried it with him. The others came out to meet him and said to him, 'What is this, Father?' The old man said to them, 'My sins run out behind me, and I do not see them, and today I am coming to

judge the errors of another.' When they heard that they said no more to the brother but forgave him."

Moses had plenty of experience as a sinner. He was a released slave who robbed miners in the desert near Scetis and resold their minerals. Some traditions say he committed murder as well. After his conversion, he was mentored by Abba Isidore, who had a reputation of being patient with "problem" novices. In this incident his leaking jug was not to call attention to himself but to remind his elder fathers that they, like him, have faults too and should be flexible with the novice in his weakness. Humility is looking deep within one's self in order to understand and be patient with the weaknesses of others. Self-knowledge and flexibility are keys to forgiveness.

Holding Your Tongue Is Not Weakness

"Another day when a council was being held in Scetis, the Fathers treated Moses with contempt in order to test him, saying, 'Why does this black man come among us?' When he heard this he kept silence. When the council was dismissed, they said to him, 'Abba, did that not grieve you at all?' He said to them, 'I was grieved, but I kept silence.'"

Why did Moses need to be "tested"? Is this a cruel form of racial prejudice? Moses was a Nubian, whose skin was much darker than the native Copts of Egypt. Since the desert elders were more concerned with actions than words, they often challenged a novice or abba to discern purity of heart within. Abba Poemen said, *"Teach your mouth to say that which you have in your heart."* The testing was not for the council's benefit but for Moses'. It was an opportunity for self-disclosure, which is not easy for any of us. The confrontation was an opportunity for Moses to rely on God's grace to guide his response. He was "grieved" by their contempt, not knowing it was a test. Nonetheless, he chose not to respond with a negative form of self-assertion or justification. His silence was not avoidance of conflict or weakness.

Silent Speech

"Abba Isidore of Pelusia said, 'To live without speaking is better than to speak without living. For the former who lives rightly does good even by his silence but the latter does no good even when he speaks. When words and life correspond to one another they are together the whole of philosophy.'"

The Roman society that surrounded the desert elders was filled with the eloquence of rhetoricians and philosophers. The power of the word was present in the desert as well, both in the Bible and in the sayings of the abbas and ammas. Twenty-first-century culture is also filled with language in sound bites, print media, and almost unlimited access to words via the internet. Isidore is not denying the value of verbal communication. But he is convinced that "when words and life correspond to one another," a person is really alive. Philosophers and desert elders are known for their words but become wise when their actions are congruent with their teaching. Actions speak louder than words because they are in the open and rooted in the consequences of behavior, for good or ill. "To live without speaking" is much harder than "speak[ing] without living" because it makes us transparent, vulnerable, and accountable.

A Different Language

Abba Isaac of Syria said, *"When Arsenius found that it was often impossible, because of the place of his abode, to be far withdrawn from the proximity of men and from the monks who settled in those parts—then by grace he learned this way of life: unbroken silence. And if out of necessity he ever opened his door to some of them, they were gladdened only by the mere sight of him; but conversation with words, and its employment, were rendered superfluous between them."*

As we have seen, Arsenius lived a unique and austere calling to absolute silence. Although he lived near other monks, he preferred not to speak or teach in order to devote all his being and energies to undistracted experience of God. The fruits of his efforts were not his

own because "by grace he learned this way of life: unbroken silence."
Yet, when "out of necessity he . . . opened his door" to some of his
brothers, they received an unspoken teaching rendered "only by the
mere sight of him." Arsenius, the consummate teacher, taught his
finest lessons by saying nothing. Abba Isaac's advice is sound: *"If
you love truth, be a lover of silence. Silence, like the sunlight will il-
lumine you in God."*

Avoid Being a Community of One

*"A brother questioned Abba Matoes saying, 'What am I to do?
My tongue makes me suffer, and every time I go among men, I cannot control it, but I condemn them in all the good they are doing and
reproach them with it. What am I to do?' The old man replied, 'If
you cannot contain yourself, flee into solitude. For this is a sickness.
He who dwells with brethren must not be square, but round, so as to
turn himself to all.' He went on, 'It is not through virtue that I live in
solitude, but through weakness; those who live in the midst of men
are the strong ones.'"*

Matoes's fellow monk was edgy and overly critical, especially when
his brothers were doing fruitful tasks. His need to be right isolated
him from other monks because his world was the only world. Yet he
was honest enough to seek advice for a helpless situation that was
causing him pain, a crucial aspect of humility. Matoes suggested that
he stay by himself or learn to be a "round" monk. Speaking from his
own experience of weakness, Matoes comments that "those who live
in the midst of men are the strong ones." Humility requires restraint
by shaving off the sharp edges of self-assertion that isolate a person
from recognizing and honoring collegial needs, relationships, and
responsibilities.

Humility Holds a Community Together

"Abba Poemen heard of someone who had gone all week without eating and then had lost his temper. The old man said, 'He could do without food for six days, but he could not cast out anger.'"

Poemen knows that strict ascetic discipline does not produce automatic results. Unless fasting is linked with and supports patience and respect, it becomes as empty as the stomach of the one who fasts. Monastic art is the integration of all the virtues, not necessarily their individual perfection. The catalyst binding the virtues and holding them together is humility. The monk who lost his temper allowed anger to overcome the patience he exercised through fasting. He could not be as patient with his brothers. Humility is not a virtue that lives by itself; a person does not acquire humility through personal effort or training. It is embodied in specific behavior and thoughts. Humility holds and directs human behavior and thinking. It is a container bringing patience, respect, and compassion to each situation. The monk's anger replaced patience and respect with the unrestrained desire of his ego to be in control of a situation. This loss of humility ate away part of the pillars of his community.

Fasting from Pride

Abba Isidore the Priest said, *"If you fast regularly, do not be inflated with pride, but if you think highly of yourself because of it, then you had better eat meat. It is better for a man to eat meat than to be inflated with pride and to glorify himself."*

Isidore was a no-nonsense, streetwise monk. This gave him the patience and perception to work with young monks no one else could tolerate. He could see possibilities in a person because he knew that truculent, vain, and uncooperative behavior were masks that, in time, could be removed. Perhaps this saying was prompted by memory of a monk in his care whose problem was not orneriness but vainglory. Walking around with your head in the clouds always results in leaving yourself behind. Isidore was not fooled. He demanded honesty.

"It is better for a man to eat meat than to be inflated with pride and to glorify himself." Humility, in this case, is knowing who you are and being honest about yourself and your limitations. This does not leave out room for fruitful change but reflects a willingness to depend on God for everything. False and conjured pride limits a person to his or her own self-creation and inhibits the fulfillment of God's image.

Relying on God's Faithful Presence

Abba Paul of Tamma said, *"Allow yourself only one out of a thousand as an advisor and you will be at peace all the days of your life. . . . You shall test the teaching that you follow, walking alone with God at your side. . . . For Elijah was at the river Chorath alone, God was with him, and the raven ministered to him. . . . Now then, God will remain with you as you walk alone and he will look for you in your cell and the mysteries of God will be revealed to you there as they were to Cornelius in his house. . . . Therefore, if you wear poverty in this world and humility, you will be with the Son of God in his kingdom."*

Abba Paul reminds us that in order to depend on God, we must spend time in God's presence. "Wearing poverty" is letting go of everything that keeps us or distracts us from the company of God. Easily satisfied needs help us "wear" what is most fundamental in our lives. We can "overdo" retreats, books by popular authors, revered teachers and prefer them to taking time for intimacy with God. It is wise to seek guidance from human mentors, but their wisdom and example should not become a substitute for our experience of God. In the midst of your daily life God "will look for you," both in your solitude and prayer as well as in your daily activities. When Elijah's life was in danger, God's presence sustained him in peace (see 1 Kgs 17).

Asking for God's Guidance

Amma Mary of Egypt left her home in Alexandria and lived for seventeen years *"as a fire for public depravity."* During a visit to the Church of the Holy Sepulchre, she was overcome with a desire to venerate the wood of the cross of Jesus and experienced a profound awareness of her need for repentance. A mysterious power, perhaps her own sense of unworthiness, prevented her from entering the church. She prayed to the Virgin Mary for help, promising to *"go wherever you as my mediator for salvation shall order and lead."* The next day she was able to enter and in the presence of the cross *"understood the promises of God and realized how God receives those who repent."* As she was leaving the church, she prayed again to the Virgin, saying, *"Now therefore, lead me wherever you please; lead me to salvation, teach me what is true, and go before me in the way of repentance."* Mary was led into the Palestinian desert, where she remained a hermit, with only one visitor, for forty-seven years. Mary's prayer is an inspired understanding of the process of repentance. It displays a spirit humbled by awareness of sins and a desire for new life. Her prayer is a paradigm of our spiritual journey.

"Now therefore, lead me wherever you please; lead me to salvation, teach me what is true, and go before me in the way of repentance."

Traveling the Way of Repentance

Amma Mary of Egypt prayed, *"Now therefore, lead me wherever you please; lead me to salvation, teach me what is true, and go before me in the way of repentance."*

Amma Mary's prayer is a concise summary of the goal of monastic art and gives a vision of the entire Christian path. We will reflect on each part for the next five days.

"Now therefore, lead me wherever you please" shows Mary's humble desire to place her new life totally in God's hands. This act of turning toward God's desires for her is the consequence of her honest confrontation with the pattern of her previous life of hedonism.

Repentance is not a rational decision. It has deeper psychological roots. At the door to the church something inside Mary's psyche creates a tension between her passion to venerate the cross of Jesus and her sense of unworthiness. The barrier between Mary's past and her desire for God seems impossible to cross. Her old unrestrained passion now yearns for a new life and she realizes that she must place this redirected passion totally in God's hands. "Now therefore, lead me wherever you please" is her first step on the path.

A Desire for Fullness of Life

"Now therefore, lead me wherever you please; lead me to salvation, teach me what is true, and go before me in the way of repentance."

Like Arsenius, Amma Mary knows her life is incomplete and she prays, "lead me to salvation." At the door to the Church of the Holy Sepulchre, she realizes that her life of unrestrained sexual pleasures has no destination. Its colors and excitement are evaporating in relation to "something" drawing her into the church. Its focus is in the wood of the cross of Jesus. We cannot know what she was thinking or feeling as she brought her life to the cross. The intensity of her desire to enter shows a passion to leave her former life behind, to let it die. But in that emptiness Mary has no idea of what her new life will be like or where it will begin. Her words "lead me to salvation" show her desire for the Virgin Mary's help. Mary, who was in full control and certainly self-assertive in her former life, is now placing her life in God's hands. She has turned completely toward God to fulfill her desire for fullness of life. Her request for "salvation" is a present need, not something for the future. She places the weight of her emptiness in God's hands and is willing to wait for God's love.

A Desire for What Is True

"Now therefore, lead me wherever you please; lead me to salvation, teach me what is true, and go before me in the way of repentance."

A humble spirit is not full of its own wisdom. Mary of Egypt has forsaken everything that was futile and self-destructive in her life. She has an "empty slate." Like so many women and men who were led to the desert, Mary could have rewritten her life with a self-constructed pattern of ascetic disciplines. But a self-help program was not her desire. She had spent seventeen years choosing her own destiny and found it empty. As she leaves the church in Jerusalem, she wants a very different form of life. She desires "what is true" and now relies on God, rather than herself, to be her teacher. Mary wants a life that is real, that is truly herself, and is authentically human. She is willing to let God show her these things and learn to see life and herself through God's eyes.

A Desire to Remain in God's Presence

"Now therefore, lead me wherever you please; lead me to salvation, teach me what is true, and go before me in the way of repentance."

What is "the way of repentance"? The desert elders experienced repentance as a daily renewal of their lives and their dependence on God. It is a pathway leading to transformation where each step is guided by God's Spirit. All aspects of the "monastic art" are disciplines that help each person discern God's presence on the path and rely on God's strength and guidance. Mary of Egypt knew she must rely on God to lead her to fullness of life. At the same time she knew the power and enticement of the memories of her former life. She was honest about her weakness, and "the infamy of her deeds" brought her "shame and contrition." She feared God's judgment but was rescued by God's love. "Filled with faith," Mary of Egypt accepts the Virgin Mary as an exemplar who will help her accept God's desires for her life. It is not coercion; it is a genuine self-emptying that makes room for God's love. The only way to experience that love is to remain in God's presence.

Continuing on the Way

"When Abba Macarius was returning from the marsh to his cell one day carrying some palm leaves, he met the devil on the road with a scythe. The latter struck at him as much as he pleased, but in vain, and he said to him, 'What is your power Macarius, that makes me powerless against you? All that you do, I do; you fast, so do I; you keep vigil, and I do not sleep at all; in one thing only do you beat me.' Abba Macarius asked what that was. He said, 'Your humility. Because of that I can do nothing against you.'"

Abba Poemen said, *"To throw yourself before God, not to measure your progress, to leave all self-will; these are the instruments for the work of the soul."*

Amma Sarah said, *"If I prayed that all men should approve of my conduct, I should find myself a penitent at the door of each one, but I shall rather pray that my heart may be pure towards all."*

Amma Syncletica said, *"Just as one cannot build a ship unless one has some nails, so it is impossible to be saved without humility."*

The desert elders all agree. We can do nothing by ourselves. They took Jesus' wise words seriously. "For those who want to save their life will lose it, and those who lose their life for my sake will find it" (Matt 16:25). But they realized his wisdom was not enough. It was his life that spoke most eloquently. Jesus embodied his relationship with his Abba. He lived each day in God, surrounded and filled with his Abba. "Very truly, I tell you, the Son can do nothing on his own, but only what he sees the Father doing; for whatever the Father does, the Son does likewise" (John 5:19). The desert mothers and fathers learned that in order to follow Jesus, they too must depend totally on God.

OCTOBER

Facing the Reality of Sin, Lack of Progress, and Hardships

When desert monastic life is not romanticized or abused, it embodies what it means to be a human being. The manner of life itself is definitely not the model for everyone, but its vision of authentic human life is a valid aspiration for any person. Although unapologetically Christian, it shares wisdom and practices with other religious traditions, especially Judaism and Buddhism. At first glance the austerities of the desert elders may seem unreasonable, if not abusive, simplistic, and self-serving. It is possible to view their ascetic life as a denial of the goodness of human life and society with a myopic focus on the individual at the expense of other people. When viewed through the lenses of modern society and religious experience, the lives of the desert mothers and fathers can be misunderstood. Some critics claim that their desire to guard their souls against influences that scatter life with God is based on an assumption that human life itself is evil and must be transformed to something good. This is not true. A second and more patient glance at the lives and teaching of the desert elders will reveal a positive understanding of the original nature of human life as well as a mature and honest realization that it is possible to reject that original nature. The desert elders accepted Jesus' invitation to die to self in order to find one's self. The first steps were to find solitude and silence and, through various forms of praxis, acknowledge the reality of sin in their lives. They learned that continuing to carry the burdens of recurring memories of unrestrained pleasures, sinful behavior, and temptations inhibited their openness to and the possibility for transformation of their lives. This aspect of the monastic art was difficult and demanded

191

honesty, guidance from elders, and persistence in remaining rooted in God's presence and power. It required self-reflection, brutal honesty about one's self, and trust in God's grace.

Men and women were attracted to desert monastic life for many reasons. But sooner or later they learned that they shared a common path. That path included emphasis on self-knowledge, letting go of the self-centered desires of an unrestrained ego (a false self), and depending solely on God to guide and empower the path toward transformation and restoration of one's authentic (true) self. A noble path! But sometimes it seemed as though it was getting nowhere. There were roadblocks like harboring anger, pride, self-righteousness, bearing malice, frustration with and doubt about the path itself, and lack of hope. There were new temptations, failures, and sinful behavior in the midst of monastic life. Actually, life in the desert could look very much like the life they had left behind. So why bother?

All these difficulties along the path were ground in the pestle of maintaining praxis, learning from others who walked the same path, and remaining focused on Christ. During October we will reflect on how the desert elders encountered and lived through these difficulties.

OCTOBER 1

Daily Warfare

Amma Syncletica said, *"If love is a great good, conversely, anger is a great evil. This is because anger darkens the soul, makes it savage, and misleads us with fallacious reasoning. Therefore, our Lord, Who ever makes provision for our salvation, left no part of the soul unprotected and unguarded. When the enemy attacks with fornication, the Lord has armed us with self-control. If the enemy attacks with pride, humility is not far. If the enemy suggests hatred, we may find love close by. Though the enemy wages war by strategically moving weapons against us, our Lord, for the sake of our salvation, fences us about with greater weapons to ensure our victory."*

In the twenty-first century, warfare may seem like an inappropriate metaphor for the human spiritual journey. But as we have seen, the desert elders came from a materialistic and hedonistic society where most relationships were self-serving and the sanctity of human life was profaned daily. Even in the desert, seeking a life dedicated to

God was a life-and-death struggle. The desert itself was known as the place where the evil powers lived. As Syncletica points out, entering the desert was a huge risk because one would be confronted with the dark side of her or his life. The daily battle was within each monk as he or she tried to overcome anger, fornication, pride, hatred, and a host of other human temptations. They faced their weaknesses openly, but how did they cope?

OCTOBER 2

Anger's Hold

Amma Syncletica said, *"If love is a great good, conversely, anger is a great evil. This is because anger darkens the soul, makes it savage, and misleads us with fallacious reasoning."*

Anger is dangerous because it distorts our thinking and actions. It is a cloud that hides our desire to love and severs restraints that keep our relationships civil. We forget who we are and impulsively guard our self-interest. Abba Agathon said, *"A man who is angry, even if he were to raise the dead, is not acceptable to God."* Yet anger returns over and over again. Abba Ammonas said, *"I have spent fourteen years in Scetis asking God night and day to grant me victory over anger."* The elders sought God's help in a variety of ways. Abba Nilus said, *"Prayer is the seed of gentleness and the absence of anger."* Once, when Abba Moses was being mistreated by his brothers in a council, he remained silent. After the meeting, they said, *"'Abba, did that not grieve you at all?' He said to them, 'I was grieved, but I kept silence.'"* Amma Syncletica realized that anger is an emotion that can be used at an appropriate time but never as a weapon to wield against others. She said, *"If we cannot put anger away, then we must continually repent of it."*

OCTOBER 3

Keeping Anger from Taking Root

Amma Syncletica said, *"If we cannot put anger away, then we must continually repent of it."*

How does a person turn away from anger? Syncletica advises, *"Hearken to the words of the Apostle Paul: 'Do not let the sun go down on thy wrath.' Therefore it is good never to be angry. To remember wrongs for a twenty-four hour day is not permitted by the divine Paul. Hence, do not let the sun, which rules by day, abate until thy wrath against anyone has subsided. Why, O nun, dost thou wait until thy declining years to promote friendship with her whom thou hast confounded or frustrated?"* It is easy to enjoy being angry and hang on to its demonic power. The possibility for healthy relationships suffers when efforts to resolve an anger-producing situation are delayed. Abba Paul the Barber and his brother Timothy learned that anger makes it impossible to listen to and respect another person during an agreement. *"They often used to argue. Abba Paul said, 'How long shall we go on like this?' Abba Timothy said to him, 'I suggest you take my side of the argument and I will take your side when you oppose me.' They spent the rest of their days in this practice."*

Learning from Anger

"A brother questioned Abba Poemen saying, 'What does it mean to be angry with your brother without a cause?' He said, 'If your brother hurts you by his arrogance and you are angry with him because of it, that is getting angry without a cause. If he plucks out your eye and cuts off your right hand, and you get angry with him, you are angry without cause. But if he separates you from God, then be angry with him.'"

On another occasion, *"A brother questioned Abba Poemen saying, 'I am losing my soul through living near my abba; should I go on living with him?' The old man knew that he was finding this harmful and he was surprised that he even asked if he should stay there. So he said to him, 'Stay if you want to.' The brother left him and stayed on there. He came back again a third time and said, 'I really cannot stay there any longer.' Then Abba Poemen said, 'Now you are saving yourself; go away and do not stay with him any longer,' and he added, 'When someone sees he is in danger of losing his soul, he does not need to ask advice.'"*

Poemen learned that anger is warranted when a person's relationship with God is placed in danger. Anger can reveal harm to one's soul. Poemen's wisdom reveals anger as an emotion of discernment. In the first example, the brother wants to know when to respond to anger and when to acknowledge its presence, but control his response. The elders knew that anger can lead to judgment and violence. In the second example, a brother is frustrated with his abba and feels he is being harmed by the relationship. While anger is not mentioned specifically, it lurks in the shadows of frustration. Poemen suggests that patience will help the brother discern whether reconciliation of the relationship is possible. Once again, the primary issue is, "when someone sees he is in danger of losing his soul, he does not need to ask advice."

OCTOBER 5

Resisting Anger

Abba Hesychios of Sinai said, *"Just as snow will not produce a flame, or water a fire, or the thorn bush a fig, so a person's heart will not be freed from demonic thoughts, words, and actions until it has first purified itself inwardly, uniting watchfulness with the Jesus Prayer, attaining humility and stillness of soul, and eagerly pressing forward on its path. . . . The soul's true peace lies in the gentle name of Jesus and in its emptying itself of impassioned thoughts."*

The greatest resistance to anger lies within us. A quiet soul, centered on Jesus, will watch for "demonic thoughts, words, and actions" and not be overcome by their power. A habit of remaining in God's presence will recognize an impulse toward anger and not let it take control, "eagerly pressing forward on its path." Alternatives to anger become a pattern when they are consciously desired. Abba Isidore of Pelusia said, *"To live without speaking is better than to speak without living. For the former who lives rightly does good even by his silence but the latter does no good even when he speaks. When words and life correspond to one another they are together the whole of philosophy."* We are truly alive when our inner life is the source of our outer speech and behavior.

A Sure Foundation

A brother asked Abba Isidore the Priest, *"Why are the demons so frightened of you?' The old man said to him, 'Because I have practiced asceticism since the day I became a monk, and not allowed anger to reach my lips.'"*

"Watch your heart always" became a way of life for Isidore. By setting his soul in "quietness" through his practice of asceticism, there was no room for anger to take hold in his thoughts and relationships. He does not list his personal pattern of monastic art, but it framed each day of his life. He would be the first to admit that it was not his personal power that drove away the demon of anger. His openness to God's grace was all he needed, day after day. Isidore confirms that each person's life of prayer needs a disciplined pattern. Like any exercise program, intermittent spurts of energy will not provide solid conditioning and may even do harm. Resistance to anger begins with a foundation of prayer.

Bearing Malice Damages the Soul

Amma Syncletica describes how anger can lead to a more serious inner struggle: *"Anger is a much smaller sin when compared to the remembrance of past injuries. To bear malice is the gravest of all sins. Anger, like smoke, for a while will perplex and cloud the soul; but holding a grudge is to be compared to a hammered stake in the soul that renders it more brutal than a beast."*

As Abba Hesychios declared earlier, the path toward transformation is meant to free the soul from burdens that restrain its progress. Constant prayer will *"set your soul in quietness."* But the gifts of freedom of soul and quietness of heart can be rejected by clinging "to the remembrance of past injuries." Syncletica makes the bold statement that bearing malice will hammer a stake through the soul into the ground. She is speaking about deep and serious psychological dysfunctions that "will perplex and cloud the soul." The emotional and mental energy wasted on bearing malice block our receptivity to the movement of the Spirit's grace in our lives and relationships. Syncletica is saying that this does "brutal" malice to ourselves and to other persons. Where will this lead?

Malice Leads to Spiritual Illness

Amma Syncletica said, *"We must, therefore, take precautions to avoid remembering wrongs, because, through it, many other evils are introduced. I speak of envy, grief, babbling, and other evils which bring death, though they appear small and few. Often, such grievous sins as fornication, murder, and greed are healed by the saving remedy of repentance, but the remembrance of wrongs undermines spiritual health."*

Amma Syncletica learned how easy it is to deceive ourselves. Even though we may not be consciously "remembering wrongs" on a daily basis, they still take their toll and lead to "other evils which bring death, though they appear small and few." When malice takes control, we can easily justify a few words of gossip or complaining here and there. Soon a pattern develops that competes with our openness to the Spirit that will eat away at the foundation of our spiritual life. We may pride ourselves and thank God that we are not murderers, thieves, or adulterers while at the same time these other "invisible" evils are eating away at our life with God and other people. Malice, murmuring, gossip, and harboring misinformation can tear at the fabric of community. The desert elders contended with all these dangers to the soul.

Desiring Good for All

Amma Syncletica continues her advice for stewardship of the soul. *"We must not rejoice at the calamities of others, though they be great sinners. We should not behave as those without understanding who, when they see a sinner, thrash and imprison such a one, and recite the worldly proverb, 'Whoever makes a bad bed, then badly shall that*

*one sleep.' . . . All the earthborn travel on the same path though they
have different conducts of life. None are exempt from encountering
misfortune. How then dost thou rejoice in the calamities of others?"*

One of the greatest temptations of monastic life is self-righteousness.
As a monk or nun pursues the difficult path of holiness, it is easy to
look down upon persons who live by self-centered values and feel
justified when they experience calamities. But Syncletica reminds us
that gloating in the misfortunes of sinners creates our own misfortune
by severing the solidarity with all persons that God desires. When we
reject this possibility, we "behave as those without understanding"
and forget that none of us "are exempt from encountering misfortune." Celebrating the failures of other people makes it impossible for
us to "travel on the same path." Syncletica mirrors St. Paul's words
in 1 Corinthians 13:4-6: *"Love is patient; love is kind; love is not
envious or boastful or arrogant or rude. It does not insist on its own
way; it is not irritable or resentful; it does not rejoice in wrongdoing,
but rejoices in the truth."* Both Syncletica and Paul show what living
according to the Great Commandment looks like.

OCTOBER 10

Encouraging the Wayward

Amma Syncletica reminds her nuns that desiring good for all includes both an attitude of inclusion and encouragement to change:
*"Just as we are not to hate our enemies, likewise we should not avoid
and hold in contempt the careless and reluctant. Some, however, will
put forward the following verse of the Prophet (Psalm 17:26): 'With
the perverse Thou shalt turn aside (διαστρέψεις [in Greek]).' They
strongly contend that they bypass such people, so as not to be sinners, too. However, they do the opposite of what was written by the
Prophet through the inspiration of the Holy Spirit. The verse does not
tell us to be perverse with the perverse, but to remedy their perversity;
for the [Greek] verb (διαστρέψεις) means to turn a different way.
Hence this verse declares unto us that we should draw the froward to
us that we might turn them aside to a different way, that is to bring
them from the evil to the good."*

It is easier to let the careless, reluctant, and perverse continue to
"sleep in their own beds." Syncletica reminds us that this judgmental

attitude encourages us "to be perverse with the perverse." We become like the ones we want to avoid rather than "turn them aside to a different way." We take on their "vision" of life rather than lure them to a change of consciousness. Amma Syncletica reveals that the motive behind repentance and conversion is love, not judgment. She knows that "the careless and reluctant" need help and inspiration to look at their lives in a different way. By "draw[ing] the froward to us that we might turn them aside to a different way," we help God's love for them become tangible.

Overcoming the Grip of Hearsay

"A provincial priest went to visit an anchorite to offer the Eucharist for him. Now someone went to the anchorite and spoke against the priest, so when the latter came according to custom to give him communion, the anchorite, who had been shocked, did not let him in, and the priest went away. Then, behold, a voice came to the anchorite, saying, 'Men have taken my judgment away from me.' The anchorite was as though in ecstasy, and he saw a well of gold and a rope of gold and a jug of gold and much water of surpassing quality. Then he saw a leper draw the water and pour it out, and would gladly have drunk but could not because he who drew the water was leprous. Again a voice came to him saying, 'Why do you not drink the water? What does it matter if he who draws it is leprous? He only draws it and pours it out.' Returning to himself and perceiving the meaning of the vision, the anchorite sent for the priest and let him give him communion as usual."

Rather than see the goodness the priest was offering, the anchorite judged and rejected him on the basis of his ego's assessment of hearsay. In his prayer he "returned to himself" and put judgment away. We have seen that often the desert elders were plagued by demonic voices determined to lead them astray. This time the first voice the anchorite heard was very human! By accepting the slander about the priest, he dishonored him without cause and rejected the opportunity for the priest to give him the gift of the Eucharist. But there was another voice to hear. Rather than a voice leading him astray, it was a voice that helped him "return to himself" and seek the offering of one who cared for him.

Beware of Overlooking Weaknesses

Amma Syncletica uses the monastic tonsure to illustrate the need to remove what covers inward corruption of life: *"We have cut the hairs of our head in the holy Tonsure; let us also remove the lice and worms that infest our heads. If we allow them to remain on our heads, without hair, they will prick us even more. The hairs that we have shorn bespeak the cutting away of worldly life, that is, honor, glory, wealth, splendid dresses, bathing, and good food. Though we have cast off all these things, let us throw off the soul-corrupting worms, that is, talkativeness, avariciousness, lying, swearing, and whatever other passions we detect in our souls. These parasitical passions did not appear since they were covered by hair, that is, the material things of the world. However, now that we have been denuded of worldly things, all the passions appear clearly. Therefore, the smallest sin is manifest to the monastic, just as in a clean house the smallest vermin is noticed by all."*

The desert elders knew the danger of ignoring our weaknesses. Syncletica warns her nuns not to be smug about how much of the "worldly life" they have given up. Their tonsure is a reminder that monastic life will continue to uncover "soul-corrupting worms" that were sources of their former worldly values and pleasures. The desert elders knew the danger of sublimating or ignoring smoldering temptations, malice, pride, and other personal demons or sins (past or present) that inhabit our souls. These are dangerous because these "parasitical passions" eat away the opportunity for a person to be open to the transformative power of God's spirit. As always, Syncletica uses mundane images to unveil the role of honest self-knowledge in the path to transformation. Knowing one's self is a preliminary step to a change of consciousness.

A Common Call to Holiness

Amma Syncletica said, *"When the Lord made the world He placed two ranks of beings to dwell therein: Those who wisely conduct their lives within the boundaries of marriage and childbearing, and those who enter pure into life and are commanded to remain virgin, so as to be equal to the angels. . . . Those who live in the world lurk about in the hidden holes of great and unclean caves with poisonous snakes. However, these caves and snakes are concealed, that is, cloaked with many worldly trappings. Hence, we must clean the house of our souls and give strict attention that no soul-damaging vermin creeps inside. What is meant by 'vermin' is passion hidden in the recesses of our souls. We must also perpetually burn incense over our hearts, that is, offer up the divine incense of prayer. As the most pungent incense repels poisonous creatures, so our prayer, coupled with fasting, dispels pernicious thoughts."*

Although Syncletica claims that monastic life is the highest human vocation, she honors the sanctity and call to holiness of persons who remain within conventional society. Her stark images of worldly "soul-damaging" influences on the human soul are reminders of the need for "strict attention." This is a need shared by both "ranks of beings." Syncletica's point is that our common call to holiness takes place by "clean[ing] the house of our souls." When desire for worldly pleasures leads to external vices and sinful behavior, the same "vermin" can take up residence in our souls. If they are not restrained, they will become the "pernicious thoughts" that infect external behavior. The remedy is a pattern of spiritual praxis that will help us pay strict attention to the way we live and repel the "poisonous creatures."

OCTOBER 14

A Venue for Strict Attention

Abba Isaiah the Solitary said, *"Stand guard, then, over your heart and keep a watch on your senses, and if the remembrance of God dwells peaceably within you, you will catch the thieves when they try to deprive you of it. When a man has an exact knowledge about the nature of [his] thoughts, he recognizes those that are about to enter and defile him, troubling the intellect [our capacity to experience God] with distractions and making it lazy. Those who recognize these evil thoughts for what they are remain undisturbed and continue in prayer to God."*

Isaiah, a fifth-century monk of Scetis, like Syncletica, points to the heart as the place for discernment of influences that will inhibit our life with God. The beginning of "strict attention" is for a person to have "an exact knowledge about the nature of [his] thoughts" so that he or she becomes aware of "those that are about to enter and defile" the heart and, therefore, interfere with a person's capacity to experience God's presence and grace. This capacity of the soul was called the *nous* (translated "intellect") and was distinguished from another faculty called *dianoia*, rational thought. Together they form a venue for the "strict attention" that is necessary to guard and care for the realm of the heart.

OCTOBER 15

Fill Your Attention with Awareness and Experience of God

Abba Theodoros the Great Ascetic said, *"While we are oppressed and imprisoned by the passions, we are often at a loss to know why we suffer from them. We must, therefore, realize that it is because we allow ourselves to be diverted from the contemplation of God that we are taken captive in this way. But if a man fixes his intellect without distraction on our Master and God, then the Savior of all can himself be trusted to deliver such a soul from its impassioned servitude."*

Theodoros is very streetwise. We are influenced by the company we keep. When we can't figure out why we are "imprisoned by the passions," we should examine the pattern of our thoughts and behavior. When we see that they distract us "from the contemplation of God," we should return to the One who "can himself be trusted to deliver such a soul from its impassioned servitude." Theodoros echoes Abba Moses: *"Go, sit in your cell, and your cell will teach you everything."* A modern desert abba, Fr. Thomas Hand, SJ, reminds us that "where attention goes, energy flows." If our attention is on "our Master and God," the energy of Christ will free us from the prison of unrestrained passions and the suffering they cause. We should not neglect time in our cell, wherever that may be.

Paying Attention to Thoughts

Abba Evagrius said, *"If there is any monk who wishes to take the measure of some of the more fierce demons so as to gain experience in his monastic art, then let him keep careful watch over his thoughts. Let him observe their intensity, their periods of decline, and follow them as they rise and fall. Let him note well the complexity of his thoughts, their periodicity, the demons which cause them, with the order of successions and the nature of their associations. Then let him ask from Christ the explanations of these data he has observed."*

Evagrius is speaking about human consciousness. Freedom from inner desires that lead to sinful behavior begins with paying attention to our thoughts. The monk who desires honest self-knowledge must "keep careful watch over his thoughts," remember when they appear and how they relate to each other. The desert elders learned that all behavior has its origins in the human heart and psyche. Many of these thoughts come from an unrestrained ego that is able to mask malicious desires so that they appear benign. Part of the monastic art is the discernment of thoughts, and Evagrius, knowing how easy it is to deceive ourselves, recommends that we rely on the mind of Christ to inform our consciousness.

What to Look For and Avoid

Abba Evagrius gave very specific advice about discernment of passions and thoughts: *"Of the demons opposing us in the practice of the ascetic life, there are three groups who fight in the front line: those entrusted with the appetites of gluttony, those who suggest avaricious thoughts, and those who incite us to seek the esteem of men. All the other demons follow behind and in their turn attack those already wounded by the first three groups. For one does not fall into the power of the demon of unchastity, unless one has first fallen because of gluttony; nor is one's anger aroused unless one is fighting for food or material possessions or the esteem of men. And one does not escape the demon of dejection, unless one no longer experiences suffering when deprived of these things. Nor will one escape pride, the first offspring of the devil, unless one has banished avarice, the root of all evil, since poverty makes a man humble, according to Solomon (cf. Proverbs 10:4). In short, no one can fall into the power of any demon, unless he has been wounded on the front line."*

Spiritual maturity depends on honest self-knowledge. Taking stock of what fills our minds, desires, and actions is the place to begin, as well as knowing what will harm us the most. If we fail to see the beginning of patterns that will lead us away from love of God and our neighbor, it will be harder to overcome those patterns when they have taken root in our souls. Care of the soul begins "on the front line." What we take into our lives will affect the way we live.

OCTOBER 18

Recognizing the Nature of Objects that Fill Our Minds

Evagrius continues by showing the dangers of malign images that occupy our minds: *"All the thoughts inspired by the demons produce within us conceptions of sensory objects; and this is the way the intellect, with such conceptions imprinted on it, bears the forms of these objects within itself. So, by recognizing the object presented to it, the intellect knows which demon is approaching. For example, if the face of a person who has done me harm or insulted me appears in my mind, I recognize the demon of rancor approaching. If there is a suggestion of material things or of esteem, again it will be clear which demon is troubling me. In the same way with other thoughts, we can infer from the object appearing in the mind which demon is close at hand, suggesting that object to us. I do not say that all thoughts of such things come from the demons; for when the intellect is activated by man it is its nature to bring forth the images of past events. But all thoughts producing anger or desire in a way that is contrary to nature [the goodness of human beings] are caused by demons. Thus [the intellect] cannot receive the vision of God, who sets us in order; for the divine splendor only appears to the intellect during prayer, when the intellect is free from conception of sensory objects."*

It is worth repeating: what we take into our lives will affect every aspect of our being. Self-knowledge is a difficult discipline. Without being obsessive about every thought or action, we can learn to recognize patterns that are "contrary to nature." If anger recurs, we should pay attention because anger, like any disruptive influence, can take over our behavior. Evagrius's advice is sound, obviously based on his own experience. Know who you are!

Ways to Resist Demonic Images

Evagrius has some practical suggestions for eliminating malign images so that we may *"receive the vision of God, who sets us in order"*: *"Man cannot drive away impassioned thoughts unless he watches over his desire and incensive power. He destroys desire by fasting, vigils and sleeping on the ground, and he tames his incensive power through long-suffering, forbearance, forgiveness and acts of compassion. For with these two passions [gluttony/desire for material and sexual pleasures and pride] are connected almost all other demonic thoughts which lead the intellect to disaster and perdition. It is impossible to overcome these passions unless we can rise above attachment to food and possessions, to self-esteem and even to our very body, because it is through the body that the demons often attempt to attack us."*

Evagrius creates parallel forms of praxis that will "set us in order." The first (fasting, vigils, and limiting bodily pleasure by sleeping on the ground) will help us "rise above attachment to food and possessions." The second relates to eliminating pride by reforming our relationship with other people through "long-suffering, forbearance, forgiveness and acts of compassion." Here we see "down-to-earth" praxis. Not easy, but real. Fasting helps us be grateful for what we have and not desire more than we need. Vigils, such as recitation of psalms, takes attention away from ourselves and malign thoughts or temptations that plague us. Sleeping on the ground, while not a popular twenty-first-century form of praxis, may be "translated" into any discipline that takes our mind away from excessive pleasure. Not easy, but real!

Avoid Letting Thoughts and Desires Get the Upper Hand

Abba Maximos the Confessor said, *"If you wish to master your thoughts, concentrate on the passions and you will easily drive the thoughts arising from them out of your intellect. With regard to unchastity, for instance, fast and keep vigils, labor, and avoid meeting people. With regard to anger and resentment, be indifferent to fame, dishonor, and material things. With regard to rancor, pray for him who has offended you and you will be delivered."*

Influenced by Evagrius, Maximos knew that unrestrained passions give birth to thoughts that lead to sinful consequences. Therefore, be aware of what causes passions to arise and you "will easily drive the thoughts arising from them out of your intellect." His advice is very practical. If unchastity is a problem, avoid situations that bring on physical temptation and replace impure thoughts with disciplined prayer and meditation. If anger is easily aroused, leading to rancor, let go of the need to defend or promote yourself and pray for those who cause you grief. This too is prayer.

More on Discernment of Thoughts

Abba Theodoros the Great Ascetic said, *"One of the ancients spoke wisely and simply about thoughts. Judge thoughts, he said, before the judgment seat of the heart, to discern whether they are ours or those of the enemy. Place those that are good and properly our own in the inmost shrine of the soul, keeping them in this inviolable treasury. But chastise hostile thoughts with the whip of the intelligence and banish them, giving them no place, no abode within the bounds of your soul. Or, to speak more fittingly, slay them completely with the sword of prayer and divine meditation, so that when the robbers have been destroyed, their chief may take fright. For, as he says, a man who examines his thoughts strictly is one who also truly loves the commandments."*

Theodoros acknowledges the reality of an inner warfare taking place in "the judgment seat of the heart." Only the heart, that "inmost shrine of the soul," can discern, from its experience of God, what is truly congruent with God's desires. The soul's dependable "weapon" against hostile thoughts is "the sword of prayer and divine meditation." These transpersonal experiences lead us beyond the control of the unrestrained ego and help us replace its desires with authentic love of God's desires. This advice is graphic and simple. Keep good and helpful thoughts "in the inmost shrine of the soul" and cut up and discard malign thoughts. This is not easy, but Theodoros is willing to embrace the hard, psychological part of the monastic art.

OCTOBER 22

Stillness Is a Place to Begin to Look for the Mind of Christ

Peter of Damaskos, writing in the twelfth century, echoes the advice of Evagrius to persons troubled by the power of their sins: *"Nothing so benefits the weak as withdrawal into stillness, or the man subject to the passions and without spiritual knowledge as obedience and stillness. Nor is there anything better than to know one's own weakness and ignorance, nor anything worse than not to recognize them. . . . If we want to perceive our lethal condition, we must abandon our own desires and all the preoccupations of this life. Through this flight from everything, let us assiduously devote ourselves to God with a devotion that is truly blessed and divine. Let each of us seek his own soul through studying the divine Scriptures, either in perfect obedience of soul and body or in stillness following the angelic way. This is especially important for those who are as yet subject to the passions and cannot control their own desires, whether great or small. . . . This is to prevent their mindless and impassioned inertia from dragging them down into what is even worse."*

When we feel weak and helpless, we can turn to Christ in stillness and meditation. In the silence we will hear the mind of Christ. Abba Peter points to two of the three essential spiritual disciplines that have nourished monastic life and the lives of all Christians for two thousand years. "Nothing so benefits the weak as withdrawal into stillness." Contemplative prayer and meditation are opportunities to experience God "firsthand." Jesus' experience of his Abba in prayer was the source of his words and actions. Second, "let each of us seek his own soul through studying the divine Scriptures." The Bible was a constant mentor in the lives of desert elders. It was their window into the life and mind of Christ as well as a constant companion enabling them to listen to God's voice. The third basic discipline was the Eucharist, Holy Communion.

Do Not Abandon Your Hope in God

Peter of Damaskos continues his encouragement and advice on overcoming sin and spiritual weakness by emphasizing the need to turn toward God with hopefulness: *"It is always possible to make a new start by means of repentance. . . . And if you fall again, then rise again, without despairing at all of your salvation, no matter what happens. As long as you do not surrender yourself willingly to the enemy, your patient endurance, combined with self-reproach, will suffice for your salvation. 'For at one time we ourselves went astray in our folly and disobedience,' says St. Paul. ' . . . Yet he saved us, not because of any good things we had done, but in his mercy.' (Titus 3:5) So do not despair in any way, ignoring God's help, for he can do whatever he wishes. On the contrary, place your hope in him and he will do one of these things: either through trials and temptations, or in some other way which he alone knows, he will bring about your restoration; or he will accept your patient endurance and humility in the place of works; or because of your hope he will act lovingly toward you in some other way of which you are not aware, and so will save your shackled soul. Only do not abandon your Physician. "*

No person in his or her right mind will walk away from what gives and sustains one's life. At times, God may seem distant, but it is we who have walked away, not God. Peter reminds us that God is merciful and patient. The danger is to "surrender yourself willingly to the enemy." Every effort, no matter how small, will be transformed by God for he desires to "bring about your restoration." The really good news, according to Abba Peter, is that we can place our hope in God's desires for us even when things seem bleak, for "because of your hope he will act lovingly toward you in some other way of which you are not aware, and so will save your shackled soul."

Let the Life of God Flow in You

Abba Gregory of Sinai said, *"The energy of the Holy Spirit, which we have already mystically received in baptism, is realized in two ways. First—to generalize—this gift is revealed, as St. Mark the Ascetic tells us, through arduous and protracted practice of the commandments [of Christ]: to the degree to which we effectively practice the commandments, its radiance is increasingly manifested in us. Second, it is manifested to those under spiritual guidance through the continuous invocation of the Lord Jesus, repeated with conscious awareness, that is, through mindfulness of God. In the first way, it is revealed more slowly, in the second more rapidly, if one diligently and persistently learns how to dig the ground and locate the gold."*

Abba Gregory reminds his monks that the remedy for slavery to their weaknesses and sins has already been given in their baptism. His advice for reopening this flow of the "energy of the Holy Spirit" includes a persistent desire to practice the commandments to love God and neighbor, placing one's self in constant "mindfulness of God," and seeking the spiritual guidance of an abba. All these disciplines open a flow of energy between the monk and God that manifests itself through a balance between praxis and silent awareness. Abba Gregory demonstrates that prayer is a flow of energy between God and each person. Our task is to remain open to that flow of energy.

Open the Door of Your Soul

A monk expressed concern to Abba Barsanuphius about the attraction of blasphemous thoughts. The old man said, *"For a long time has the demon of blasphemy been waging war against you—a demon who slays the souls of those who accept him. He has caught you by your neck-chain [unrestrained passions] to put you to death. Oh, may my God not let him take you captive at his will! [Cf. 2 Tim 2:26.] But do not despair. Behold, God stands before you, accepting your penitence. Awake from the beguilement of captivity—but first extinguish anger and irritability, knowing that they lead a man to soul-destroying blasphemy against God. Acquire humility, which scorches the demons, obedience, which opens the door for the Son of God to enter a man, faith which saves a man, hope which makes him unashamed; and love which lets not a man fall away from God. You took no care of these virtues, but have chosen the opposite—anger, irritability and what is total ruin: blasphemy. Strive to mend your ways, looking at the goodness of God and meditating how good the Lord is."*

The monk's desire for guidance opens a door that will lead him toward transformation. Abba Barsanuphius gives a remarkable summary of how interrelated demonic thoughts can be. The main cause of blasphemy is anger at God. Unrestrained anger is a symptom of wanting to be in control of a situation and shows unwillingness to be obedient (that is, to listen to others, especially God). This shows a clear lack of humility. This monk is really in trouble! But the trouble is with himself and not with God. Turning away from himself in humility "opens the door for the Son of God to enter a man." The first step is to look again toward God. The rest will follow.

OCTOBER 26

A Wealth of Goodness Comes through the Open Door of the Soul

Theoleptus, a fourteenth-century monk in Greece, said, *"Thus, sitting in your cell, remember God; and, moreover, withdrawing your mind from everything, prostrate it speechlessly before God. Pouring out your heart to Him, cleave to Him with love. Remembrance of God is contemplation of God, Who attracts to Himself the vision and striving of the mind and illumines it with His light. Having cut off all images of existing things and turning to God, the mind sees Him without form or image, and thus has its vision cleared despite its imperfect comprehension of the Object of its contemplation. Whose glory is utterly inaccessible. Although it cannot comprehend the Object of its contemplation, since He is incomprehensible, the mind then truly knows that it is He alone Who is, and alone has transubstantial being. Feeding its love for Him and satisfying its striving by the wealth of goodness pouring out of God, it is granted eternal and blessed rest in Him."*

A thousand years after Antony, Theoleptus affirms a deep psychic and spirit-filled flow of energy from a person's heart toward God and "the wealth of goodness pouring out of God." This transference of being gives birth to transformation. Theoleptus tries to articulate a reality that is beyond words. He uses the image of the mind being "prostrate . . . speechlessly before God" to describe an experience of God where "images of existing things" are cast aside. This opens the soul for an experience of God that "it cannot comprehend" yet is real. Since the mind is not "working" to define or control the experience, the person is free to experience "He alone Who is." This "emptiness" is a flow of "the wealth of goodness pouring out of God" into the monk's soul.

OCTOBER 27

Praxis Purges the Soul of Demons

Abba Evagrius said, *"Fast before the Lord according to your strength, for to do this will purge you of your iniquities and sins; it exalts the soul, sanctifies the mind, drives away the demons, and prepares you for God's presence. Having eaten once, try not to eat again the same day, in case you become extravagant and disturb your mind. In this way you will have the means for helping others and for mortifying the passions of your body. But if there is a meeting of the brethren, and you have to eat a second and third time, do not be disgruntled and surly. On the contrary, do gladly what you have to do, and when you have eaten a second and third time, thank God that you have fulfilled the law of love and that He himself is providing for you."*

Evagrius was known for confronting the demons head-on with a variety of forms of prayer and meditation. In this example he recommends fasting "according to your strength" because it "prepares you for God's presence." It is God's presence and power that will "purge you of your iniquities and sins" and focus your attention on helping others. But fasting never takes precedence over "fulfill[ing] the law of love" when we are needed by others. In this example the monk, who is fasting for his own spiritual need, will not diminish his need by fulfilling his responsibility to his brothers, even when that means breaking his fast. The demons cannot compete with love.

The Foundation of Constant Prayer

"Some of the monks who are called Euchites [whose piety was focused only on mental prayer to the exclusion of manual labor] went to Enaton [in Syria] to see Abba Lucius. The old man asked them, 'What is your manual work?' They said, 'We do not touch manual work but as the Apostle [St. Paul] says, we pray without ceasing.' The old man asked them if they did not eat and they replied they did. So he asked them, 'When you are eating, who prays for you then?' Again he asked them if they did not sleep and they replied they did. And he said to them, 'When you are asleep, who prays for you then?' They could not find any answer to give him. He said to them, 'Forgive me, but you do not act as you speak. I will show you how, while doing my manual work, I pray without interruption. I sit down with God, soaking my reeds and plaiting my ropes, and I say, "God, have mercy on me; according to your great goodness and according to the multitude of your mercies, save me from my sins."' So he asked them if this were not prayer and they replied it was."

As we saw earlier through this example, Lucius demonstrates how work and prayer become one unceasing action. He prays "without interruption" by soaking and plaiting reeds while his heart awaits the continued presence of God, whose "great goodness" will renew his life. His sins, distracting thoughts, and the difficulties and work of monastic life will not scatter or diminish Abba Lucius's path to salvation as long as his commitment to a life of prayer is constant.

Watchfulness Cleanses the Heart through the Presence of Jesus Christ

Abba Hesychios the Priest said, *"We will travel the road of repentance correctly if, as we begin to give attention to the intellect, we combine humility with watchfulness, and prayer with the power to rebut evil thoughts. In this way we will adorn the chamber of our heart with the holy and venerable name of Jesus Christ as with a lighted lamp, and we will sweep our heart clean of wickedness, purifying and embellishing it."*

Hesychios knows that humility is necessary for repentance because it is the attitude Jesus described when he said, "Blessed are the poor in spirit." Humility recognizes our need for God. Its partner on "the road of repentance" is watchfulness. Knowing our need for God is the first step. Watchfulness is the attitude of waiting and looking for God's presence. The third companion on the road is "prayer with the power to rebut evil thoughts." Earlier this year Abba Isaac described "prayer" as personal movement toward God "with utter earnestness of heart." These three aspects of praxis, when persistently practiced, will "adorn the chamber of our heart with the holy and venerable name of Jesus Christ" and "sweep our heart clean of wickedness."

OCTOBER 30

Simple, Uncluttered Experience of Jesus Christ

"Abba Macarius was asked, 'How should one pray?' The old man said, 'There is no need at all to make long discourses; it is enough to stretch out one's hands and say, "Lord, as you will, and as you know, have mercy." And if the conflict grows fiercer say, "Lord, help!" He knows very well what we need and he shows us his mercy.'"

Macarius's advice is to "keep it simple" and to pray with words *and* body. Later, he recommended a similar prayer to Evagrius that became a prototype of the Jesus Prayer: *"Abba Evagrius said, 'I visited Abba Macarius, distressed by my thoughts and the passions of the body. I said to him, "My father, tell me a word so I may live." Abba Macarius said to me, "Bind the ship's cable to the mooring anvil and through the grace of our Lord Jesus Christ the ship will pass through the diabolical waves and tumults of this murky sea and the deep darkness of this vain world." I said to him, "What is the ship . . . the ship's cable . . . the mooring anvil?" Abba Macarius said to me, "The ship is your heart. . . . The ship's cable is your spirit; bind it to our Lord Jesus Christ, who is the mooring. . . . For it is not easy to say with each breath, Lord Jesus, have mercy on me. I bless you, Lord Jesus."'"*

It is hard to believe that this simple prayer is enough. Modern life, including corporate worship, is filled with words and activities. Some church services have no room for silence and simple reflection. Many published resources to support our spiritual lives, including this book of meditations, are filled with words. Macarius reminds us that behind all this, and giving it life, is a simple, life-giving, and two-way relationship. "Lord Jesus, have mercy on me. I bless you, Lord Jesus." This simple prayer will go with us day and night. It is the foundation of all other experiences and relationships.

OCTOBER 31

The Prayer of the Heart

To drive away the demons, Abba Evagrius exhorted monks to "pray without ceasing." He learned this from his own abba, Macarius the Great: *"Concentrate on this name of our Lord Jesus Christ with a contrite heart, the words welling up from your lips and drawing you to them. And do not depict him with an image in your mind but concentrate on calling to him: 'Our Lord Jesus, have mercy on me.' Do these things in peace and you will see the peace of his divinity within you; he will run off the darkness of the passions that dwell within you and he will purify the inner person [2 Cor 4:16; Eph 3:16] just as Adam was pure in paradise."*

Macarius taught his disciples to keep prayer simple with few words. The short prayer "Lord Jesus, have mercy on me. I bless you, Lord Jesus" became a prototype for a later monastic discipline called "the Jesus Prayer" in Eastern Orthodox traditions. Macarius learned that by persistent use of this short prayer, without imaging Jesus, you will be drawn into the words and Jesus "will run off the darkness of the passions that dwell within you and he will purify the inner person." In November we will begin our reflections with a focus on the Jesus Prayer.

NOVEMBER

Human Transformation in Christ: Following the Path from Image to Likeness

Watchfulness

"For nothing is hidden that will not be disclosed, nor is anything secret that will not become known and come to light. Then pay attention to how you listen" (Luke 8:17-18).

Transformation

"The glory that you have given me I have given them, so that they may be one, as we are one. I in them and you in me, that they may become completely one, so that the world may know that you have sent me and have loved them even as you have loved me" (John 17:22-23).

"His divine power has given us everything needed for life and godliness, through the knowledge of him who called us by his own glory and goodness. Thus he has given us, through these things, his precious and very great promises, so that through them you may escape from the corruption that is in the world because of lust, and may become participants of the divine nature" (2 Pet 1:3-4).

Now that we have reflected for almost a year on the lives and wisdom of the desert mothers and fathers, it is legitimate to ask, Why bother? What has all this to do with life in the twenty-first century? Before responding, we must reflect on why the desert elders persisted in the monastic art themselves. Was there something more specific than "going to heaven" or "following the path to salvation"? How did these general "goals" relate to individual men and women in the desert? During November we will look at sayings that reflect the "end" or "purpose" of desert monastic life. Although different elders would give a variety of responses, centuries of experience and wisdom coalesced into a single purpose: human transformation in Christ. With few exceptions the desert elders agreed that their lives were incomplete. What were they looking for? Jesus' promise was "abundant life." The first step was to listen and develop the virtue of watchfulness. This would lead each person to the frontiers of full and abundant human life. They were seeking nothing less than transformation of their lives.

NOVEMBER 1

Constant Watchfulness

In the fifth century, two hundred years after Evagrius and Macarius, there is evidence that a pattern similar to the modern form of the Jesus Prayer had become a rich part of monastic prayer. By the eighth century that form was an essential part of monastic spiritual formation. It was and remains very simple: "Lord Jesus Christ, Son of God, have mercy on me, a sinner." Abba Hesychios of Sinai taught the following: *"Those who lack experience should know that it is only through the unceasing watchfulness of our intellect and the constant invocation of Jesus Christ, our Creator and God, that we, coarse and coddish in mind and body as we are, can overcome our bodiless and invisible enemies, for not only are they subtle, swift, malevolent, and skilled in malice, but they have an experience in warfare gained over all the years since Adam. The inexperienced have as weapons the Jesus Prayer and the impulse to discern what is from God. The experienced have the best method and teacher of all: the activity, discernment, and peace of God himself."*

The Jesus Prayer empowers both "inexperienced" and "experienced" persons through watchfulness for the faithful presence and power of God, who alone is the source of our transformation. The path toward making the likeness of God tangible in our lives begins with a desire to be in God's presence and an attitude of listening. Use of the Jesus Prayer places each person in a state of watchfulness and expectation.

Biblical Cries for Health and Wholeness

Abba Epiphanius, a Palestinian monk whose abba was Hilarion of Egypt, said, *"The Canaanite woman cries out, and she is heard; (Matt. 15) the woman with the issue of blood is silent, and she is called blessed; (Luke 8) the pharisee speaks, and he is condemned; (Matt. 9) the publican does not open his mouth, and he is heard. (Luke 18)"* He also said, *"God remits the debts of sinners who are penitent, for example, the sinful woman and the publican, but of the righteous man he even asks interest. This is what he says to his apostles, 'Except your righteousness exceed that of the scribes and pharisees, you will never enter the kingdom of heaven.' (Matt. 5.20)"*

As we have seen, the Bible was the focus of meditation for the desert elders, especially the psalms and the gospels. They are also the seed giving birth to Macarius's prayer for mercy and the Jesus Prayer. The "Canaanite woman cries out," "Have mercy on me, O Lord, Son of David"; "the publican" (a tax collector) prays silently, "God, be merciful to me, a sinner"; and "the woman with the issue of blood" touches Jesus and explains, trembling, that she knew his energy would heal her. All these cries for forgiveness and healing rely on God's merciful presence in Jesus. They represent a common, internal, and mysterious desire for abundant life that only God can give. They are echoed in the Jesus Prayer. What do these cries tell us?

The Meekness of Moses

Amma Syncletica said, *"Imitate the publican, and you will not be condemned with the Pharisee. Choose the meekness of Moses and you will find your heart which is a rock changed into a spring of water."*

Syncletica knows her Bible at its deepest level. Like her peers, she also knows the value of humility and our need for God. Her reference to the publican and his cry for mercy is another example of how the origins of the Jesus Prayer lie in the desert elders' awareness of people in the Bible, who in their great needs sought saving help from Jesus. It is their constant and persistent prayers and cries for help that initiated their relationships with Jesus. Their cries were physical outpourings of inward, deeply spiritual awareness and knowledge that Jesus could heal and save them. Jesus discerned that awareness and responded by saying, "your faith has made you whole." Syncletica recognizes this same dynamic in Moses' dependence on God. In the wilderness, when people were dying of thirst, he trusted God's promise to stand with him; as he struck a rock face, a flow of water gushed out. Syncletica realized that the meekness of both the publican and Moses will transform thirsting hearts into "a spring of water."

The Humility of Two Biblical Women

"Abba Poemen said, 'The reason why we are so greatly tempted is because we do not guard our name and status, as Scripture says. Do we not see that the Saviour gave peace to the Canaanite woman, accepting her as she was? (cf. Matt. 15) And the same for Abigail, because she said to David, "Upon me alone be the guilt," (1 Sam. 25.24) the Lord heard her and loved her. Abigail stands for the soul and David for God. So when the soul accuses herself before the Lord, the Lord loves her.'" Abba Poemen also said, *"I will tell you why we have so much difficulty; it is because we do not care about our brother whom Scripture tells us to receive. Moreover we do not remember the woman of Canaan (cf. Matt. 15.22) who followed the Lord crying and begging for her daughter to be cured, and the Lord heard her and gave her peace."*

Jesus' first-century culture was based on a strict hierarchy of leaders, power, and patronage. The Canaanite woman accepted her status as one not deserving the blessings of Jesus, a Jewish healer. Yet she persisted with her cry, "Have mercy on me, O Lord, Son of David," believing that Jesus had the power to heal her daughter, regardless of who she was. Jesus accepted her desire to entrust her daughter's health to him. Poemen realizes that in the midst of temptations, he and his disciples can learn from her humility and faith. They should claim God's love by constantly seeking the mercy and peace of Jesus.

Rising to the Occasion

Abba John the Dwarf said, *"I am like a man sitting under a great tree, who sees wild beasts and snakes coming against him in great numbers. When he cannot withstand them any longer, he runs to climb the tree and is saved. It is just the same with me; I sit in my cell and I am aware of evil thoughts coming against me, and when I have no more strength against them, I take refuge in God by prayer and I am saved from the enemy."*

The Bible was at the heart of the desert elders' prayer. We have seen that Syncletica, Poemen, and Epiphanius used specific examples in their teaching. Yet, biblical images influenced their thought in figurative and unintentional ways as well. Perhaps John the Dwarf was thinking of Zacchaeus, a short man and chief tax collector in Jericho, who climbed a tree to see Jesus as he passed by. Jesus discerned that Zacchaeus wanted more than a good view and said, "Zacchaeus, hurry and come down; for I must stay at your house today" (Luke 19:5). Something in Zacchaeus knew his life needed healing and by letting Jesus into his home, his soul's "household" was transformed. He decided to repay those he had defrauded and Jesus said to him, "Today salvation has come to this house" (Luke 19:9).

The Soul's Household

"[Abba John the Dwarf] also said this to a certain brother about the soul which wishes to be converted, 'There was in a city a courtesan who had many lovers. One of the governors approached her, saying, "Promise me you will be good, and I will marry you." She promised this and he took her and brought her to his house. Her lovers, seeking

her again, said to one another, "That lord has taken her with him to his house, so if we go to his house and he learns of it, he will condemn us. But let us go to the back, and whistle to her. Then, when she recognizes the sound of the whistle she will come down to us; as for us, we shall be unassailable." When she heard the whistle, the woman stopped her ears and withdrew to the inner chamber and shut the doors.' The old man said that this courtesan is our soul, that her lovers are the passions and other men; that the lord is Christ; that the inner chamber is the eternal dwelling; those who whistle are the evil demons, but the soul always takes refuge in the Lord."

John gives further context for the evolution of the Jesus Prayer. His image of the woman retreating "to the inner chamber" echoes Jesus' advice: "Whenever you pray, go into your room and shut the door and pray to your Father who is in secret" (Matt 6:6). This is the soul's true sanctuary. In this sanctuary the soul becomes aware of its true image and will not respond to external influences that will distract it from and blaspheme its sanctity. The inner chamber of prayer is where the soul may safely rest in God. But the inner chamber, through the discipline of the Jesus Prayer, is not a static place. It moves with us throughout our daily lives.

NOVEMBER 7

Listening in the Heart

Abba Philimon said, *"Pay strict attention to your heart and watch over it, so that it does not give admittance to your thoughts that are evil or in any way vain and useless. Without interruption, whether awake or asleep, eating, drinking, or in company, let your heart inwardly and mentally at times be meditating on the Psalms, at other times be repeating the prayer, 'Lord Jesus Christ, Son of God, have mercy on me.' And when you chant, make sure that your mouth is not saying one thing while your mind is thinking about another."*

Even though every human being has an inner room, Philimon reminds us that each person should "pay strict attention to your heart and watch over it." We will experience God's presence within ourselves by intentionally spending time in our inner sanctuary "without interruption." Listening to God's voice requires careful discipline so that we do not "give admittance to . . . thoughts that are evil or in any way vain and useless." Philimon suggests two ways to pray in our inner room, available during every aspect of daily life. The psalms, chanted aloud or silently, and repetition of the Jesus Prayer each have advantages at different times of the day. Each may be recited with a rhythm that eventually will unite words and thoughts without distraction.

NOVEMBER 8

The Threshold Leading toward Listening

Saint Peter of Damaskos said, *"If from the start we had wanted to keep the commandments and to remain as we were baptized, we would not have fallen into so many sins or have needed the trials and tribulations of repentance. If we wish, however, God's second gift of grace—repentance—can lead us back to our former beauty. But if we fail to repent, inevitably we will depart with the unrepentant demons into agelong punishment, more by our own free choice than against our will. Yet God did not create us for wrath but for salvation (1 Thessalonians 5:9), so that we might enjoy his blessings, and we should therefore be thankful and grateful toward our Benefactor. But our failure to get to know his gifts has made us indolent, and indolence has made us forgetful, with the result that ignorance lords it over us. We have to make strenuous efforts when we first try to return where we fell from."*

The early church saw baptism as birth into the life God desires for each person, yet recognized the reality that all of us, in a variety of ways, have denied that gift through our sins. But we may return to our original "beauty" by experiencing "God's second gift of grace—repentance." Abba Peter echoes the wisdom of Abba Dorotheos of Gaza, who taught that the "natural state" of every human being is goodness. By taking control of our lives, it is possible to deny that goodness. The result is sinful behavior. But the goodness is always a part of who we are and, through repentance, we "return" to our natural state. All prayer, including the Jesus Prayer, begins with awareness of sin, repentance, and total dependence on God.

Awareness of What We Have Denied

It is worth returning to part of Abba Peter's wisdom. *"If we wish, however, God's second gift of grace—repentance—can lead us back to our former beauty. But if we fail to repent, inevitably we will depart with the unrepentant demons into agelong punishment, more by our own free choice than against our will. Yet God did not create us for wrath but for salvation (1 Thessalonians 5:9), so that we might enjoy his blessings; and we should therefore be thankful and grateful toward our Benefactor."*

The fourth-century expressions of our need for God's mercy used by Macarius and Evagrius and their later form known as the Jesus Prayer, taught by Abbas Philimon and Hesychios of Sinai, express the common roots of Abba Peter's emphasis on repentance. All agree that a heart aware of its rejection of grace, coupled with genuine longing for restoration "to our former beauty," is the underlying intention and integrity of the Jesus Prayer. Otherwise it becomes a prayer disconnected from its original discipline of transformation, even if well-intended. Peter reminds us that the consequences of an unrepentant heart come from "our own free choice" because "God did not create us for wrath but for salvation." Repentance is positive.

The Power of the Name

Abba Philotheos of Sinai said, *"The blessed remembrance of God— which is the very presence of Jesus—with a heart full of wrath and a saving animosity against the demons, dissolves all trickeries of thought, plots, argumentation, fantasies, obscure conjectures, and, in short, everything with which the destroyer arms himself and that he insolently deploys in his attempt to swallow our souls. When Jesus is invoked, he promptly burns up everything. For our salvation lies in Christ Jesus alone. The Savior himself made this clear when he said: 'Without me you can do nothing.' (John 15:5)"*

The name of God in the Hebrew Scriptures and the New Testament is not simply a way to describe or identify the God of Abraham and Jesus.

Middle Eastern culture, which included and still includes most of the desert elders, asserted that a "name" embodies both the characteristics and presence of the one who is named. To invoke the name of a person, or God, is to invoke that person's presence and the energies of his or her being. Philotheos, who emphasized the crucial virtue of watchfulness in prayer, demonstrates the power of combining the invocation of God, "which is the very presence of Jesus," with the soul's desire for mercy. Jesus' presence will bring forth transformation.

Transmitting a Shared Treasure

The biographer of St. Dosithy, a disciple of Dorotheos of Gaza (ca. 506–60), tells of the close relationship between Dosithy and his abba. Dosithy assisted Dorotheos in the infirmary at the monastery in Thawatha. Dosithy was diligent in his renunciation of self-will, obedience to his abba, and placing himself always in God's presence. Toward the end of his life, dying of tuberculosis, his biographer describes his use of an early version of the Jesus Prayer, combining the name of Jesus with supplication for mercy. It speaks for itself: *"For [Dosithy] lived in continual remembrance of God. [Dorotheos, his spiritual father] had handed down to him the rule that he should always repeat these words: 'Lord Jesus Christ our God, have mercy on me! Son of God, save me!' He therefore said this prayer continually. When he fell ill, [Dorotheos] said to him: 'Dosithy, do not neglect your prayer. Make sure that you never let go of it.' [Dosithy] answered, 'I will do as you say, Father, only pray for me.' Later when he was almost completely worn out [by the disease, Dorotheos] said to him: 'How are you now, Dosithy? How is the prayer going? Do you say it all the time?' And he answered him, 'Yes, Father, thanks to your prayers.'"*

This narrative shows an intimate relationship between an abba and his disciple. The relationship was based on shared work, teaching, discipline, and prayer. It also shows the fundamental bond between abba and disciple: the transmission of treasure through example. Dorotheos was not simply giving Dosithy important knowledge and praxis; he was sharing a way of life that has its roots in Jesus. The transmission was so complete that when Dosithy was too weak to pray by himself, he prayed through his abba's words.

Remaining in the Presence of God

Saint Dosithy's use of the Jesus Prayer demonstrates how it was becoming a fundamental part of monastic praxis. The experience of the prayer itself encapsulated the present and future goals of monastic life. *"When he fell ill, [Dorotheos] said to him: 'Dosithy, do not neglect your prayer. Make sure you never let go of it.'"*

"Later, when he was so bad he had to be carried on a stretcher, he was asked, 'How is the prayer now, Dosithy?' He said, 'Pardon me, Father, I have no longer the strength to keep it going.' Dorotheos said to him, 'Never mind, leave your prayer now, just remember God and think that he is there at your side.'"

Dosithy's final days reflect his disciplined use of the Jesus Prayer throughout his monastic life of prayer. "For [Dosithy] lived in continual remembrance of God." He placed his whole being in the presence of God who filled his soul with the energies (grace) of God. Jesus said, "Abide in me, as I abide in you." Even when Dosithy's strength to speak is gone, the presence remains because his goal of future union with God had always been present in each recitation of the prayer throughout his life.

A Path to Original Beauty

Abba Theodoros, a ninth-century monk of the monastery of Sabas, near Jerusalem, said, *"Everything may be understood in terms of its purpose. It is this that determines the division of everything into its constituent parts, as well as the mutual relationship of those parts. Now the purpose of our life is blessedness or, what is the same thing, the kingdom of heaven or of God. This is not only to behold the Trinity, supreme in kingship, but also to receive an influx of the divine, as it were, to suffer deification, for by this influx what is lacking and is imperfect in us is supplied and perfected."*

Peter of Damaskos described repentance as a desire for restoration "to our former beauty." Theodoros shares this awareness and acknowledges that the image of God in every person is indelible and is the sign of the ultimate meaning and purpose of human life. Disciplines, like the Jesus Prayer, provided a genuine taste of the fruition of their lives in the midst of the groans and travails of daily life. They experienced "God's time" (eternity, without time) within the limitations of human life. The Jesus Prayer, and similar disciplines, are timeless experiences in which we "become participants in the divine nature" (2 Pet 1:4).

Entering Uncharted Territory

By the eleventh century the Jesus Prayer was used throughout the Middle East. There were several patterns for its use, but *The Method of Sacred Prayer* was common and eventually influenced use of the Jesus Prayer in monasteries on Mount Athos, Greece, and in Russia. Attributed to Symeon the New Theologian, its origin is uncertain.

"Then sit down in a quiet cell, in a corner by yourself, and do what I tell you. Close the door, and withdraw your intellect from everything worthless and transient. Rest your beard on your chest, and focus your physical gaze, together with the whole of your intellect, on the center of your belly or navel. Restrain the drawing-in of breath through your nostrils, so as not to breathe easily, and search inside yourself with your intellect so as to find the place of the heart, where all the powers of the soul reside. To start with, you will find there darkness and an impenetrable density. Later, when you practice this task day and night, you will find, as though miraculously, an unceasing joy. For as soon as the intellect attains the place of the heart, at once it sees things of which it previously knew nothing. It sees the open space within the heart and it beholds itself entirely luminous and full of discrimination."

Modern mentors in the use of the Jesus Prayer, such as Orthodox Bishop Kallistos Ware, suggest that *The Method of Sacred Prayer* be learned in a small community of persons who have used the practice for a long time. There is nothing secret about it, but it is so unique and full of power that it is best to begin in the company of others. It is not simply a "technique" to be mastered. It is an experience of total entrustment to the divine presence.

Simplicity and Flexibility

The Jesus Prayer has become a fundamental part of the spirituality of the Eastern Orthodox churches. Its roots lie in the prayer of the desert elders, but it also spread to Christian faith communities in the West with the English publication of *The Way of the Pilgrim.* Yet it remains simple, as Bishop Kallistos Ware describes: *"The Invocation of the Name is a prayer of the utmost simplicity, accessible to every Christian, but it leads at the same time to the deepest mysteries of contemplation. . . . No specialized knowledge or training is required before commencing on the Jesus Prayer. To the beginner it is sufficient to say: Simply begin. . . . The outward form of the prayer is easily learnt. Basically it consists of the words 'Lord Jesus Christ, Son of God, have mercy on me.' There is, however, no uniformity. We can say, '. . . have mercy on us,' instead of 'on me.' The verbal formula can be shortened: 'Lord Jesus Christ, have mercy on me.' Or 'Lord Jesus,' or even 'Jesus' alone, although this is less common. Alternatively, the form of the words may be expanded by adding 'a sinner' at the end, thus underlining the penitential aspect. . . . The one essential and unvarying element is the inclusion of the divine Name 'Jesus.'"*

Simple yet Legendary

Theoliptos of Philadelphia said, *"And as Adam, molded by God's hands from dust, became through divine spiration a living soul, so the intellect molded by the virtues and repeatedly invoking the Lord with a pure mind and an ardent spirit, is divinely transformed, quickened, and deified through knowing and loving God."*

Theoliptos says it all. The lives and prayer of the desert elders were so uncomplicated yet their hearts were opened to legendary frontiers of human experience. Words were less important than behavior. Their goal was nothing less than full maturation (perfection) as human beings through total dependence on God. They accepted Jesus' invitation to die to self in order to be "divinely transformed, quickened, and deified through knowing and loving God." This is the true self God intends for every person. The legacy of the desert mothers and fathers is nothing less than showing that each person is created in the image of God and called to make that image tangible in her or his life.

Sharing God's Image and Likeness

Peter of Damaskos said, *"This is the beginning of our salvation; by our free choice we abandon our own wishes and thoughts and do what God wishes and thinks. If we succeed in doing this, there is no object, no activity or place in the whole of creation that can prevent us from becoming what God from the beginning has wished us to be: that is to say, according to his image and likeness, gods by adoption through grace, dispassionate, just, good, and wise, whether we are rich or poor, married or unmarried, in authority and free or under obedience and in bondage—in short, whatever our time, place, or activity. That is why, alike before the Law, under the Law and under grace, there have been many righteous men—men who preferred the knowledge of God and his will to their own thoughts and wishes."*

Peter echoes the awareness of Dorotheos of Gaza that all humans, monks or laypersons, are created in the image and likeness of God. Our original state is goodness and this is what God has always desired for each of us. The "beginning of our salvation" is freely letting go of "our own wishes and thoughts." In this way we open our soul to manifest the likeness of God in the way we live: deification. The audacious truth that there is "no activity or place in the whole of creation that can prevent us from becoming what God from the beginning has wished us to be: that is to say, according to his image and likeness" is not commonly taught among modern Christians, yet it is the most fundamental treasure of Christian experience.

The Mystery of Deification

Abba Pachomius said, *"But all the same, hear about a great vision. For what is greater than such a vision, to see the invisible God in a visible man, his temple?"*

The desert fathers and mothers placed great emphasis on dying to self, as Jesus exhorted his disciples, so that their desires would be congruent with what God desires for themselves, for their neighbor, and the world. This self-emptying and openness of heart makes room for the presence of God and takes place through total dependence on God's grace. Abba Pachomius, echoing Saint Paul, describes what this looks like: *"to see the invisible God in a visible man, his temple."* Three hundred years later, St. Maximos gives a similar description of deified human life. *"God and the Saints had one and the same energy. . . . The Saints participate in God; not only do they participate, but they also communicate him. . . . They not only live, but also bring to life, and that is not the attribute of a created faculty."* A miracle?

The Mystery of Coinherence

Saint Maximos, who was influenced by Abba Evagrius and Origen of Alexandria, speaks of God's desire for each person to share in God's unique presence in Jesus of Nazareth. This radical claim declares that God's incarnation in Jesus proclaims the sanctity and ultimate purpose of human life: to share in the life of God. This is a gift of grace, made possible through the life of Jesus and the work of the Holy Spirit. Maximos said, *"the power of this reciprocal gift which deifies man for God through the love of God, and makes God man for man through his love for man, making through this noble exchange God to become man for the deification of man, and man to become God for the humanisation of God. For the Word of God who is God wills always and in all things to work the mystery of his embodiment."*

As we have seen, the desert elders learned that the venues for human transformation are ordinary daily life and individual human beings. The goal of monastic life is not to escape the nature and limitations of our lives but to discover and reclaim our true nature within those limitations because "the Word of God who is God wills always and in all things to work the mystery of his embodiment."

Divine Embodiment

Saint Maximos wrote, *"He who is perfect in love and has attained the summit of detachment knows no difference between 'mine and thine,' between faithful and unfaithful, between slave and freeman, or indeed between male and female. Having risen above the tyranny of the passions and looking to nature, one in all men, he considers all equally and is disposed equally towards all. For in him there is neither Greek nor Jew, neither male nor female, neither slave nor freeman, but everything and in all things Christ."*

Human deification, as experienced and taught in the earliest periods of Christianity, is often misunderstood and held in suspicion. It does not declare that humans become God but expresses a mysterious reality that a human being may share in God's divine life. Like Dorotheos of Gaza, Maximos declares that through God's gift of deification we become what we were created to be. What does this look like? Maximos, echoing St. Paul in Galatians 3:28 and Ephesians 2:21-22, describes one aspect of deification. When a person has become a dwelling place for God, the lives of all persons are approached and treated as equal.

Fully Engaged with the Life of the World

Father Dumitru Staniloae, a Romanian theologian and one of the best modern interpreters of St. Maximos's teaching, describes the primary consequence of human deification.

"The most shining demonstration of the action of grace within us is in our sympathetic awareness of our neighbor. By grace we long to make those who are in need at home with us, as we wish to make

God at home with us. Nothing contributes so much to our growth in righteousness, to our drawing close to God, to our deification, as compassion showed to those in need."

Father Staniloae's words, "to make those who are in need at home with us," bring to mind images of Jesus being at meals with tax collectors and sinners, touching the sick and blind, and reassuring persons in his society who had been shamed and marginalized that they have integrity because they are loved by God. Jesus was very clear that his intimate relationship with his Abba was the source of his words and actions. Toward the end of his ministry he exhorted those who had entrusted their lives to him that they "will also do the works that I do and, in fact, will do greater works than these, because I am going to the Father" (John 14:12). The audacity of deification has its roots in Jesus.

Living the Embodiment

These words of Peter of Damaskos are worth repeating. They show that deification is neither abstract nor dualistic. *"There is no object, no activity or place in the whole of creation that can prevent us from becoming what God from the beginning has wished us to be: that is to say, according to his image and likeness, gods by adoption through grace, dispassionate, just, good, and wise, whether we are rich or poor, married or unmarried, in authority and free or under obedience and in bondage—in short, whatever our time, place, or activity."*

Deification does not transcend or escape the limitations of human life. At the same time, deification endows a human life with the eternal energies and nature of God's mysterious being. Peter gives a picture of this amazing coinherence that is available to *everyone*: a person who shares God's nature is able to share God's goodness (Jesus said, "There is only one who is good"), will desire the wealth of God's goodness for everyone (justice), will discern and prefer knowledge of God and God's will to personal thoughts and wishes (wisdom), and will not be attached to anything in a possessive or controlling way (dispassion), "whatever our time, place, or activity."

The Fundamental Reality of All Creation

Saint Maximos continues, *"God made us so that we might become 'partakers of the divine nature' (2 Peter 1:4) and sharers in His eternity, so that we might come to be like him (1 John 3:2) through deification by grace. It is through deification that all things are reconstituted and achieve their permanence, and it is for its (deification's) sake that what is not is brought into being and given existence."*

Deification is not an option for a select few. Nor is it something we strive to achieve. Maximos declares that human beings are created "so that we might come to be like him . . . through deification by grace." We were "given existence" to share in the eternal dimension of God's life. But this is not only for human life. Maximos uses language similar to St. Paul to say that it is "through deification that all things are reconstituted and achieve their permanence." (See Rom 8:18-25.) All this is a gift because God knows who we really are and wants us to have what is truly our own. The gift matches the fundamental reality of who we are.

The Work of God in Christ

Saint Symeon the New Theologian (949–1022) wrote, *"What is the purpose of the Incarnation of the Divine Logos, which is proclaimed throughout the Scriptures, about which we read and that yet we do not recognize? Surely it is that he has shared in what is ours so as to make us participants of what he is. For the Son of God became the Son of man in order to make us human beings sons [and daughters] of God, raising us up by grace to what he is by nature, giving us a new birth in the Holy Spirit and leading us directly into the kingdom of heaven. Or, rather, he gives us grace to possess this kingdom within ourselves (Luke 17:21), so that not merely do we hope to enter it, but being in full possession of it, we can affirm: 'Our life is hid with Christ in God.' (Colossians 3:3)"*

Symeon stands on the shoulders of the early desert elders in bearing witness to the essential biblical roots of deification as the natural state of human life. He ties deification directly to the incarnation of God in Jesus of Nazareth. The presence and union of God, the creator of all life, in the human life of Jesus makes it possible for us to be "participants of what he is." The result is also "to possess this kingdom within ourselves" so that our life is not our creation but lived "with Christ in God." The good news in this truth is that because the kingdom is within us, we have the opportunity to manifest that same kingdom in the desires, words, and actions of our daily lives.

NOVEMBER 25

Becoming Fully Human

Saint Theodoros the Great Ascetic said, *"Everything must be understood in terms of its purpose. It is this that determines the division of everything into its constituent parts, as well as the mutual relationship of those parts. Now the purpose of our life is blessedness or, what is the same thing, the kingdom of heaven or of God. This is not only to behold the Trinity, supreme in kingship, but also to receive an influx of the divine and, as it were, to suffer deification, for by this influx what is lacking and imperfect in us is supplied and perfected."*

Theodoros is saying that deification is nothing less than the completion of the creation of a human life. It is something we suffer in the sense that we must yield what we want to be to what God desires us to become. When Abba Arsenius prayed, "What must I do to be saved?" he knew in his heart that his influential, entitled, and fancy life in Constantinople was "lacking and imperfect." The answer he received, "flee, find solitude, and pray," was an invitation to an alternative lifestyle that would enable him "to receive an influx of the divine." His choice of the life of a hermit was his way (not everyone's way) to "suffer deification," that is, to cooperate with God's grace in a "mutual relationship" that completes his life of "blessedness."

Living in the Present

Amma Theodora said, *"Let us strive to enter by the narrow gate. Just as the trees, if they have not stood before the winter's storms cannot bear fruit, so it is with us; this present age is a storm and it is only through many trials and temptations that we can obtain an inheritance in the kingdom of heaven."*

The "narrow gate" does not imply that only a few will enter the realm of God. Its "narrowness" refers to the firm, yet voluntary, decision that must be made in order to cross its threshold. The opportunity to accept the gift of sharing God's nature requires a choice to let go of all the other "doors" that lure us away from the realm of God. And Theodora reminds us that this new life in Christ takes place within our daily lives. The mystery of deification does not eliminate the "many trials and temptations" we face. Theodora is saying that through the storms of "this present age" our inner transformation will become manifest and mature. Like Syncletica, she has seen tree buds, tightly closed and dark in color, withstand the cold storms of winter. But in this harsh environment lies the promise of spring blooms and fall's fruit. Theodora exhorts us to respond to the lure of divine love and pass through the narrow gate.

Discerning Priorities

"In his youth Abba John the Eunuch questioned an old man, 'How have you been able to carry out the work of God in peace? For we cannot do it, even with our labor.' The old man said, 'We were able to do it, because we considered the work of God to be primary, and bodily needs to be subsidiary; but you hold bodily needs to be primary and the work of God to be secondary; that is why you labor, and that is why the Savior said to the disciples, 'Seek first his kingdom and his righteousness, and all these things shall be yours as well.' (Matt. 6:33)"

Sharing the nature of God's life includes sharing God's desires for you, your neighbor, and the world. This was not easy for Abba

John when he was young because he was so earnest about the hard work of becoming a monk and his "bodily needs." He was unable "to carry out the work of God in peace" even though it was God's work. Something was missing. His heart was not at peace. The abba he consulted could see right away that John had placed material needs, even though necessary, above what God desired for him at this time in his life. The abba reminded him that Jesus exhorted his disciples to seek what God desires first and trust that our authentic needs will be satisfied.

Patience and Persistence

Abba Antony said, *"Having therefore made a beginning, and set out already on the way to virtue, let us press forward to what lies ahead. And let none turn back as Lot's wife did, especially since the Lord said, 'No one who puts his hand to the plow and turns back is fit for the Kingdom of heaven.' Now 'turning back' is nothing except feeling regret and once more thinking about things of the world. But do not be afraid to hear about virtue, and do not be a stranger to the term. For it is not distant from us, nor does it stand external to us, but its realization lies in us, and the task is easy if only we shall will it."*

Sharing in the nature of God (deification) is a gift that enables us to look forward and see ourselves as God sees us. It requires a forward-looking spirit that trusts that what God desires for us is possible. Antony learned from personal experience that sharing in God's nature includes a firm desire for the virtues (disciplines of thought and action) that will make our transformation tangible. Although this may seem like a distant goal, it already lies within if we will claim it. When Jesus declared that "the realm of God is here," he was showing Galileans who were oppressed by the wealthy, political leaders, and some religious leaders, that they have integrity in God's eyes. God loves and cares about them. They no longer have to live in shame. Even though Jesus did not solve all their problems during his lifetime, the integrity of their lives was restored. This gave them hope and resilience in the face of difficult lives.

Lasting Peace

"It was said of Abba Netras, the disciple of Abba Silvanus, that when he dwelt in his cell on Mt. Sinai, he treated himself prudently, with regard to the needs of his body; but when he became bishop of Pharan, he curbed himself with great austerities. His disciple said to him, 'Abba, when we were in the desert, you did not practice such asceticism.' The old man said to him, 'There in the desert, I had interior peace and poverty and I wished to manage my body so as not to be ill and not need what I did not have. But now I am in the world and among its cares and even if I am ill here, there will be someone to look after me and so I do this in order not to destroy the monk in me.'"

Interior peace flowed into the daily life of Abba Netras wherever he lived and sustained his passion to manifest God's presence faithfully.

"Abba Lot went to see Abba Joseph and said to him, 'Abba, as far as I can I say my little office, I fast a little, I pray and meditate, I live in peace and as far as I can, I purify my thoughts. What else can I do?' Then the old man stood up and stretched his hands towards heaven. His fingers became like ten lamps of fire and he said to him, 'If you will, you can become all flame.'"

Most people today live "in the world and among its cares." We are not monks and cannot live a traditional monastic lifestyle. But each of us can share Abba Netras's desire to pay attention to "the monk in me." Being a monk means having a single-minded (*monakos*) desire to live an undivided life, where our desires are congruent with God's desires for ourselves and the world. Like the desert elders, we are challenged to ask, how can I be a good steward of my soul so that the image of God in me becomes tangible in my life? Instead of leaving towns and cities for the desert, we are called to bring the wisdom of the desert elders into our towns and cities.

A Rich Legacy

In the sixth century Benedict of Nursia developed a rule of life for his newly formed monastic community. The Rule of Benedict has influenced the formation and life of most Christian monastic communities ever since and has become a fundamental part of Christian spirituality. In chapter 73 of his Rule, Benedict cites the wisdom and lives of the desert elders as a crucial source of wisdom and example for the lives of Benedictine monks.

"But for someone who is in a hurry to reach the fullness of monastic life, there are the teachings of the Holy Fathers. Anyone who carries them out will arrive at the pinnacle of perfection. For what page or even what word of the divinely inspired Old and New Testaments is not a completely reliable guidepost for human life? Or what book of the holy Catholic Fathers does not teach us how to reach our Creator by the direct route? And then there are the Conferences *of the Fathers and their* Institutes *and* Lives, *along with the Rule of our holy Father Basil. What else are they for monks who live upright and obedient lives but tools of virtue?"*

Benedict's influence goes far beyond the walls of monastic communities into the worship and piety of many Christian denominations. Thousands of Christians have become "oblates" of monastic communities, living rules of life that are congruent with their monastic brothers and sisters yet appropriate for their lives in conventional society.

In December we will look at more examples of the continuing legacy of the desert elders.

DECEMBER

The Legacy of the Desert Fathers and Mothers

Wisdom is the desire to speak or act, or to refrain from speech and action, in the present moment in a manner that is congruent with what a person or group discerns to be truly real and life-giving. Wise speech and action or wise silence and restraint from action evolve from a person's pattern of interior listening to God as well as the crucible of past circumstances and experience. This combination of inner perception of truth (experience of God in prayer) and exterior insights about what is fruitful in daily life is the source of wisdom.

Wisdom is not a body of knowledge. It cannot be acquired through mastery of "right thinking." Wisdom, like humility, becomes tangible in a person's way of living. Wise sayings point toward a manner of life that embodies wisdom. Words and sayings by themselves, while edifying, are lifeless until they become manifest in individual human lives.

The desert mothers and fathers learned the inner wisdom of their abbas and ammas by observing their lives. Their teaching was empty without their example. Their exemplar was Jesus who said, "I am the way, and the truth, and the life" (John 14:6). His life embodied both inner perception of truth through his experience of his Abba and the life-giving presence of God in his words and engagement with society. His wisdom reveals what is real and sustains life. It is practical because it inspires human life with the presence and power of God.

Amma Syncletica said, *"It is dangerous for anyone to teach who has not first been trained in the 'practical' life."*

The wisdom of the desert mothers and fathers did not arise from a vacuum or "come down from heaven." It was not doctrine or

instructions formulated by groups of abbas and ammas and then applied to their lives. Although there were revered teachers and, eventually, rules governing the lives of men and women living in community,
this teaching and guidance for communal life evolved from years of
solitude, struggles with demonic thoughts and temptations, patient
and persistent disciplines of praxis, honest self-reflection, work, relationships with other people, experience of God's presence and grace,
failure and impatience with lack of progress, study and meditation
on the Bible, common worship, sharing experience, and opportunities to love one's neighbor. Authority and integrity for teaching and
influencing others were rooted in the tangible presence of God in an
amma or abba.

Yet, as Abba Evagrius learned, even though they were physically
separated from all, at the same time they were united to all. The world
around them hungered for the wisdom that was visible in the fruits
of their way of life and articulated so simply in their teaching. When
Athanasius of Alexandria published his *Life of Antony*, he opened a
floodgate of interest in the lives of the desert elders that spread into
almost every aspect of the same societies the desert elders had left.
Just as Antony and Syncletica withdrew to the desert to encounter
God in solitude, the wisdom of their way of life is returning to societies all over the world that are yearning for God's presence and
transforming power.

In December we will examine the rich legacy of the desert mothers
and fathers.

DECEMBER 1

Welcome the Implanted Word

*"Every generous act of giving, with every perfect gift, is from
above, coming down from the Father of lights, with whom there is no
variation or shadow due to change. In fulfillment of his own purpose
he gave us birth by the word of truth, so that we would become a kind
of first fruits of his creatures. You must understand this, my beloved:
let everyone be quick to listen, slow to speak, slow to anger; for your
anger does not produce God's righteousness. Therefore rid yourselves
of all sordidness and rank growth of wickedness, and welcome with
meekness the implanted word that has the power to save your souls.*

*But be doers of the word, and not merely hearers who deceive them-
selves. For if any are hearers of the word and not doers, they are like
those who look at themselves in a mirror; for they look at themselves
and, on going away, immediately forget what they were like. But
those who look into the perfect law, the law of liberty, and persevere,
being not hearers who forget but doers who act—they will be blessed
in their doing. If any think they are religious, and do not bridle their
tongues but deceive their hearts, their religion is worthless. Religion
that is pure and undefiled before God, the Father, is this: to care for
orphans and widows in their distress, and to keep one's self unstained
by the world" (James 1:17-27).*

The desert elders did not invent their legacy. They lived what
they learned from the Bible. This quotation from the Letter of James
clearly mirrors a Galilean remembrance of the teaching and life of
Jesus and could be seen as a "job description" for the desert elders'
way of life. God is the source of "every perfect gift" (action), God's
"word of truth" is born in us, and God's righteousness emerges from
our lives from being "quick to listen." Jesus asked, "Why do you call
me 'Lord, Lord,' and do not do what I tell you?" (Luke 6:46). James
exhorts his readers to "be doers of the word, and not merely hearers
who deceive themselves." Perseverance, humility in speech and action,
purity of heart "before God," and love of one's neighbor are biblical
images that were integrated into the lives of the desert elders. They
took the Bible very seriously.

DECEMBER 2

The Priority of Hospitality

*"Abba [John] Cassian related the following: 'The holy Germanus
and I went to Egypt, to visit an old man. Because he offered us hospitality we asked him, "Why do you not keep the rule of fasting, when
you receive visiting brothers, as we have received it in Palestine?"
He replied, "Fasting is always to hand but you I cannot have with
me always. Furthermore, fasting is certainly a useful and necessary
thing, but it depends on our choice while the law of God lays it upon
us to do the works of charity. Thus receiving Christ in you, I ought
to serve you with all diligence, but when I have taken leave of you,
I can resume the rule of fasting again. For 'Can the wedding guests*

fast while the bridegroom is with them, but when the bridegroom is taken from them, then they will fast in that day.'"' (Mark 2.19-20)"

Here "an old man" declares that receiving guests is not only polite but it is also receiving Christ in the guest. He is also clear that a rule is not an end in itself. The law of charity must prevail. After he left Egypt, John Cassian founded two monasteries near Marseilles in 415. He wrote *Institutes* to describe the life of the desert monks and guide the formation of new monasteries. The *Institutes* influenced Benedict of Nursia, and in his Rule he declares that "all guests who arrive should be received as Christ." Hospitality is not an interruption to the flow of our lives. Nor is it simply a practical aspect of "being a good neighbor." It is an opportunity to recognize and celebrate the sacred image in another person. Hospitality is the gift of mutual presence.

DECEMBER 3

A Fourfold Path to Transformation

"Listen, O my son, to the teachings of your master, and turn to them with the ear of your heart. Willingly accept the advice of a devoted father and put it into action. Thus you will return by the labor of obedience to the one from whom you drifted through the inertia of disobedience. Now then I address my words to you: whoever is willing to renounce self-will, and take up the powerful and shining weapons of obedience to fight for the Lord Christ, the true king."

In the prologue to his sixth-century Rule for monks, Benedict of Nursia describes a fourfold path to holiness that mirrors the teachings of the desert mothers and fathers. Everything begins with *listening* and not simply to words but with "the ear of your heart." Then he advises *turning* toward the teachings of a master, a father or abba. The turning is a desire to reorient the focus of your life to a person whose life and wisdom authentically incarnate the presence of Christ. But turning is not enough. This is not an academic experience. Along with the turning comes a genuine desire to "willingly accept" a mentor's advice and, finally, "put it into action." This is a whole-hearted decision.

The Path Begins with Listening

"Listen, O my son, to the teachings of your master, and turn to them with the ear of your heart."

The path to the gift of union with God begins with listening. The Rule of St. Benedict, influenced by the teaching of the desert elders, is filled with both references to and direct quotations from the Bible. In Deuteronomy 6:4 the Hebrew Scriptures exhort: "Hear, O Israel . . . " and when God's unique presence in Jesus is manifested to Peter, James, and John on the mountain of transfiguration, a voice declares, "This is my Son, the Beloved; listen to him!" (Mark 9:7). Jesus' ministry was filled with listening. "In the morning, while it was still very dark, he got up and went to a deserted place, and there he prayed" (Mark 1:35). Jesus himself declared, "Anyone who hears my word and believes him who sent me, has eternal life" (John 5:24). Like the desert elders, Benedict invites his monks to listen "to the teachings of your master." The role of a master, abba, or amma is to transmit the experience and wisdom of God in their lives, not to call attention to themselves. But their role is crucial in a person's vocation of listening. God speaks both in the silence of our hearts and in the life and teaching of our mentors.

The Courage to Change Our Lives

"Listen, O my son, to the teachings of your master, and turn to them with the ear of your heart."

Turning "to the teachings of your master" carries a double meaning for Benedict and echoes words of Abba John Cassian. In the prologue to his Rule, Benedict's monks are urged to renounce sins and self-will and return to the graced-filled life given at baptism. The "teachings of your master" may refer both to Jesus and to a monastic teacher or mentor. As we have seen in the lives of the desert elders, the integrity of an abba's or amma's teaching is that it manifests the presence of Jesus. Ultimately we are called to listen to the teachings of Jesus. But there is more. We are to *"turn to them* with the ear of your heart." The teachings will reorient our lives only if we embrace them. A choice must be made. It seems possible that Benedict, like Cassian, has Psalm 45:10-11 in mind. The psalm describes a bride leaving her father's house to marry a king: "Hear, O daughter, consider and incline your ear; forget your people and your father's house, and the king will desire your beauty" (45:10-11). Reorienting one's life is never easy.

The Grace of Obedience

"Willingly accept the advice of a devoted father and put it into action. Thus you will return by the labor of obedience to the one from whom you drifted through the inertia of disobedience."

The desert elders and Benedict place great stock in "obedience" because it enables us to listen and follow someone besides ourselves. Fullness of life is not possible if we are the center of our lives. But Benedict emphasizes that obedience is "willingly" accepted. Both he and the desert elders value obedience because it was the hallmark of the life of Jesus, who, in St. Paul's words, "humbled himself and became obedient to the point of death" (Phil 2:8). Amma Syncletica said, *"It is dangerous for anyone to teach who has not first been trained in the 'practical' life,"* and Abba Dorotheos taught that we need assistance and guidance in addition to God's grace. The value of "the labor of obedience" is that it directs us away from "the inertia of disobedience" of self-will. Later in the prologue Benedict says, *"And so, brothers, we have queried the Lord about what is required of a dweller in his tent, and we have received the teaching about dwelling there. . . . Therefore we must prepare our hearts and bodies to wage the battle of holy obedience to his precepts."* Obedience is freedom.

Words without Action Are Useless

Saint Benedict writes, *"Willingly accept the advice of a devoted father and put it into action."*

Amma Syncletica said, *"Because humility is good and salutary, the Lord clothed himself in it. . . . For he says, 'Learn from me, for I am gentle and humble of heart' [Matt 11:29]. Notice who it is who is speaking; learn his lesson perfectly. Let humility become for you the beginning and end of virtues. He means a humble heart; he refers not to appearance alone, but to the inner person, for the outer person will also follow after the inner."*

Jesus' life was his message. He exhorted those around him to listen to his words, but he made it clear that the vocation of a disciple is to *follow him.* He invited those who wanted to follow him to *share his life, including his actions,* regardless of the outcomes. An emphasis on personal example, embodied in humble charity, is the greatest legacy of the desert elders and appears as the core of the Rule of Benedict. *"An old man said, 'Every evening and every morning a monk ought to render an account of himself and say to himself, "What have we done of what God does not want, and what have we done of that which God wills."'"* We can ask ourselves each day, how has my "inner person" been given the opportunity to speak and act today?

DECEMBER 8

Solitude and Community

Benedict's genius was to integrate the wisdom and praxis of two great forms of monastic life from the desert elders: the life of individual *solitude* and life in a *community.* Like Antony and Pachomius had done in the East, Benedict had a formative influence on monastic life and spirituality as Christianity developed in the West.

"When [a novice] is to be received, he comes before the whole community in the oratory and promises stability [commitment to a specific community], fidelity to monastic life [the manner of life in the community], and obedience [to Christ, through the abbot, and the community]. This is done in the presence of God and his saints to impress on the novice that if he ever acts otherwise, he will surely be condemned by the one he mocks."

Within this community life Benedict also provides for the solitude and personal prayer of each monk. *"Monks should diligently cultivate silence at all times, but especially at night."* Like the desert elders, he associates solitude as a means of *"refusing to indulge evil habits and by devoting ourselves to prayer with tears, to reading, to compunction of heart and self-denial."*

In what ways do you combine life in a faith community and personal silence and prayer?

Work, Study, and Prayer

Benedict's Rule is a pattern of monastic life that integrates body, mind, heart, soul, and spirit. Notice how he wove virtues and activities into the life of his communities that mirror the lives of the desert mothers and fathers.

"Idleness is the enemy of the soul. Therefore, the brothers should have specified periods for manual labor as well as for prayerful reading. . . . Let us consider then, how we ought to behave in the presence of God and his angels, and let us stand to sing the psalms in such a way that our minds are in harmony with our voices."

"Abba Poemen said, 'Life in the monastery demands three things: the first is humility, the next is obedience, and the third which sets them in motion and is like a goad is the work of the monastery.'"

Speaking about steadfastness of heart, Abba Isaac told Abba John Cassian, *"There are three things that stabilize a wandering mind—namely, vigils, mediation, and prayer. Being faithful and constantly attentive to them produces a solid firmness of soul. . . . For whoever is in the habit of praying only at the hour when the knees are bent prays very little. But whoever is distracted by any sort of wandering of heart, even on bended knee, never prays. And therefore we have to be outside the hour of prayer what we want to be while we are praying."*

What is your pattern of work, study, and worship? In what ways does your life of prayer influence your work and relationship with other people?

The Primacy of Love

As we have seen, the desert elders gave first priority to what they called the Great Commandment. Jesus summed it up as loving God and loving your neighbor. Benedict agrees. In chapter 4 of his Rule he says, *"First of all,* love the Lord God with all your heart, your whole soul and all your strength, and love your neighbor as yourself. . . . *Then the following:* You are not to kill, not to commit adultery; you are not to steal nor to covet . . . ; you are not to bear false witness. . . . You must honor everyone . . . , *and* never do to another what you do not want done to yourself. . . . Renounce yourself in order to follow Christ . . . ; discipline your body . . . ; *do not pamper yourself, but love fasting. You must relieve the lot of the poor,* clothe the naked, visit the sick . . . , *and bury the dead. Go to help the troubled and console the sorrowing. Your way of acting should be different from the world's way; the love of Christ must come before all else."*

"Abba John the Dwarf said, 'A house is not built by beginning at the top and working down. You must begin with the foundations in order to reach the top.' They said to him, 'What does this mean?' He said, 'The foundation is our neighbor, whom we must win, and that is the place to begin. For all the commandments of Christ begin with this one.'"

Total Dependence on God

"We must, then, prepare our hearts and bodies for the battle of holy obedience to [the Lord's] instructions. What is not possible for us by nature, let us ask the Lord to supply by the help of his grace."

Benedict reminds us that our exterior obedience to the Lord's teaching will flow from our interior life with God. "We must, then, prepare our hearts and bodies" echoes the words of Abba Arsenius: *"A brother questioned Abba Arsenius to hear a word of him and the old man said to him, 'Strive with all your might to bring your interior activity into accord with God, and you will overcome exterior passions.'"* The desert elders were firm in their dependence on God's grace because they knew their own weaknesses very well. *"Once the spirit of fornication attacked [Amma Sarah] more insistently, reminding her of the vanities of the world. But she gave herself up to the fear of God and to asceticism and went up onto her little terrace to pray. Then the spirit of fornication appeared corporally to her and said, 'Sarah, you have overcome me.' But she said, 'It is not I who have overcome you, but my master, Christ.'"* Benedict learned that the preparation of "our hearts and bodies" is knowing our weaknesses and depending on God to do what we cannot do ourselves.

Praise Unites Our Voices and Minds with God's Presence

In his vision for community life Benedict continues the desert elders' emphasis on reciting and chanting the psalms: *"We must always remember, therefore, what the Prophet says:* Serve the Lord with fear *(Ps 2:11), and again,* Sing praise wisely *(Ps 46[47]:8); and,* In the presence of the angels I will sing to you *(Ps 137[138]:1). Let us consider, then, how we ought to behave in the presence of God and his angels, and let us stand to sing the psalms in such a way that our minds are in harmony with our voices."*

Benedict devotes three chapters in his Rule to protocols for reciting and chanting the psalms in community worship. He provides a method for including all 150 psalms in one week while commenting, *"We read, after all, that our holy Fathers, energetic as they were, did all this in a single day. Let us hope that we, lukewarm as we are, can achieve it in a week."* Behind his "lukewarm" schedule is his understanding that experiencing the wide range of human experience, emotions, and prayers expressed in the Psalter is essential for the spiritual health of his monastic community. The recitation is not an end in itself. It is an opportunity to listen with and be guided by an interior consciousness.

A Spacious Heart

"Do not be daunted immediately by fear and run away from the road that leads to salvation. It is bound to be narrow at the outset. But as we progress in this way of life and in faith, we shall run on the path of God's commandments, our hearts overflowing with the inexpressible delight of love."

The "battle of holy obedience to [the Lord's] instructions" can be a daunting prospect, especially for younger monks. Benedict, like the desert elders, encourages his monks not to "fear and run away from the road that leads to salvation." At the same time "it is bound to be narrow at the outset." But progress will be made because of the common life and support of the monastic community. Benedict is saying, "We are in this together." His intent is similar to that of Abba Pachomius's foundations that lived together in harmony. Pachomius established a rule that provided a manner of life and stability that formed and nurtured the soul of every person in the community. The lifestyles of both Pachomius and Benedict are designed to develop a spacious and flexible heart in each monk. Like abbas Evagrius and Cassian, Benedict knows that "hearts overflowing with the inexpressible delight of love" are hearts that do not seek their own will but are open and desire only what God desires. Rather than limiting a person's life, it brings forth joy and freedom that are the offspring of love.

A More Accessible and Less Austere Monastic Life

"Therefore we intend to establish a school for the Lord's service. In drawing up its regulations, we hope to set down nothing harsh, nothing burdensome. The good of all concerned, however, may prompt us to a little strictness in order to amend faults and to safeguard love."

Benedict "establish[es] a school for the Lord's service" to provide a community whose goal is profitable for souls. He seems familiar with a pattern of life in the communities of Abba Pachomius. The Greek *Life* of Pachomius describes a pattern of teaching called "conferences" at the end of each day's work, following a light meal. After the teaching, there was common prayer, discussion, and reflection. The genius of Pachomius is that each monk is given opportunities to be "formed" by the wisdom and experience of an elder and, at the same time, contributes his wisdom, experiences, and concerns to the whole community. Benedict's innovation is that he moderates some of the austerity of the desert elders yet retains the need for formation in a context of basic rules and strictness. Modern congregations would profit from this kind of formation. Where does your formation take place?

The Beginning and End of All Virtues

"Accordingly, brothers, if we want to reach the highest summit of humility, if we desire to obtain speedily that exaltation in heaven to which we climb by the humility of this present life, then by our ascending actions we must set up that ladder on which Jacob in a dream saw angels descending and ascending (Gen 28:12). Without doubt, this descent and ascent can signify only that we descend by exaltation and ascend by humility. Now the ladder erected is our life on earth, and if we humble our hearts the Lord will raise it to heaven. We may call our body and soul the sides of this ladder, into which our divine vocation has fitted the various steps of humility and discipline as we ascend."

Like the desert elders, Benedict knows that a humble heart is the key to human transformation. Abba Poemen said, *"As the breath which comes out of his nostrils, so does a man need humility and the fear of God."* Benedict spends the rest of chapter 7 describing twelve steps of humility. He warns that attitudes that place us ahead of God and our neighbor will destroy the harmony between our inner prayer and our actions. The desert elders were adamant about this. Abba Moses said, *"When someone is occupied with his own thoughts, he does not see those of his neighbor. If a man's deeds are not in harmony with his prayer, he labors in vain."*

The twenty-first century places great value on self-assertion and "pulling your own strings." Benedict declares that what conventional wisdom defines as "moving up" is, in reality, stepping down. Progress can leave our "divine vocation" behind.

Finding God in Each Other

About forty-five years after Benedict's death in 547, Pope Gregory the Great commends Benedict's example of holy living in a way that reflects the insistence of the desert elders on personal example: *"Anyone who wishes to know more about his life and character can discover in his Rule what he was like as an abbot, for his life could not have differed from his teaching."*

One way of "listening" to others is to discern God's presence in them. Abba Pachomius said, *"For I have truly seen the treasure of God hidden in human vessels."* Yet a person's "speech" enables God's presence to be "heard." Abba Isidore of Pelusia said, *"To live without speaking is better than to speak without living. For the former who lives rightly does good even by his silence. . . . When words and life correspond to one another they are together the whole of philosophy."* Most of the chapters in Benedict's Rule demonstrate that it is in the variety of relationships, labor, worship, tensions, and responsibilities of community life that each monk will discover God's presence. As Abba Macarius said, *"I have not yet become a monk, but I have seen monks."*

A Different Kind of Desert

Almost one hundred years before the birth of Benedict and only fifty years after the death of Abba Antony, the influence of the Egyptian desert elders spread west to Gaul and Britain. Martin of Tours (316–97) established a simple monastic community in rural Gaul and his piety and disciplines spread to the British Isles. Ninian (b. 360), a native of the Solway Firth in Scotland, studied in Rome and visited Martin's communities on his way back to Scotland. He established a monastery and school at Whithorn in Galloway. The deserts of Egypt became the *dysarts* of Scotland, Ireland, and Wales: islands, rugged mountains, fertile valleys, and forests.

"[Martin] lived in a small cell made of wood and a number of the brothers lived in a similar manner, but most of them had shelters for themselves by hollowing out the rock of the mountain which

overlooked the place. . . . No one there possessed anything of his own, everything was shared. . . . It was rare for anyone to leave his own cell except when they gathered at the place of prayer. They all received their food together after the period of fasting."

These Celtic-speaking monks and laypersons found cells close to home. They called their places of solitude "places of resurrection." Their small monastic communities and the individual hermitages of solitaries were places of sanctuary that influenced the lives of people struggling for survival in the presence of greedy and abusive local rulers. They witness to a different way of life.

Where are our "deserts" today? Where is yours?

DECEMBER 18

A Unique Monastic Presence in Society

After Abba John Cassian left the Egyptian desert, he founded two monastic communities in 415, near Marseilles, Gaul. He documented the experiences, disciplines, and wisdom of the desert elders in his *Conferences* and the *Institutes*, as guides for the formation of other monasteries. A Breton soldier of fortune named Illtud left a battlefield in Wales to become a monk and was mentored by Germanus of Auxerre in one of Abba Cassian's monasteries in Gaul. After a period as a hermit, in 450 he founded a monastery at Llantwit Major in southeast Wales. It became a blending of monastery, local church, and university. Its monastic life was similar to the communities of Abba Pachomius and it offered courses in Old Testament, New Testament, science, geometry, rhetoric, grammar, arithmetic, philosophy, and reading. Like Pachomius, Illtud organized the monastery in "houses" of twenty monks and each had its own oratory, refectory, and classroom. Residents included students, scholars, bards-poets, historians, clergy, missionaries, monks, and persons preparing for ordination and/or monastic life.

In the twenty-first century we now have monastic communities, schools of theology, seminaries, and programs of religious studies at colleges and universities that offer substantive spiritual formation. But most people do not have the opportunity to participate in their programs. There are not many local congregations that have the same priority for spiritual formation that was available at Illtud's community. Where do you find opportunities for your spiritual formation?

A Monastic Alternative
to Violence and Greed

The withdrawal of Roman legions and internal authority from Britannia in the early fifth century began almost two hundred years of political conflict and internal dissensions. This extended period of sometimes vicious civil wars ate away at the stability ensured by the Roman forts and urban centers. It was a dark age of hard work, tragedy, terrorism, cruelty, greed, unrestrained passions, and injustice as a way of life. A historian of Llantwit Major writes, *"No wonder men in the fifth century fled from the world and tried to be alone with God. Europe was a chaos; Rome had been sacked; the Teutonic tribes were growing stronger and stronger; bands of robbers infested the land; the amusements of the people were either tasteless or brutal; and all around were tawdry luxury, cunning intrigue, and bloody warfare. Here [at Llantwit Major] members of the schools, warm-hearted Celtic youths, knelt side by side with older men who had come to Llantwit to find a haven of refuge away from the strife, anger, and jealousy of the heathen world around them."*

In contrast, Celtic monastic life offered an alternative manner of life in this description of the monk and abbot Samson: *"ineffable in the work of God . . . renewed daily . . . ever bent on fasting and exercised unceasing prayers, also very often immersed in searching and learning Holy Scriptures, without any pause he went on praying . . . he cultivated himself by a stricter rule of abstinence . . . studied to be humble and more courteous."*

Daily Life and Community Rooted
in Work, Worship, and Prayer

When Roman legions left Britain in the early fifth century, ancient sea routes connecting Ireland and Wales with the eastern Mediterranean opened once more. This meant direct contact between Celtic monastic life and the Egyptian desert elders. This influence is seen in glimpses of the sixth-century monastic community of St. David in southwest Wales, where lives were rooted in prayer.

"Labor in the fields once ended they would return to the cloister of the monastery, and they spent the whole of the day until the evening in reading, writing or praying. . . . When evening was come, the stroke of the bell was heard . . . and so, in silence, without any empty talk or chatter they repair to the church. When they had finished chanting the psalms, during which the voice and heart were in complete accord, they humble themselves on bended knees until the appearance of the stars. . . . [After a meal] they go to the church . . . and there they give themselves up to watchings, prayers, and genuflexions for about three hours."

Life in St. David's monastery is very similar to the description we read earlier of monastic life at Scetis, Egypt, by seven visiting monks from Palestine in the late fourth century. Prayer gave meaning and sanctity to work; and work was the venue for putting prayer into action. The emphasis is on a persistent rhythm that supports the different aspects of each day. The purpose of a "rule of life" is to provide a stable guide for individual or communal living. It centers one's life and prevents intentional or unintentional scattering of a person's or a community's life with God.

DECEMBER 21

Love Is in the Little Things

In the morning after Matins Abbot David spent *"the whole of the day . . . in teaching, praying, genuflecting and in care of the brothers; also in feeding a multitude of orphans, wards, widows, needy, sick, feeble, and pilgrims . . . he imitated the monks of Egypt, and lived a life like theirs."*

David was a faithful abbot to his monks, but like the desert elders, he knew that the goal of monastic life and prayer is to make Christ tangible in the society that surrounded their community. Without love of neighbor, prayer is incomplete.

As David was dying, laity and monks came from the surrounding areas to honor his life and mourn his passing. Just prior to his death, he addressed them, saying, *"Lords, brothers and sisters; be joyful, and keep your faith and your belief, and perform the small things which you have heard and seen with me, and I will go the road which our fathers have travelled. Be courageous while you are on earth, for you will not anymore see me in the world."*

David accepted one of the greatest legacies of the desert fathers and mothers. How will that legacy become manifested in our lives today?

"The Training of All Training"

The Rule of the sixth-century Irish monk Columbanus also echoes the teaching of the desert elders, especially abbas John Cassian and Evagrius. Here, Columbanus speaks of the essential role of self-knowledge and discernment. *"How necessary discernment is for monks is shown by the mistake of many and the ruin of some who, lacking discernment at the beginning, continue without guiding knowledge and thus cannot live a praiseworthy life. Just as error overtakes those who have no path, so for those who live without discernment excess is near at hand, always contrary to the virtues, which lie between the extremes. Its onset is dangerous when beside the straight path of discernment our enemies place the stumbling block of wickedness and the temptations of various kinds of errors."*

In his Monks Rule, Columbanus outlines a monastic ascetic life that parallels the desert elders. The monastic virtues leading to transformation and sanctification are obedience, silence, temperance in food and drink, poverty, humility, chastity, the choir office, discretion, discernment, mortification, and the monk's perfection. These lead toward love of God and neighbor. In a sermon to his monks Columbanus referred to this as the *disciplina disciplinarum*, "the training of all training." This training must take place in the presence of wise and experienced elders and requires withdrawal from the world to avoid "bodily temptations" and "distractions." Columbanus echoes Abba John Cassian. *"Therefore it is better for us to go after, with unbroken constancy, the very small fruit of the desert, which no worldly concerns or earthly distractions or swelling of vainglory or vanity can nibble away at."* How do you care for your soul and life with God? Who are your mentors? How do you find solitude?

A Living Legacy

When St. Benedict wrote his Rule, there were already over forty monastic foundations in Wales and Scotland. Celtic foundations were appearing in Ireland as well. While all Benedictine monasteries followed the same rule of life, the monasteries in Celtic-speaking lands did not follow a common rule. Yet the evolving Benedictine and Celtic communities shared a strong influence from the desert elders.

During this period their legacy was moving through the eastern Mediterranean world as well. Saint Catherine's monastery in the Sinai was a link in spreading the desert legacy to Greece. The life, example, and writings of Symeon the New Theologian (949–1022) and Gregory of Sinai (1255–1346) integrated the life of hesychasts with larger monastic communities. This was the pattern that developed at Mount Athos, where settlements of hermits (with disciples) shared worship, affiliation, and support with monastic communities. Gregory of Sinai summarizes the life of the hesychast: *"Stillness gives birth to contemplation, contemplation to spiritual knowledge, and knowledge to the apprehension of the mysteries. The consummation of the mysteries is theology [experience of God], the fruit of theology is perfect love, of love humility, of humility dispassion, and of dispassion foresight, prophecy and foreknowledge."*

Can We Know an Unknowable God?

In the fourteenth century a Greek philosopher and scholar named Barlaam challenged the contemplative praxis of hesychast monks, especially their use of the Jesus Prayer. He claimed that if God cannot be known, then the hesychastic experiences of God in prayer cannot be real. This controversy clouded the future of monastic contemplative experience. It was settled by a Greek hesychast and bishop of Thessalonika named Gregory Palamas. Following the wisdom of Maximos the Confessor (seventh century), Gregory distinguished between the "essence of God" that is unknowable and the "energies of God" that are the uncreated source of creation, God's grace, and the transformation of human beings. The position of Gregory was affirmed by a church council and this "settlement" validated the hesychast tradition and enabled it to become the hallmark of Eastern Orthodox prayer and experience of God. It ratified the authenticity of experience of God in contemplative prayer and the reality of deification. Palamas wrote, *"The grace of deification is . . . above nature, virtue, and knowledge and according to St. Maximos all things fall infinitely short of it. . . . Through grace, God in his entirety penetrates the saints in their entirety, and the saints in their entirety penetrate God entirely . . . for he embraces them as the soul embraces the body, enabling them to be in him as his own members."* Palamas mirrors Jesus, who said, "Abide in me as I abide in you" (John 15:4).

Giving Birth to God

The legacy of the desert elders still exists in the deserts of Egypt. Saint Macarius Monastery is halfway between modern Alexandria and Cairo. The life of its monks is a chalice holding the wisdom of the ancient fathers and mothers and a modern community that includes hermits and monks who are substantively engaged with the world around them. These monks have degrees in science, medicine, and education. They are committed to making Christ tangible by enriching the lives of other people. Their spiritual father for half a century was Matthew the Poor (Abba Matta), who wrote, *"Union with God is not a subsidiary issue in faith or doctrine. It is the basis of all faith and doctrine. It is the ultimate aim of God for sending his only Son to the world to become human: 'For he has made known to us in all wisdom and insight the mystery of his will, according to his purpose which he set forth in Christ as a plan for the fullness of time, to unite all things in Christ, things in heaven and on earth.' (Ephesians 1:9-10) So the mystery of union between humankind and Christ is the ultimate aim of the incarnation, the crucifixion, the resurrection—nay, of creation in full."*

Abba Matta also said, *"Prayer, then, is a mystery forming an integral part of our being and psychic consciousness. Mystically, it is God's perpetual call within us drawing us toward the fulfillment of the ultimate purpose of our creation, our union with God."*

What would happen if this became the highest priority in our lives?

United through Participation in God

In the Christian West, A.M. Donald Allchin, an Anglican scholar and contemplative theologian, was a faithful guide connecting the legacy of the desert elders with our modern world. As director of the St. Theosevia Centre for Christian Spirituality at Oxford University, he was an advocate for dialogue and mutual praxis between the Anglican and Eastern Orthodox traditions. He called attention to the need for Christians to pay attention to the desert's emphasis on deification.

"At a moment of such intense conflict in human history, how is the light of God to be perceived? How is the joy of God, the delight of God in humankind and in creation to be made known? How can that joy become at this moment in history, [after] the century of Auschwitz and Hiroshima, the reality which dwells not only in the heart of each one of us but also at the heart of the whole of humankind, how can it inhabit the central place of the whole of the human family? . . . This is why, while there can be no place among Christians for an abandonment of our share in responsibility for the public issues of our day, there is also an urgent need for a rediscovery of the inner depth in each one, that inner depth in which we find the presence of God within us, and finding that, find our fellow women and men in it. . . . For the things which belong to the story of Jesus are not yet completed."

The challenges that face us in the twenty-first century call for more than human ingenuity and economic, military, and institutional resources. We need a change of consciousness expressed through "a rediscovery of the inner depth in each one, that inner depth in which we find the presence of God within us, and finding that, find our fellow women and men in it." It seems clear that this is part of an ongoing transformation of human life. "For the things which belong to the story of Jesus are not yet completed."

"Word into Silence"

How can Donald Allchin's words be put into practice? John Main was a twentieth-century Roman Catholic Benedictine monk who founded a Benedictine priory in Montreal, a community dedicated to bringing the legacy of the desert elders to laypersons and clergy in modern society. Through the World Community for Christian Meditation, his successors make contemplative prayer accessible to thousands of people. In *Word Into Silence* John Main writes, *"But we can only turn to the Other, we can only make this movement of self, if we leave self behind, that is, if we take our consciousness away from its involvement with me and direct it on the thou. Self-obsession is the means of restricting and limiting the self. Self-renunciation, on the other hand, is the means of liberating the self for its real purpose which is loving the Other. Meditation is a simple and natural process. It is the process that reveals our real being as a state of openhearted receptivity to the Spirit of Jesus who dwells in our hearts. This revelation dawns when we renounce, step aside from, the external manifestations of our consciousness such as thoughts, words, and images and when instead we move into the level of consciousness itself. We then become silent because we have entered silence and we are wholly turned toward the Other. In this fully conscious, fully free silence, we naturally open ourselves to the Word that proceeds from the silence, God's own Word, in whom we are called into being, and in whom we ourselves are spoken by the Creator."*

The challenge of silence is to be vulnerable to be "spoken by the Creator." It is this self that will manifest God's unconditional love in the world. In what ways are you willing to be "spoken" by God?

DECEMBER 28

Leading a Centered Life

After the Second Vatican Council in the 1960s, Fr. Thomas Keating, a Cistercian monk, dedicated himself to opening the "deep rest" of contemplative prayer to laity and clergy from all walks of life and cultures. Father Keating became the guiding spirit and mentor behind Contemplative Outreach, an international organization of laity and clergy committed to sharing the art of "centering prayer" because it "gradually brings about the liberation of whatever prevents the presence of God from becoming part of our constant awareness." In *The Better Part* Fr. Keating writes of the need for centering prayer.

"What can the Christian contemplative tradition offer to the world in the coming millennium? What might be the major elements of a spiritual life rooted in the Christian tradition and at the same time in dialogue with the other world religions, modern science, and the healing arts? The great gift that contemplative persons offer is the experience of the divine presence. Who is going to bring this realization into society if not those who are experiencing it? To be in dialogue with the other world religions requires the contemplative experience because all in their fully developed spiritual disciplines have experienced it. This fact suggests that the members of other world religions must henceforth be fully accepted as brothers and sisters, greatly loved by God and blessed with resources of immense value to contribute to us and to the world at large."

Being Ourselves

Thomas Merton was a twentieth-century monk, hermit, and spiritual guide to countless monks and seekers. A social activist, poet, and writer, his books have influenced the lives of persons from a variety of backgrounds. He describes the desert elders' legacy: *"These monks insisted on remaining human and 'ordinary.' This may seem to be a paradox, but it is very important. If we reflect a moment, we will see that to fly into the desert in order to be extraordinary is only to carry the world with you as an implicit standard of comparison. The result would be nothing but self-contemplation, and self-comparison with the negative standard of the world one had abandoned. Some of the monks of the desert did this, as a matter of fact: and the only fruit of their trouble was that they went out of their heads. The simple men [and women] who lived their lives out to a good old age among the rocks and sands only did so because they had come into the desert to be themselves, their ordinary selves, and to forget a world that divided them from themselves. There can be no other valid reason for seeking solitude or for leaving the world. And thus to leave the world, is, in fact, to help save it in saving one's self. This is the final point, and it is an important one."*

Merton articulates the fundamental desire of Jesus of Nazareth: human transformation. This was the heart of the monastic lives of the desert elders. Everything else looked toward this reality. Merton's "final point" sums it all up. The transformation of the world begins with the transformation of each individual. Each of us is called to become who we really are in order for God's will to be done "on earth as it is in heaven." This requires a "leaving" (Jesus called it "dying") of the self we have created in order to find our true self. This journey, as the desert elders discovered, will take us to the frontiers of human life. It takes courage and is risky only if we do not depend on God.

DECEMBER 30

Embracing the Unknown

Thomas Merton continues his description of the legacy of the desert elders: *"The Coptic hermits, who left the world as though escaping from a wreck, did not merely intend to save themselves. They knew that they were helpless to do any good for others as long as they floundered about in the wreckage. But once they got a foothold on solid ground, things were different. Then they had not only the power but even the obligation to pull the whole world to safety after them. This is their paradoxical lesson for our time. It would perhaps be too much to say that the world needs another movement such as that which drew these men [and women] into the deserts of Egypt and Palestine. Ours is certainly a time for solitaries and hermits. But merely to reproduce the simplicity, austerity and prayer of these primitive souls is not a complete or satisfactory answer. We must transcend them, and transcend all those who, since their time, have gone beyond the limits which they set. We must liberate ourselves, in our own way, from involvement in a world that is plunging to disaster. But our world is different from theirs. Our involvement in it is more complete. Our danger is far more desperate. Our time, perhaps, is shorter than we think."*

Some readers may think it is hyperbolic to say that Merton describes a situation that is a matter of life and death. Yet the desert elders embraced a life in the desert that stood in sharp contrast to the futility of life in the late Roman Empire. They chose life. They "got real." We face similar choices today. The legacy of the desert mothers and fathers is rarely taught in schools of theology and even less available in local congregations of every denomination. Their legacy is rooted solidly in the life and example of Jesus who said, "Follow me." We can learn from the desert elders, but we must take our own steps into the future of human living.

Our Life's Work

Mother Mary Clare is a cloistered member of the Anglican Sisters of the Love of God in Oxford, England. She is a modern "desert amma." Like most of the ancient desert fathers and mothers, her community combines lives of solitude with community life that is sustained by the regular celebration of the Eucharist (Holy Communion). The sisters welcome visitors and pilgrims to share their life. Mother Mary Clare's union with Christ in her silence and the Eucharist gives birth to a voice that can guide "the work of God" wherever it is lived.

"In the outpouring of love there is only one life to live—the life of charity; and for all of us it springs from the altar, as we offer and are united in Christ with the Father through the Holy Spirit. United with him we are bound to one another. For some of us this oblation will take us out into the highways and hedges; for some of us in enclosure, no less in contact with the world, though in a different way, oblation will hold the needs of the world to God's mercy for healing; for some of us, it will be the closeness and the discipline of ordinary family living. The recognition that the Christian community is the praying community unites the whole Church to the spiritual bond of charity. It is our bounden duty and responsibility to sound the trumpet clearly with no uncertain note. . . . Many people think that living and dying for God is one thing, living and dying for each other another; but the Christian truth is that in our love of God is contained our love of humanity."

In an age that images progress in exponential terms, are simplicity in prayer and living and personal charity still possible? What can one person do? Is *doing* the primary task? It is exciting that in the twenty-first century the lives, voices, and wisdom of ancient and modern desert elders are reentering society. Antony, Syncletica, Arsenius, and Theodora are returning from the desert! Their voices ring out with Matthew the Poor, Thomas Merton, Donald Allchin, Mother Mary Clare, and Thomas Keating. The "monastic art" is being sought and practiced in a variety of ways by persons who are not monks and nuns. In fact, today's monastic communities are encouraging and supporting persons who want to live the "monastic art" in the midst of families, the workplace, politics, and society at large. Our world can use a change of consciousness and the desert elders can still be our mentors. It all begins with listening . . .

"Go, sit in your cell, and your cell will teach you everything."

ABBREVIATIONS
of Sources

ALH (A Listening Heart)	Brother David Steindl-Rast. *A Listening Heart.* New York: Crossroad Publishing Company, 1999.
BF (Becoming Fire)	Tim Vivian, ed. *Becoming Fire: Through the Year with the Desert Fathers and Mothers.* Trappist, KY: Cistercian Publications, 2008.
BP (The Better Part)	Thomas Keating. *The Better Part: Stages of Contemplative Living.* New York: Continuum, 2002.
BR (Benedict's Rule)	Terrence G. Kardong. *Benedict's Rule: A Translation and Commentary.* Collegeville, MN: Liturgical Press, 1996.
CS (Columba Stewart)	Columba Stewart, OSB, trans. *World of the Desert Fathers*: Stories and Sayings from the *Apophthegmata Patrum*. Oxford: SLG Press, 1986.
CSp (Celtic Spirituality)	Oliver Davies, trans. *Celtic Spirituality.* Mahwah, NJ: Paulist Press, 1999.
CSQ (Cistercian Studies Quarterly)	Tim Vivian. "The Ascetic Teaching of Stephen of Thebes." *Cistercian Studies Quarterly* 34:4 (1999).
DC (Desert Christians)	William Harmless, SJ. *Desert Christians: An Introduction to the Literature of Early Monasticism.* New York: Oxford University Press, 2004.

DDL (Day-to-Day Life)   Lucien Regnault. *The Day-to-Day Life of the Desert Fathers in Fourth-Century Egypt.* Petersham: St. Bede's Publications, 1999.

DG (Dorotheos of Gaza)   Dorotheos of Gaza. *Discourses and Sayings.* Translated by Eric P. Wheeler. Kalamazoo, MI: Cistercian Publications, 1977.

DW (Desert Wisdom)   Yushi Nomura, trans. *Desert Wisdom: Sayings from the Desert Fathers.* Maryknoll, NY: Orbis Books, 2001.

ED (Encountering the Depths)   Mother Mary Clare, SLG. *Encountering the Depths: Prayer, Solitude, and Contemplation.* Oxford: SLG Press, 1993.

EP (Evagrius, Praktikos)   Evagrius Ponticus. *The Praktikos & Chapters on Prayer.* Translated by John Eudes Bamberger, OCSO. Kalamazoo, MI: Cistercian Publications, 1972.

FCU (Fifth Century University)   Alfred C. Fryer. *A Fifth Century University.* London: Elliot Stock, 1893.

FD (Fathers of the Desert)   Marcel Driot. *Fathers of the Desert.* Middlegreen Slough, UK: St. Paul Publications, 1992.

FHC (Five Hundred Chapters)   Maximos the Confessor. *Five Hundred Chapters.* In *Patrologia Graeca*, vols. 90–91. Edited by J. P. Migne. Paris: Petit-Montrouge, 1857–86.

FSH (Fifty Spiritual Homilies)   Pseudo-Macarius. *The Fifty Spiritual Homilies and the Great Letter.* Translated by George A. Maloney. New York: Paulist Press, 1992.

G (Gerontikon)   P. B. Paschos, ed. *Gerontikon.* Athens: 1961.

GFP (Guidelines for Prayer)   Matta El-Meskeen. *Guidelines for Prayer.* Scetis, Egypt: The Monastery of St. Macarius the Great, 2004.

HD (Harlots of the Desert)   Benedicta Ward. *Harlots of the Desert: A Study of Repentance in Early Monastic Sources.* Kalamazoo, MI: Cistercian Publications, 1987.

IWG (Intoxicated with God)   *Intoxicated with God: The Fifty Spiritual Homilies of Macarius.* Translated by George A. Maloney, SJ. Denville: Dimension Books, 1978.

JCC (John Cassian, Conferences)	John Cassian. *The Conferences.* Translated by Boniface Ramsey, OP. New York: Paulist Press, 1997.
JD (John of Damascus)	John of Damascus. *Three Treatises on the Divine Images.* Translated by Andrew Louth. Crestwood, NY: St. Vladimir's Press, 2003.
LA (Life of Antony)	Athanasius. *The Life of Antony and the Letter to Marcellinus.* Translated by Robert C. Gregg. Mahwah, NJ: Paulist Press, 1980.
LAM (Life and Miracles)	Gregory the Great. *Life and Miracles of St. Benedict* (Book Two of the *Dialogues*). Translated by Odo J. Zimmerman, OSB, and Benedict R. Avery, OSB. Collegeville, MN: Liturgical Press, 1949.
LBS (Life of Blessed Syncletica)	Pseudo-Athanasius. *The Life of Blessed Syncletica.* Translated by Elizabeth Bryson Bongie. Toronto: Peregrina, 1999.
LD (Life of David of Wales)	Rhigyfarch. *Life of David.* Translated by J. W. James. Cardiff: University of Wales Press, 1967.
LDA (Ladder of Divine Ascent)	John Climacus. *The Ladder of Divine Ascent.* Translated by Colm Luibheid and Norman Russell. Notes by Norman Russell. Introduction by Kallistos Ware. New York: Paulist Press, 1982.
LDF (Lives of the Desert Fathers)	Norman Russell, trans. *The Lives of the Desert Fathers.* Introduction by Benedicta Ward, SLG. Kalamazoo, MI: Cistercian Publications, 1981.
LH (Lausiac History)	*The Lausiac History of Palladius.* Willits, CA: Eastern Orthodox Books, n.d.
LM (Life of St. Martin)	Sulpicius Severus. *Life of St. Martin.*
LOA (Letters of Ammonas)	Derwas J. Chitty, trans. *The Letters of Ammonas.* Revised with an introduction by Sebastian Brock. Fairacres, Oxford: SLG Press, 1995.
LS (Life of Samson of Dol)	Thomas Taylor, ed. *The Life of Samson of Dol.* Felinfach, Wales: Llanerch Publishing, 1991.
LSA (Letters of St. Antony)	Samuel Rubenson. *The Letters of St. Antony: Monasticism and the Making of a Saint.* Minneapolis: Fortress Press, 1995.

LSM (Lives of the Spiritual Mothers)	*The Lives of the Spiritual Mothers.* Translated and compiled from the Greek of *The Great Synaxaristes of the Orthodox Church.* Buena Vista, CO: Holy Apostles Convent, 1991.
MATER (Matericon)	*Matericon: Instructions of Abba Isaiah to the Honorable Nun Theodora.* Safford, AZ: St. Pasius Serbian Orthodox Monastery, 2001.
MC (Maximus the Confessor)	Maximus the Confessor. *Selected Writings.* Translated by Paul C. Berthold. London: SPCK, 1985.
MLP (Making Life a Prayer)	Keith Beasley-Topliffe, ed. *Making Life a Prayer: Selected Writings of John Cassian.* Nashville, TN: Upper Room Books, 1997.
MS (Macarius the Spiritbearer)	Tim Vivian, trans. *St. Macarius the Spiritbearer: Coptic Texts Relating to Saint Macarius the Great.* Crestwood, NY: St. Vladimir's Press, 2004.
NJ (Name of Jesus)	Irénée Hausherr. *The Name of Jesus.* Kalamazoo, MI: Cistercian Publications, 1978.
OPL (Orthodox Prayer Life)	Matthew the Poor. *Orthodox Prayer Life: The Interior Way.* Crestwood, NY: St. Vladimir's Seminary Press, 2003.
OW (The Orthodox Way)	Bishop Kallistos Ware. *The Orthodox Way.* Crestwood, NY: St. Vladimir's Seminary Press, 1990.
P1	G.E.H. Palmer, P. Sherrard, and Kallistos Ware, trans. and eds. *The Philokalia*, Vol. 1. London: Faber and Faber Ltd., 1979.
P2	G.E.H. Palmer, P. Sherrard, and Kallistos Ware, trans. and eds. *The Philokalia*, Vol. 2. London: Faber and Faber Ltd., 1981.
P3	G.E.H. Palmer, P. Sherrard, and Kallistos Ware, trans. and eds. *The Philokalia*, Vol. 3. London: Faber and Faber Ltd., 1984.
P4	G.E.H. Palmer, P. Sherrard, and Kallistos Ware, trans. and eds. *The Philokalia*, Vol. 4. London: Faber and Faber Ltd., 1995.

PG (Patrologia Graeca)	J. P. Migne, ed. *Patrologia Graeca*. 166 vols. Paris: Petit-Montrouge, 1857–86.
PIG (Participation in God)	A. M. Allchin. *Participation in God.* Wilton, CT: Morehouse-Barlow, 1988.
PK1 (Pachomian Koinonia Vol. 1)	Armand Veilleux, trans. *Pachomian Koinonia: The Life of Saint Pachomius*, Vol. 1, "The Life of Saint Pachomius." Kalamazoo, MI: Cistercian Publications, 1980.
PK2 (Pachomian Koinonia Vol. 2)	Armand Veilleux, trans. *Pachomian Koinonia: The Lives, Rules, and Other Writings of Saint Pachomius and His Disciples*, Vol. 2, "Pachomian Chronicles and Rules." Kalamazoo, MI: Cistercian Publications, 1981.
PN (Power of the Name)	Bishop Kallistos of Diokleia. *The Power of the Name*. Oxford: SLG Press, 1986.
RB (The Rule of St. Benedict)	Timothy Fry, OSB, ed. *RB 1980: The Rule of St. Benedict*. Collegeville, MN: Liturgical Press, 1981.
SDF (Sayings of the Desert Fathers)	Benedicta Ward, SLG, trans. *The Sayings of the Desert Fathers: The Alphabetical Collection.* Kalamazoo, MI: Cistercian Publications, 1975.
SF (Spiritual Friendship)	Aelred of Rievaulx. *Spiritual Friendship.* Translated by Mary Eugenia Laker, SSND. Introduction by Douglass Roby. Kalamazoo, MI: Cistercian Publications, 1977.
SFP (Syriac Fathers on Prayer)	Sebastian Brock, trans. *The Syriac Fathers on Prayer and the Spiritual Life*. Kalamazoo, MI: Cistercian Publications, 1987.
SGP (Study of Gregory Palamas)	John Meyendorff. *A Study of Gregory Palamas.* Crestwood, NY: St. Vladimir's Seminary Press, 1998.
SMC (St. Maximus the Confessor)	*St. Maximus the Confessor: The Ascetic Life and the Four Centuries on Charity.* New York: The Newman Press, 1955.
SWI (Spiritual World of Isaac)	Hilarion Alfeyev. *The Spiritual World of Isaac the Syrian.* Kalamazoo, MI: Cistercian Publications, 2000.

WD (Wisdom of the Desert)   Thomas Merton. *The Wisdom of the Desert.* New York: New Directions Books, 1960.

WDF (Wisdom of the Desert Fathers)   Benedicta Ward, SLG, trans. *The Wisdom of the Desert Fathers: Apophthegmata from the Anonymous Series.* Foreword by Anthony Bloom. Oxford: SLG Press, 1975, 4th impression 2001.

WH (Way of Humility)   Andrew Louf, OCSO, trans. *The Way of Humility.* Introduction by Lawrence S. Cunningham. Kalamazoo, MI: Cistercian Publications, 2007.

WIS (Word Into Silence)   John Main. *Word Into Silence.* New York: Paulist Press, 1981.

WP (Writings from the Philokalia)   E. Kadloubovsky and G. Palmer, trans. *Writings from the Philokalia on Prayer of the Heart.* London: Faber & Faber, 1951.

S O U R C E S
by Month

Introduction

January

25   SDF Sisoes 26
26   DC Macarius the Egyptian 191
27   LOA 19; See SF
28   SDF Anthony 33
29   LSA Letter Three 206
30   SDF Anthony 27; SDF Psenthaisius 1
31   SDF Arsenius 3

February

1   SDF Moses 6
2   SDF Anthony 10
3   SDF Daniel 5
4   SDF Rufus 1
5   SDF Rufus 1
6   SDF Rufus 1
7   LH V.1, 2, 3, 27–28
8   SDF Theodore of Pherme 14; SDF Sarah 5; SDF Poemen 63
9   SDF John the Dwarf 12
10   SDF John the Dwarf 12
11   SDF Alonius 1
12   SDF Alonius 3; SDF Alonius 2
13   SFP 68
14   SDF John the Dwarf 27
15   SDF John the Dwarf 27
16   SDF Sisoes 27
17   SDF Paul 4
18   SDF Ammonas 27; EP 76
19   JCC 10. VII.3, p. 376
20   SDF Poemen 81
21   SDF Silvanus 11
22   SDF Theodora 3
23   SDF Poemen 135; SDF Poemen 29
24   SDF John the Dwarf 12
25   SDF Anthony 10
26   SDF Syncletica 6
27   SDF Moses 7
28   SDF Moses 6

March

1   MS 101–2
2   MS 101
3   SDF Poemen 46
4   LBS 22, p. 20; 29, p. 24
5   SDF Ares 1

April

17	PK2 Precepts 49, pp. 152–53
18	PK2 Precepts 49, p. 152
19	PK2 Precepts 49, p. 153
20	LSA 208
21	PK2 Precepts 49, p. 153
22	SDF John the Dwarf 34
23	SDF John the Dwarf 34
24	SDF John the Dwarf 34
25	SDF John the Dwarf 34
26	SDF John the Dwarf 34
27	SDF John the Dwarf 34; LA 45; SDF Evagrius 1
28	MATER 58, p. 56
29	MATER 67, p. 59
30	SDF John the Dwarf 39

May

1	GFP 33–34
2	GFP 33
3	GFP 33–34
4	LDA 121; OW 87
5	GFP 33–34
6	SDF Poemen 119
7	SDF Poemen 119; SDF John the Dwarf 34
8	SDF Elias 3, 5; unpublished comment by Fr. Thomas Hand, SJ
9	SDF Sarah 5; SDF Syncletica 1
10	SDF Macarius 27; SDF Benjamin 4
11	GFP 13
12	FSH 116
13	SFP 262
14	SDF Syncletica 9
15	WH 14
16	MS 117
17	MS 117
18	DDL 184
19	LA 58
20	LA 58
21	PK1 82
22	SDF Poemen 30
23	SFP 72; EP 106
24	EP 77
25	EP 18–19
26	MLP 61
27	SDF Anthony 1
28	SDF Anthony 1

29   EP 59
30   SDF Isaac the Theban 1
31   LA 61

June

Intro. SDF Isidore 4
 1   EP 29–30
 2   LDF II On Abba Or 7, p. 64
 3   SDF Joseph of Panephysis 7
 4   DG 122
 5   SWI 78
 6   SDF John the Dwarf 34
 7   WDF XV, 1975 edition
 8   LA 46
 9   SDF Syncletica 16
10   SDF Poemen 65
11   SDF Ammonas 11
12   SDF Rufus 2
13   SDF Theodora 5
14   SDF John the Dwarf 1
15   DW 61
16   LDF VIII Apollo 50–54, passim
17   SDF Psenthaisius 1
18   PK1 301–2
19   SDF Longinus 1
20   SDF Lot 2
21   SDF Lot 2
22   SDF Lot 2
23   SDF Moses 2
24   SDF Isidore 1; SDF Isidore 9
25   SDF Poemen 174
26   SDF Ammoes 1
27   SDF Elias 8
28   SDF Syncletica 12
29   SDF Silvanus 2
30   PK1 121

July

 1   None
 2   WDF XVIII, 1975 edition
 3   WDF 78, p. 25, 4th impression, 2001
 4   WDF 78, p. 25, 4th impression, 2001
 5   G Ammonas 5, 120 CD
 6   G Ammonas 6, 120D–120A

7	LDF I John of Lycopolis, p. 145
8	FD 17
9	WDF 38, p. 9, 4th impression, 2001
10	CSQ 425–54
11	SDF Syncletica 6
12	SDF Paul the Great 2; SDF Paul the Great 3
13	SDF Arsenius 11
14	SDF Theodora 3
15	MLP 57
16	SDF Syncletica 27
17	SDF Anthony 1
18	EP 12, pp. 18–19
19	EP 12, pp. 18–19
20	SDF Syncletica 27
21	SDF Serapion 1
22	SDF John the Dwarf 35
23	SDF Theodore of Enaton 3
24	WDF 5, p. 2, 4th impression, 2001
25	IWG Homily 11, p. 82
26	DDL 106–7; SDF An Abba of Rome 1; LH 32
27	SWI 193
28	JCC 10. XI.5, pp. 384–85
29	JCC 10. XI.5, p. 385
30	ALH 6
31	SDF An Abba of Rome 2

August

Intro.	SDF Syncletica 27; CS 35
1	SDF Syncletica 27; SFP 71
2	SFP 70
3	SFP 70
4	SDF Moses 7
5	SFP 71
6	SFP 70–71
7	IWG Homily 11, p. 82
8	SDF Agathon 8; LDF Prologue 3, p. 49
9	IWG 116
10	IWG 270–71
11	SDF Silvanus 8
12	SDF Poemen 103
13	SDF Arsenius 5
14	SDF Agathon 27
15	SDF Daniel 5
16	SDF John the Dwarf 2

17	LDF 102
18	LH 27–28
19	SDF Megethius 1
20	SDF Lucius 1
21	SDF Eucharistus the Secular 1
22	SDF Anthony 24
23	CS 35
24	SDF Arsenius 1
25	SDF Arsenius 2
26	SDF Arsenius 3
27	SDF Arsenius 4; SDF Arsenius 18; SDF Arsenius 6
28	SDF Arsenius 13; SDF Arsenius 9; SDF Arsenius 10
29	SDF Arsenius 19; SDF Arsenius 30; SDF Arsenius 27
30	SDF Arsenius 8; SDF Arsenius 22
31	SDF Arsenius 36

September

Intro.	LBS 39–40; DG 101
1	SDF Anthony 7
2	DG 101
3	DG 98–99
4	LBS 39–40
5	WH II 32
6	SDF Sisoes 1
7	WH 29
8	SDF Tithoes 7
9	SDF Motius 9
10	SDF Anthony 17
11	SDF Sisoes 17
12	SDF Theodora 5
13	SDF Poemen 8
14	LSM 26
15	LSM 26
16	LSM 43
17	SDF Moses 2
18	SDF Moses 3; SDF Poemen 63
19	SDF Isidore of Pelusia 1
20	SWI 78
21	SDF Matoes 13
22	SDF Poemen 203
23	SDF Isidore 4
24	BF 53
25	HD 27; all others HD 48
26	HD 48

27	HD 48
28	HD 48
29	HD 48
30	SDF Macarius 11; SDF Poemen 36; SDF Sarah 5; SDF Syncletica 26

October

1	LSM 29
2	LSM 29; SDF Agathon 19; SDF Ammonas 3; SDF Nilus 2; SDF Moses 3; LSM 29
3	LSM 29; LSM 30; SDF Paul the Barber 1
4	SDF Poemen 118; SDF Poemen 189
5	P1, p. 183, 122; SDF Isidore of Pelusia 1
6	SDF Isidore the Priest 2
7	LSM 29–30
8	LSM 31
9	LSM 32
10	LSM 33
11	WDF 122, pp. 35–36, 4th impression, 2001
12	LSM 38–39
13	LSM 36, 39
14	P1, p. 24, 12
15	P2, p. 34, 90; SDF Moses 6
16	EP 29–30
17	P1, p. 38, 1
18	P1, pp. 38–39, 2
19	P1, p. 39, 2–3
20	P2, pp. 84–85, 13
21	P2, p. 29, 70
22	P3, p. 161, 106
23	P3, p. 170
24	P4, p. 259, 3
25	WP 360–61
26	WP 387–88
27	P1, p. 36
28	SDF Lucius 1
29	P1, p. 189, 152
30	SDF Macarius 19; MS 117–18
31	MS 117

November

1	P1, p. 169, 42
2	SDF Epiphanius 6; SDF Epiphanius 15
3	SDF Syncletica 11
4	SDF Poemen 71; SDF Poemen 204

5   SDF John the Dwarf 12
6   SDF John the Dwarf 16
7   P2, p. 348
8   P3, p. 84
9   P3, p. 84
10   P3, p. 25, 22
11   NJ 268
12   NJ 268; DG 43
13   P2, p. 43
14   P4, pp. 72–73
15   PN 4–5
16   P4, p. 189, 2
17   P3, pp. 76–77
18   PK1 330–31; SGP 175
19   Quoted in PIG 70
20   SMC 158
21   Quoted in PIG 71
22   P3, p. 76
23   P2, p. 173, 42
24   P4, p. 48, 108
25   P2, p. 43
26   SDF Theodora 2
27   SDF John the Eunuch 1
28   LA 46
29   SDF Netras 1; SDF Joseph of Panephysis 7
30   BR 603

December
Intro. SDF Syncletica 12
1   None
2   SDF Cassian 1
3   BR 3
4   BR 3
5   BR 3; see JCC 123–24
6   BR 3; SDF Syncletica 12; BR 4
7   BR 3; LBS 39–40; WDF 132, p. 39, 4th impression, 2001
8   RB 269; RB 243; RB 253
9   RB 249; SDF Poemen 103; JCC 386–87
10   RB 181–83; SDF John the Dwarf 39
11   RB 165; SDF Arsenius 9; SDF Sarah 2
12   RB 217; RB 215
13   RB 165
14   RB 165
15   RB 193; SDF Poemen 49; SDF Moses 13

16   LAM 74; LDF 49; SDF Isidore of Pelusia 1; SDF Macarius 2
17   LM X:1–9
18   None
19   FCU 23–24, p. 89; LS 21–22
20   LD 35–38 passim
21   LD 38; CSp 211
22   CSp 252; CSp 246–56 passim
23   P4, p. 254, 5
24   P4, p. 420, 2
25   OPL 108; OPL 22
26   PIG 75–77 passim
27   WIS 59–60
28   BP 121–22
29   WD 22
30   WD 23
31   ED 72; ED 74; SDF Moses 6

A SHORT METHOD OF
Lectio Divina

Lectio Divina means "divine or sacred reading" and is an ancient form of contemplative prayer found in many religious traditions. In the Christian tradition it has been an essential part of monastic prayer and is now common for Christians in all walks of life. It is a method for using the Bible or other spiritual writings as paths to contemplation through listening and responding to God's voice. This method is adapted for use with *Desert Banquet.*

Find a relatively quiet place and sit with your back straight but not rigid. Find the saying for the day and read it slowly, out loud if possible, four times with a period of silence after each reading (I recommend at least two minutes). After the first reading, listen for a word or phrase that may attract you in a special way. After the second reading, try to enter into what you have read as if it was happening right now. Let it become your own experience. After the third reading, let the saying speak to you personally and respond to what you may hear God saying to you in the passage. After the final reading, simply sit in silence for five or ten minutes, without further reflection on the saying, and rest in God's presence and wisdom. When your silent period is ended, express simple thanks to God.

BLACK SEA

Constantinople
Chalcedon
Nicaea

GREECE

ASIA MINOR

Site of household monastic community led by Macrina the Younger, who influenced her brothers, Basil the Great and Gregory of Nyssa
+ •Nyssa

•Nazianzus

Athens

•Ephesus

•Antioch
+*Female community of virgins led by the deaconess Publia*

SYRIA

MEDITERRANEAN SEA

Caesarea
Jerusalem PALESTINE
Gaza + DEAD SEA

Alexandria
Bethlehem
Site of monastic communities of Jerome and Paula
Nitria +
Scetis+ + Cellia
Mt. Sinai
+ + +
Antony
+
Oxyrhynchus•
•Antinoë
ARABIA

EGYPT

Lycopolis•
Tabennesi RED SEA

• Town or city
+ Monastic site
•Thebes
Latopolis•

1. The Worlds of the Desert Fathers and Mothers

Maps by David G. R. Keller

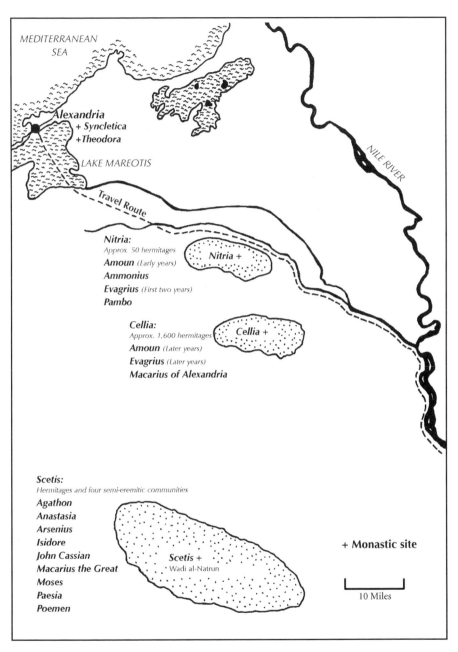

MEDITERRANEAN
SEA

Alexandria
+ Syncletica
+Theodora

LAKE MAREOTIS

NILE RIVER

Travel Route

Nitria:
Approx. 50 hermitages
Amoun (Early years)
Ammonius
Evagrius (First two years)
Pambo

Nitria +

Cellia:
Approx. 1,600 hermitages
Amoun (Later years)
Evagrius (Later years)
Macarius of Alexandria

Cellia +

Scetis:
Hermitages and four semi-eremitic communities
Agathon
Anastasia
Arsenius
Isidore
John Cassian
Macarius the Great
Moses
Paesia
Poemen

Scetis +
Wadi al-Natrun

+ **Monastic site**

10 Miles

2. Lower Egypt
Hermits and Semi-eremitic Sites

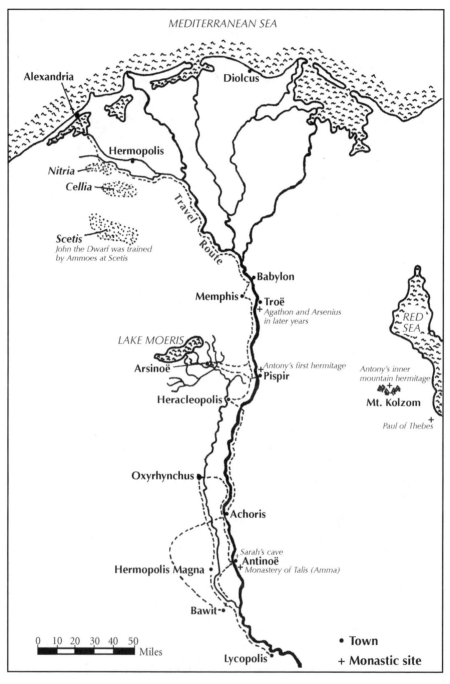

MEDITERRANEAN SEA

Alexandria

Diolcus

Hermopolis

Nitria

Cellia

Scetis
*John the Dwarf was trained
by Ammoes at Scetis*

Travel Route

Babylon

Memphis

Troë
+ *Agathon and Arsenius
in later years*

LAKE MOERIS

Arsinoë

Heracleopolis

Antony's first hermitage
+ Pispir

*Antony's inner
mountain hermitage*

RED SEA

Mt. Kolzom

+
Paul of Thebes

Oxyrhynchus

Achoris

Sarah's cave
Antinoë
+ *Monastery of Talis (Amma)*

Hermopolis Magna

Bawit

0 10 20 30 40 50
Miles

Lycopolis

• Town
+ Monastic site

3. Lower and Middle Egypt Monastic Sites